ALSO BY KATHLEEN MEYER

How to Shit in the Woods: An Environmentally
Sound Approach to a Lost Art

BAREFOOT-HEARTED

VILLARD · NEW YORK

BAREFOOT-HEARTED

A Wild Life
Among
Wildlife

KATHLEEN MEYER

All rights reserved under International and Pan-American Copyright
Conventions. Published in the United States by Villard Books, a division of
Random House, Inc., New York, and simultaneously in Canada by
Random House of Canada Limited, Toronto.

VILLARD BOOKS is a registered trademark of Random House, Inc.
Colophon is a trademark of Random House, Inc.

Grateful acknowledgment is made to HarperCollins Publishers for
permission to reprint a text selection from *Nora's Room* by Jessica Harper.
Text copyright © 2001 by Jessica Harper. Used by permission of
HarperCollins Publishers.

Library of Congress Cataloging-in-Publication Data

Meyer, Kathleen
Barefoot-hearted : a wild life among wildlife / Kathleen Meyer.
p.   cm.
ISBN 0-375-50438-9
1. Natural history—Montana—Anecdotes.   2. Country life—
Montana—Anecdotes.   I. Title.
QH105.M9 M48 2001
508.786—dc21   2001022237

Villard Books website address: www.villard.com
Printed in the United States of America on acid-free paper

9 8 7 6 5 4 3 2

FIRST EDITION

Never to be forgotten, ever to be missed,
Imogen Foster Sahi
Gujjard Sahi
Suzanne Lipsett

In boundless thanks to Jean Hayes

For Patricio

com•plex (käm•pleks'), *adj*. [L. *complexus*]: entwined round, hence intricate; not simple; entangled, plaited.

For the animals shall not be measured by man. In a world older and more complete than ours . . . they are not brethren, they are not underlings; they are other nations.

—HENRY BESTON,
The Outermost House, 1928.

Acknowledgments

First, in small remembrance of my mother, who was a reference librarian, I pay tribute to the parade of librarians, library workers, and historical-society caretakers who steered me through card catalogs and stacks and interlibrary loans, answered innumerable questions long distance, tutored me time and again in the use of the ungodly (however useful) library computers, and in a few cases allowed me to check out uncheckoutable books.

I am colossally indebted to the scientists, professionals, government officials, and myriad Bitterroot residents who gave freely of their time and expertise to assist in my writing coherently and with accuracy. I mention here only people not already referred to in the book—except to further thank those who proofread and offered suggestions. To gain an understanding of the Bitterroot Valley's geological beginnings, I had assistance from research geologists Jeff Lonn and Dr. Karen Porter, at the Montana Bureau of Mines and Geology; from Dr. Donald W. Hyndman, professor of geology at the University of Montana and coauthor of *Roadside Geology of Montana;* and from Dr. James W. Sears (mentioned in the Introduction), professor of geology also at the University of Montana, who was kind enough to read over my interpretation of all the input. The other academicians who read portions of the book were wildlife biologist and bear specialist Dr. Charles Jonkel (the chapter on bears); author and chiroptologist Dr. M. Brock Fenton (the chapter on bats); and "mephitologist of infamy" Dr. Jerry Dragoo (the chapter on skunks).

Bruce Farling, director of Montana Trout Unlimited, critiqued my rendering of our conversation on the history and behavior of trout. I'm grateful to Jeff Darrah, Judy and Bob Hoy, and Tom Ruffatto for reading their respective sections and offering corrections. For the story on the Ruffatto Ranch wolves, animals otherwise referred to as the Bass Creek pack, I also drew from conversations with Joe Fontaine and Ed Bangs, of the U.S. Fish and Wildlife Service; John Shivik, with Wildlife Services; and Keith Lawrence, director of the Nez Perce Tribe's Wildlife Management Program. For furthering my education on a number of issues, I thank Les Davis, curator of archaeology and ethnology at the Museum of the Rockies. I had repeated assistance from Jerry Marks, Rob Johnson, and Margaret Sharp at offices of Montana State University's county extension. I'm grateful to Barbara Orlans, a physiologist on the faculty of the Kennedy Institute of Ethics, Georgetown University, and author of *In the Name of Science,* for sending me copies of the studies on pain in fish.

The hospitality of John Dooling, Bud and Max Lapham, and Matt Wood was critical to the success of my covered-wagon journey, as was that of all the Hirschy family, mentioned in chapter 7. It was a trip I'll never forget. Thank you!

I am majorly obliged to my neighbor Arden Cowan, who has for years cordially fielded phone calls from me at all hours of the day and night, regarding intimate aspects of the physiology and lifestyles of wildlife. Things like: Do mice swim? Where do mink live? What's wrong with that coyote's voice? Arden's knowledge of wildlife stems from his years working as a mountain hunting guide, taking part in a lynx study in the Great Bear Wilderness, and possessing a lifelong fondness for prowling the backlands of Pennsylvania, Montana, and Alaska. Another man of the mountains, the late Mike Gossi, shared with me an unusually sensitive outlook on the ways of bears.

Others to contribute information or direction were friends Kathy Witkowsky and Ben Quinters; Thomas Beck, Colorado Division of Wildlife; Henry Harlow, University of Wyoming in Laramie; Kim Dionis, Penn State University; Sharon Rippey, Hamilton College in Clinton, New York; Sheilah Nicholas, American Indian Language Development Institute at the University of Arizona; Dr. Lynn Rogers, wildlife research biologist; Sue Toth, Hearing Conservation Program in Missoula, Montana; Mark Lewing, Montana Department of Natural Resources and Conservation; Bob Hutton, U.S. Forest Service; many folks at the Big Hole National Battlefield; Barra O'Donnabhin and Traolach O'Riordan, blessed authorities on Irish language; and NASA.

For her unlimited patience, I thank Terry at the copy desk at Valley Drug. And also Leah, Gina, Bill, Diana, and Angie at One Hour Photo Plus. To Tina and Mark St. John, I owe a very special thank-you for unexpectedly, and most graciously, housing me during the final round of galleys.

Two notes now for readers. At the request of Dr. Charles Jonkel, I've steered clear of the terms *boar* and *sow* for bears, words that carry connotations of domesticated and raised-for-meat livestock. Other folks I know say flat-out, "Bears are not pigs and their babies aren't piglets." With moose and elk, I've left the references *bulls, cows,* and *calves*—same as for cattle—as they are, at least, all ungulates.

In Montana, the word *Indian,* rather than being politically incorrect, is in prominent usage in native circles—certainly,

in part, as a result of the American Indian Movement's bestowing upon it a proper respect, but also because, as I was
once told by a tribal member, the appellation *Indian* is often
preferred in that it serves to differentiate peoples of indigenous roots from Montana-born Anglos enamored of calling
themselves "natives."

I was lucky enough to have four editors for the book, one
west of the Mississippi, three east of the Hudson. At Villard:
I blow a big kiss to Oona Schmid, wherever she is now, for
first believing in a very partial manuscript; I send a huge
thank you to Pamela Cannon for seeing it into print; and I
stand in awe of, and with wholehearted gratitude for, copy-
editor Susan Brown. My editor and friend in chief was
Marnie Prange—journalist and poet, creative writing teacher
and great encourager—who supplied a wealth of explicit
suggestion and spirited discussion throughout the course of
my writing.

To my agent, Robert Stricker—dear man—I practically
owe my life.

A special Hail! to my women friends—without whom, in
this world, I couldn't keep body and heart and soul working
together. Those not already woven into the book are Susan
Adams, Fredi Bloom, Kathy Couchois, Linda Cunningham,
Ann Harding, Martha Massey, and Jan Reiter. I must only
trust that the rest, and my male friends as well, will be speaking to me after I have snatched them up—not totally indis-
criminately, I hope—for writing fodder. To Barbara Gordon,
I'm additionally grateful, for her friendship and unremitting
research of small details.

The grandest acknowledgment, without a doubt, goes to
the person who takes my spirit soaring, the person for
whom, and about whom, this book is written: My Sweet
Gypsyman, who, in his red suspenders and high-top, lace-
up, Western dancing boots, is always ready to tango!

Contents

Preface

For the largest part of my life, should I live to be eighty, I will have run barefoot, with the exceptions of taking part in some school, work, and social activities—those more formal occasions—and entering the establishments perennially posted NO ADMITTANCE WITHOUT SHIRT AND SHOES. As a youngster on Atlantic bay waters, crewing on small catboats, I pressed salty toes against a centerboard trunk, using the broader lid as a toe stopper, a bracing that with the boat's heeling allowed me to hike out and over the side until I often could view the centerboard itself rising from the water. On the West Coast, beginning at fourteen, I roamed shoeless the cornfields and arroyos of the San Fernando Valley as well as Southern California's coastal tide pools, baked beaches, long wooden piers.

Such a shoe-free penchant was not without its perils. I endured the seasonal stickers and thorns, the splinters, deep glass cuts, and frequently broken toes from stubbings on roots and stones. From March through November, the soles of my feet toughened like a street urchin's to the thickness of shoe leather. It would be New Year's before I began to molt, sloughing calluses turned soft by confinement in socks and shoes, winter's hot baths bringing on the final disintegration into sorts of rubbery crumbles, resembling detritus shed from art gum erasers. I was always a little tender of foot for the first few weeks of spring, but come June, blazing asphalt again posed no challenge.

When continuing education drew me north to Berkeley and San Francisco, I stole away from the concrete, tile, and linoleum surfaces at every opportunity, my soul aching for a closeness with dirt, pebbles, rocks—weeds caught between my toes!—those most sensual and tactile basics of walking barefoot across ground. The surest way I knew of accomplishing this was to streak for the San Joaquin Valley and there wiggle my feet into the fertile, sandy soil until buried to the arches. It would be evening by the time I reached the flatland farms, their thick, heady smells of livestock and maturing crops intermingling all along the miles to the little town of Livingston. There, old family friends owned a dairy farm and vineyard. Mornings, I was out early and into the cool, damp grass alongside the guest cottage, then a stroll down a narrow lane of compacted sand, bordered by the gnarled trunks of grape, to the farm kitchen—the most lived-in room of a house built of hand-cast bricks. The final foot-sensation of my free-soled morning sojourn came curiously from a chilly slab of concrete. I minded it little as the four-foot-square stoop at the back screen door.

Valleys to mountains. One summer, I hiked the connecting trails around Northern California's Mount Lassen with my feet clad only in wool socks, which after a few miles grew at heel and toe pleasingly holey. This once, I'd had every intention of going shod, but over the course of the first day, the newness of a pair of tennis shoes raised watery blisters on both heels. Socks afforded my insteps a measure of protection against emerging points of rocks and tough crooks of roots, in turn allowing me welcome ganders at the surrounding landscape beyond the intent business of selecting the next patch of path for a footfall.

Ensuing years brought me riverbanks, those of white-water rafting trips—terrain where my heels and toes communed in their own weird rituals with smooth, water-tumbled stones, bee stings, caked sand.

Then my shoeless life came suddenly to an end, as I traded rafts for horses. In working with the big drafts, one is inclined to don boots of leather, the thicker the better. I had heard about a horse stepping on a woman's bare foot. The hoof, freshly trimmed by a horseshoer, severed three of her toes.

Horses are not all that keep me shod these days. Snow and ice and fifty-below windchills, all barreling like double-trailered Peterbilts through a Rocky Mountain valley, and the frigid floors of the old dairy barn I call home collectively drive me into serious footwear: felt-lined winter pacs, Polar-fleece socks, cork-soled slippers of boiled wool. And then there's my podiatrist, whose assessments I've come to hate! Old, he says, I'm getting old; arches dropping; bone spurs started; orthotics required to relieve pain. The likes of duct tape will be needed to bind the $250 items to bare feet or summer sandals. My future, it seems, will brim with walking shoes, hiking boots, clodhopper beachwear, oxford bedroom slippers.

Freedom and convenience and high fashion aside, this encasement in footwear robs me most of *connection*, that instantaneous feel of how I'm woven into the grand scheme of the planet. When shoeless, one cavorts intimately with Earth's textures, its temperatures, its levels of moisture. One is party to sensations that are the makeup of Earth's personality: searing sting of nettles, soothing ooze of mud. Earth's history is imbued in its surface, and in padding along upon it, one absorbs the ages, makes them undeniably one's own: polished hardpan, volcanic ash, hayfield stubble, razorback rock chips, springy green shoots, spongy deadfall, brittle fallen leaf and twig. Shoeless, I yield to the earth's insistence, encounter it smack-on, not as a thing postponable.

Feet to earth, I am forced to remain mindful and attentive. It is I who adjusts to the ground, requiring of it in my passing no grandiose transformation for self-comfort, or whim. A close and hearty relationship develops—of earth and person—one that fosters in me vulnerability and humility, a ladder down off the towering human pinnacle of arrogance.

Naked soles and dexterous toes long served me a route into sisterhood with the planet's greater community of wildlife, as well as animated dialogue with plants and rocks. I can't help thinking that what the feet for all those years took for granted, the heart—in my present manner of living—now seeks. However blindly it began, without linear progression or startling forethought, in a kind of slow, absentminded aligning, the way a barometer might rearrange itself to a change in atmospheric pressure, oblivious to whip of prevailing wind, my preciously felt connection with Earth has swung round from foot-bottom to bosom.

Yet in transcending footwear there is no perfection. Feet are sensory appendages, while the heart has a mind of its own. The heart is a fickle organ, disposed toward standing in the way of plain sense, *taking* when it should be *giving*. Mine and yours are on a path—we can hope—a path similar to the one the author Nathaniel Branden sought to teach in his book *The Psychology of Romantic Love*, from that of immature love to healthy love. It is very much a relationship and a romance that we human creatures have with Earth, replete with love and hate and who—by God!—will be in control.

As a species so in need of a means of balance, we could do worse than stand to with our toes in the dirt, run the straightaways, the grades, the bends of our big race, hearts barefooted.

. . .

The writings in this book come out of the years following my move from an ocean state, as I saw it, to a mountain state and the burgeoning of a fresh, but wildly uncharted, romance interest—in a sense, both new partnerships. Here I have turned my gaze from the outer world—that sensory onslaught of around-the-globe wars, corporate power jockeying, failings of our political system—to those ethical, spiritual, and ecological battles closer to home. Ones I can touch with my fingers, turn over like a stone along the trail, a stone showing me only its light-bathed side and needing to be read where dark and damp, another set of teachings springing from where it cleaves tightly to the earth. Wilderness envelops our rural setting, and its grand inhabitants sally back and forth across the valley floor. Barn life has confronted me with a kind of community living: a confined space shared with mice, skunks, birds, snakes, bats, and then a full-time man. The yellow-bellied marmots have been the most brazen, flies the most despicable. I have come to think of this place where we squat as a miniature pool of biological diversity, altered somewhat from the wilds, but nonetheless with our sitting, as humans do, with the potential to be king and queen predators over all.

I did not set out with a grand and noble plan, assigning each critter a cozy nook. Any heightening of sensitivity sprang from odd sources: tenderness for one mouse, my own self-centeredness, laziness in trapping skunks, a fondness on the part of my mate for loathsome and crawly things, summer evenings of digging weeds. Only over time did we move beyond a kind of blind groping on to more purposeful intentions, as we began to see the fates of the animals and plants and insects—in and around the barn and in the adjacent countryside—as linked to a *greater* collection of species and the fate of the planet as a whole.

In the eyes of many people, the two of us lead a bizarre

life—someplace between *somewhat* and *downright.* Yet just like anyone else these days, we are out there knocking up against a world gone crazy; a world grown mega-industrial, super-high-tech, cybernated, and virtual all in half a lifetime; a world that's gained nearly five billion people and as many points of stress since I first learned to live in it. Problems now are like prairie grasshoppers, propagating exponentially on the turn of a season: the earnest voter is hard-pressed to decipher the real issues in a barrage of divisive political rhetoric; the person passionate to live gently, with cheek and ear to the ground, is mightily challenged to figure out how. A confusion of basic needs is bound up with ownership and greed. Happiness requires glitter. Wisdom and perspective come to us slowly, and only with searching effort.

There are moments when the sets of conundrums become so entangled as to pose the greatest conundrum of all: Where even to begin? The answers to my life are never immediate in their unfolding—some days pondering is all I get. This book offers up small pieces to the search, to *my* search for equilibrium ... with myself, with the changing world around me, and with an unusual man.

Introduction

Dust clouds like ground-hugging contrails billow out the backs of vehicles flying across long traverses of landscape. Breezing down a dirt road, I endeavor to follow suit. At the first washboard corner, I spin out—a one-eighty, the old pickup's tires sledding across chatter bumps as though they are ice. When I settle, the left front bumper juts over an irrigation ditch. The smell of sweet clover wafts in the window, a horse stares blankly at me from a fence post. Then a jerking of my arms tight against my ribs, a small involuntary spasm, and I know: I owe my life to the lack of traffic.

The whole of this Rocky Mountain valley is a rural fringe: an interface of sprinkled human settlement and wildlands. Morning's sunbeams play on a high, snow-polished cirque, a forested fold of slope, a crook of river, the slant of a windshield. There are parking places! A plethora of vacant slots on the broad streets of all the small towns. And an absence of queues: for the postmistress, the bank teller, the grocery checkout. This is wide country, requiring no wasting of a life in *waiting*. The muscle in my middle finger will atrophy, my voice box heal. No more of the Bay Area's gridlock, and near gridlock, that rampage of vituperatory drivers of which I'd become one, habitually engaging in my own high-decibel blasphemy (with the windows rolled up, so as not to get shot). Slackening now is the attendant urge to play amusement-park bumper car on a stalled freeway. Ka-bang! *Out of my way assholes! I'm clearing a path.*

It was a fine springlike day when I drove away from life as I had known it, as a commercial white-water rafting guide and owner of a small drywall taping company in Marin County, California. I stuffed my belongings into a twenty-six-foot U-Haul truck and piled in with a gypsy horseshoer named Patrick McCarron—a man of blinding charm, towering physique, and full Irish blood. Depositing my convertible with a friend to sell, we hitched my old Ford pickup on behind us and steered for the mountains of Montana.

While filling out the U-Haul forms, we had come under heavy pressure to check the *yes* box for insurance—what if, accidentally of course, we crunched the cab overhang on a low-slung branch? backed the long wheelbase into the side of a building? Patrick had asked, in a form of irreverent quipping I would come to know as his style, "Does this cover root canals?" Never joke with the U-Haul man: the trip unfolded without incident until the last morning, when I woke up in Salmon, Idaho, holding my jaw, in dire need of an emergency root canal. A little behind schedule, yet fittingly, we dropped into the Bitterroot Valley of western Montana on Saint Patrick's Day.

Patrick and I had first met four years earlier, when he was on tour through the Pacific Northwest as actor and farrier with the Caravan Stage Company, a professional Canadian theater troupe, rumbling from town to town by means of thirteen feathery-footed Clydesdales and five brightly painted gypsy wagons. By coincidence of fate, I had been learning to drive parade horses, a team of shire mares, under the tutelage of an eighty-year-old Italian dairyman—Petaluma, California's own Silvio Piccinotti.

The move from California to Montana held the promise of adventure curative for the mind and the soul, but especially for the nerves—a universal unjangling, as though I were unplugging my developmental self from a wall socket. To fit in, one needed only change license plates on the day of arrival; speak not of the thirty-two years residing in that lanky state twice bent against Pacific waters; mention *nothing* beyond younger years on the Jersey shore and time spent in Colorado and Wyoming. The "Californicating of Montana," if not a capital offense, remains in some folks' minds offense plain enough, deriving as is thought from a personal history marred by hot tubs and drug depravities, unnatural habits of vegetable eating and dude dressing, and godless leanings toward environmentalism, any of which cause to be thrown as wild an eye by the established resource-based community as a rattler in the grass. It behooved one in the beginning to cloud over a previous residence—particularly if it be California. It was with no real choice then that I took the calculated risk: of letting people know me first by my character.

On the outskirts of the one-block town of Victor, we settled into a temporary rental and I plunged into finishing the manuscript for my first book, *How to Shit in the Woods: An Environmentally Sound Approach to a Lost Art*. During those same weeks, in a double garage heated by woodstove, we painstakingly rebuilt a hundred-year-old wagon, while I also sewed us old-timey calico clothes and every day we put Pancho and Lefty, our newly acquired team of black draft geldings, into near-Olympic training. Our high-gear preparation had a serious deadline: the May 27 departure of the Bitterroot Centennial Wagon Train, meeting up two weeks later with the Montana Centennial Wagon Train.* A box of my books, shipped by my publisher—a lightning turnaround on production—caught up with us camped at the Beaverhead County Fairgrounds in Dillon. Out of the back of the wagon, I peddled books and Patrick shoed horses, and we generated enough income to buy oatmeal and beans and horse feed.

From each forwarded bundle of mail, we tore open reviews of my book—without exception, wildly good ones. With its success, there was the expectation for my writing career to shift into overdrive, but instead, my scribbling creaked to a standstill. Stone-struck in love, deep into the perils of full-time intimacy, thick in partnership keeping horses and wagon on the road through long days of rain, snow, hail, blistering sun, and raging dust storm, any thoughts of a book about our travels rapidly slipped away.

Our mountain states odyssey carried us as far south as Steamboat Springs, Colorado, where we stopped to drive sleigh rides over the winter. In spring, we again took to the trail: some paved, some dirt, some merely grass-grown wheel ruts. When not clip-clopping along on organized wagon trains, we rolled by whimsy on our own.

The Wyoming Centennial Wagon Train—Casper to Cody over the course of a month—was our last leg and the most trying. Early American settlers in coming west had wound alongside rivers when they could, bottomland that today is mostly fenced and given over to irrigated field crops. Our sometimes five-mile-long, snaking entourage—flags and horses and wagons and support trucks—was routed instead across high, windswept cactus barrens. With Patrick's and my having met years after our wild twenties and bearing the

---

*The organized wagon trains that I write about here were celebrations of statehood; they were not reenactments in the sense of Civil War battles, but, for authenticity, Patrick grew out his hair.

unhealed brandings from strings of failed relationships that we'd left behind like potholes in the dirt tracks unwinding at our backs, if we were ever to invest again, it was going to take a fierce bonding, something engendering far more stickum than what moving into a condo together could produce—something like the Wyoming Centennial Wagon Train. As the train's official farrier, Patrick was engaged in shoeing, starting at dawn and then again each evening, until all light faded. It was the camp chores that kept me skipping, in addition to the plains prickly pear, or *Opuntia polyacantha*, a prolific, low-growing cactus loving poor and gravelly soil and flourishing on overgrazed rangeland. Its flat, pear-shaped pads grow woolly nodes loaded with two- and three-inch spines possessed of a bootmaker's ability to pierce layers of tough leather, and skewer a tender toe. For the first hour in camp, I solely dug cactus (vaguely aware that several species of cactus, yet surely not this one, were threatened with extinction), making safe a path around the wagon, a pallet for our bedding, and an area off the tailgate where we might freely move about to cook. Mornings it was another hour, this time armed with tweezers, pulling spines out of horsehide—not such tough material when still on the animal—after the big boys had spent the night rolling in their portable paddock. One cactus spine left to fester could end the trip for us. Our journey was an endeavor of devised adventure, not one of life and death in locating a homestead, and we treated the horses accordingly.

Every evening about dinnertime, a semi truck steamed into camp stacked high with hay for the stock: saddle horses, packhorses, draft horses, mules, burros. Working to their limits—in pulling our wagonload of camp bedding, pots and pans, food boxes, coolers, Coleman stove and lantern, a trunkful of clothes (petticoats, high-button shoes, bonnets, and such), horse tack, grain, battery post-and-wire paddock, a box of my books and our maps and notebooks, large tarps and tepee poles to create sheltered work areas, a mountain bike for laundry and grocery runs into towns, a shovel, an ax, an anvil, a forge, propane tanks, Patrick's shoeing tools, and a sizable assortment of steel bar stock for turning horseshoes—our horses required the sustenance of two eighty-pound bales. Balancing the twine-bound loads awkwardly on the bicycle, one at a time, we wheeled them back to camp, sometimes seven circles away, or a distance of half a mile.

The train's water supply also arrived by truck. Two fat-bellied tankers made the rounds from circle to circle, one filling the fourteen stock tanks, the other the wagon barrels and canteens. On the hottest candy-sticky days and when the supply of people's drinking water was judged to be in surplus, the tanker driver mercifully held the big hose for large gatherings of us standing around sudsing our sweat-itchy scalps and dust-laden hair. Out of a second semi, a mobile grocery store operated. You could purchase the overpriced food conveniently offered at its back door, or do as we did and con tourists agog over visiting an authentic-looking wagon train into taking away a list of desired fresh vegetables, milk, and eggs, and delivering them to the next camp. Each afternoon about two o'clock, after the day's stint of hauling up steep sagebrush grades and filing through sandstone canyons, invariably we topped some rise and through the horses' ears I would glimpse across a sun-bleached landscape a little town of white buildings. It was the same town every day. Thirty-eight portable outhouses trucked in for the night's camp.

Beneath the big desert sun, our days unfolded in a maca-ronic version of the Wild West. There were runaways, fistfights, and failing money supplies—much like a hundred years ago. Wagons bogged down and turned over in mud holes and sandpits. Wheels broke. Horses took sick. A blond grit sifted into food containers and bedding and underwear. Old men killed rattlesnakes and roasted them over coals. All the while that folks worked together to pull every last wagon through, the train broke into warring factions. Yet people fell in love. There were weddings, and divorces. Medical crises that would have dealt certain death to our forebears were handled swiftly by today's paramedic rescue teams. And the train's accidents and injuries ran aplenty. Any Kansas farm woman crossing the prairie in 1840 would have thought hell upon her with the unscheduled halting of the wagons and the descent out of the sky of a *whomp-whomping* whirlybird—daily, it seemed, to fly out an injured person, a heart attack victim. Pancho and Lefty became rock-steady horses, accustomed to all manner of riot and commotion. Every morning the wagon train's official modern-day version of the Pony Express, with riders and flags enough to serve five states, made its way through camp, picking up and delivering mail. Greenhorn riders, cowboy wanna-bes, tore around spooking every living thing. One teenage boy, with a sadly misplaced sense of purpose, continually whipped a team of four small burros into dragging a wagon loaded down with grossly overweight adults.

Riding along was a bevy of journalists, prowling the train for stories. The crew from the *Billings Gazette*, who camped with the wagons and dispatched daily reports of our activities, soon quietly dubbed the whole operation The Wyoming Centennial Wagon Train and Bozo Extravaganza. A horseshoer friend, Jim Rieffenberger, who drove his own team and helped Patrick mornings and nights, tacked on a personal, but widely appreciated, ending: and Death March!

The train ended in Cody in a dismal, torn-down, drive-in movie theater. Before setting up the corral, we were forced to clear away shards of glass, bent nails, broken lumber. My prairie skirt and petticoats hung ragged and clay-caked, and under a droopy Stetson my frizzled hair appeared at once greased and starched beyond human recognition. A cloud, a sort of vaporousness, redolent with fresh acrid sweat on top of powerful stale sweat, hung thickly about me. Laced, as it was, with a woman's sweet musky secretions, and all gone past ripe, oddly it was a pungency I savored. Such goaty piquance though was cause to be shunned in any town setting. A creature of wild traveling, I was short only a few months of the condition of the sheepherder in Norman Maclean's *A River Runs Through It.* The man had worn his long johns until his body hair grew into the weave.

In the cool shadow of the wagon, Patrick and I stood with our arms about each other, emotionally and physically wrung out. Pancho had a fever of 102°F: dust pneumonia. We were treating it with steroids. Soon after Patrick trudged off to town on errands, a stiff wind kicked up. To hide from the blowing grit, I wrapped myself in a dusty canvas tarp and, with duffel bag of rain gear for pillow, fell dead asleep on the wagon seat. An hour later I awoke to loud snoring—I never snore—and a mild awareness that a thick stream of drool was sculpting a muddy course through my cheek grime. A strange *click-clicking* emanated from close to my ear. I opened my eyes to a semi-circle of camera-wielding tourists crowding the wagon box.

The look of my world had changed. Gone were the high-dollar designer clothes and the zipping around fabled Marin County in a candy-apple red 1966 Mustang convertible. It was true that I unfailingly sought the ironies in life and, with a kind of dual personality, shifted easily through incongruencies such as town strolls in high heels and backcountry hiking in bare feet; the bucket seats of a classic automobile and the broken-down bench of a beater truck. It was only during the years that I'd worn white overalls, taped drywall, and come home every night much like Charles Schulz's Pig Pen, flaking a cloud of dried white mud bits onto the rug, that I'd felt moved to keep my fingernails painted red. Now I was to slip farther than ever planned toward one end of my seesaw and then, incredibly, by conscious design, inch out even farther.

Our transition from vagabonds to landed gentry technically happened on a truck run back to our storage locker in Victor, a month prior to setting out on the Wyoming Centennial Wagon Train. Patrick and I stopped to visit the three Benish brothers, proprietors of the Bitterroot Carriage Company, where months before we had dragged from the tall weeds behind the milk house the driftwoodlike shell that became our wagon. We were possessed of the thought to head there at the end of summer and take up an offer once made to Patrick to set up his forge. Instead we found the brothers selling out, in fact a day or two from listing the barn, outbuildings, and four acres with a realtor. The original three-hundred-acre dairy farm had long since been whittled down to the five the brothers acquired. They then had lopped off another acre, the one with the 1920s, two-story farmhouse, and poured the money from the sale into upgrading the barn for their carriage shop.

Selling? Patrick and I probed the depths of each other's dark pupils and watched the dreaded word *mortgage* float to the surface, as though on a white signboard. Could we do this? Two people who planned never to grow up, to be gypsies for another ten years at least? A longtime dream of Patrick's, to build a horseshoeing establishment, one where the steeds would be brought to him—anything to shake himself free of gasoline-powered vehicles—looked to be a possibility here. It was a valley of horses: historically for farming, logging, and mountain packing; more recently for western pleasure and endurance riding; and lately for the French discipline known as dressage.* The barn with its property lay midvalley and fronted U.S. Highway 93, the main north-south, two-lane artery—prime spot for a business. I was drawn to the gentle, willowy river bottom that unwound out the back, and the sweeping sunsets that showcased the craggy Bitterroot Mountains. It was with my breath caught on these sights that I came to glance around the barn with a blind eye for someone well-schooled in the building trades, thinking only: Oh, a little paint and this will make dandy living quarters! We quickly placed a few phone calls to borrow money from friends, the few we thought might have any. The rest of the paperwork we finalized through the Pony Express and a couple of phone booths on the Wyoming trail.

The July day that we parked our wagon in the barnyard, Patrick climbed a ladder and pried off the white letters strung down the barn's weathered red siding, reading BITTER-ROOT CARRIAGE COMPANY. Selecting letters from the pile, and one E he trimmed into an F (he'd been thinking about this for some miles), he nailed them back up to read ROMANY FORGE (pronounced "*Rah*-ma-nee," the word for gypsy or the gypsy language). Yet in stopping here, our carefree Romany way of life took flight. It became a time for experiencing different kinds of firsts: our first mortgage, Patrick's first year-round home, my first full-time household shared exclusively with a lifemate, and my first Montana winter.

It was five weeks of hard work and September before a chance arose for solitude and a pacific communing with my new home. Patrick had driven off before dawn, to Idaho and

---

*The systematic training of a horse in gait, pace, and demeanor, in response to barely noticeable cues from the rider.

a four-day horseshoeing clinic. I tossed a few flakes of hay to the horses and plunked down on the boardwalk front porch of the barn. The barnyard spread out from my feet, its sandy surface still warm from the afternoon sun. Soon the quiet of evening teased me into thinking I could hear phantom snatches of laconic talk, the crisscrossing of footfalls that surely had accompanied years of farm chores. Close by, on the crowning board on a pile of junk lumber, a toothy, yellow-bellied marmot, species *Marmota flaviventris* (a western relative of the woodchuck), sat up perkily on the wide chunk of his brown haunches and *pipped* at me.

Strung out in a line down the porch, cocked against the barn's siding, were five white enamel drawers drying from the washing I had given them. In the morning, when I had settled down with coffee and the classified pages of the local paper, I'd come across an old freestanding kitchen cabinet, the sort with doors and drawers, and drainboards flanking a sink. Somebody was remodeling; the cabinet was offered free to anyone willing to haul it away. I had tooled twelve miles up the valley, and a man wearing a carpenter's belt had helped me load it. On the way home, I stopped at the grocery store and picked up a roll of blue calico shelf paper. By backing the truck to the porch's edge and dropping the tailgate, I managed to wiggle-walk the unwieldy piece indoors. So now I was having an evening of it—cleaning and cutting and fitting. I was more thrilled, perhaps, than the woman getting the new kitchen.

The marmot *pipped* again, his sound high, loud, and crisp—a statement, resonating with saucy challenge and lordliness, which I took to mean, "You may hold the papers on this place, but never think for a minute that the ground isn't mine!"

He was right, of course; he and his extended family did own the place, every inch of it ground level and below.

Heavily excavated holes ran under the old one-room log cabin, said to be the original homestead cabin, and the granary, a timeworn structure heeling back into the earth that I called the inside-out building, because its siding was nailed on the *inside* of the studding. With the efficiency of little backhoes, the marmots had also tunneled under the barn's rock foundation on three sides, passages all leading to the extensive, though merely foot-tall, cavity beneath the thick-timbered flooring. Only the cinder-block milk house with its slab floor discouraged their digging.

Nestled in a cluster, the barn and outbuildings lie at the lip of an embankment that drops away eastward into bottomland adjacent to the Bitterroot River. To the west, two acre-and-a-half paddocks unroll on either side of our sandy drive out to the rural two-lane highway. On westward, the scene is a pastoral one, of a few ranches and farms—beef cattle, Holstein dairy cows, horses and mules and llamas, irrigated hayfields, the tidy rows of a cherry orchard—all laid out on the almost imperceptible incline of the valley floor, running to the foot of the mountains.

Looming as the valley's western horizon are the jagged, heavily glacier-scored peaks of the Bitterroot Range—eastern front of what's geologically termed the Idaho batholith, or ten thousand square miles of granite formed when molten magma rose into the earth's crust more than 50 million years ago. Long-held geological theories have pointed to the more sedimentary substance of the Sapphire Mountains, defining the valley's eastern edge, as having formed in a great eastward slide off the front of the Bitterroots. In newer postulations, some geologists describe the magma of the Bitterroots as actually pulling westward, out from under the Sapphires, then floating like a lumpy air mattress to the top of the earth's crust. Everyone, however, agrees that the material of the Bitterroot Mountains is compatible with the term *batholith*, meaning "deep rock." After this eruption—whichever form it took—a protracted wet period set in. The newly emerged Bitterroots were wet enough, I'm told by Jim Sears, professor of geology at the University of Montana, to have made their own weather and fed the river captured in their creation. Sears believes that the Bitterroot River of today is only a "tiny remnant of a vast system" that once had its headwaters near what we know as Sun Valley, Idaho. From there it flowed north into the Bitterroot Valley. "Evidence is in the gravel itself," Sears says. Pebbles of salmon-pink quartzite that abound in a Bitterroot Valley gravel quarry,* amazingly, match Sun Valley rock types. The river then likely flowed on northward, following the great Rocky Mountain Trench into Canada.

When Patrick and I look at our *Rand McNally Road Atlas*, the one we carried in the wagon with us, we see the Montana-Idaho border forming a west-looking face and the Bitterroot Valley lying in the profiled nose. The river, with its headwaters near the tip of the nose, flows north for approximately ninety miles—a rushing mountain creek relaxing into meandering braids on the valley floor. We can follow it, running a finger along the squiggly blue line, to where it joins the Clark Fork River near Missoula, Montana, and then runs west into the Columbia drainage. This short slip of a river that we see on our map today, Sears says, is rooted in "something big" that happened 17 million years ago: A lot of faulting and the eruption of vast lava lakes in Oregon and Washington precipitated releases of carbon dioxide that brought about a global climate change. One fault pushed right through Missoula, turning the course of the ancestral Bitterroot River west. Other faults, to the

*On Airport Road in Stevensville.

south, shaping a further southern reach of the Bitterroot Range, set in place the mountains of today's Lost Trail Pass (at the base of the nose)—thus cutting off the headwaters of the ancestral river while creating the familiar headwaters of the Missouri River.

During this time, after the major forming of the mountains and the following extended wet period (which, I shouldn't fail to note, routered a canyon almost comparable in depth to the Grand Canyon, though nearer in character to Hells Canyon of the Snake River), the weather of the region swung in great arcs, from extreme wet to extreme dry. Forty million years ago, Sears tells me, the Bitterroot River ran in all its ancestral glory quite like the Nile—a north-flowing desert river. Accompanying the desert climate was a gently tipping, Serengeti-like plain that rose from today's Dakota states west to the Sapphires. Upon this plain, camels and rhinos roamed! Over the course of the dry periods, the Bitterroot Valley filled up with silt and clays and gravel, as the river's low flow continually dropped deposits. Then in the wet periods, a Mississippi-sized river carried off huge amounts of sediment and carved new channels. Well-core drillings some twelve miles south of Victor tell us the ancestral riverbed is 2,500 feet beneath the current valley floor.

To complicate matters, as the ancient river left behind its floodplain terraces, the ensuing dry periods with flash flooding brought outwashes of mud and sediment from the bordering mountain ranges, creating a layering effect in the valley's margins.

The last series of global geological events to influence greatly the look of the valley was the ice age, or ages, that began two million years ago and lasted until roughly ten thousand years ago, at which time, up in the Bitterroot Mountains the remnants of larger glaciers were still scouring U-shaped furrows in the granite. Nowadays, tributary streams—small watersheds in themselves—drain the dramatic ice-gouged canyons; they course out of the mountains at intervals of two to seven miles and wend their way through timber, pasture, and backyards to join the main river. Moose, elk, mule deer, white-tailed deer, mountain lion, and black bear commonly move along these drainages.

At the tail end of the ice age, Glacial Lake Missoula backed up into the Bitterroot Valley a number of times—no one's certain just how many—but, unlike in other areas, in this valley it left few telltale signs (or perhaps it's that few remain).* What a person sees driving into the Bitterroot today is a valley floor gently sloping from the river to the base of the mountains, overlaid by earth fingers and alluvial fans reaching back toward the valley center. The westside fans (named for their shape) are glacial outwashes. The south valley fingers are moraines, crooked into the configuration of commas—formed when glaciers, advancing onto the valley floor, melted and dumped their jumble of sediment. The jutting fingers on the east side of the valley are different in origin; they are flat-topped sedimentary benches left standing between fiercely stream-eroded draws. The subsequently exposed layerings in the eastside benches offer us viewings of the ages, and they sometimes give up treasures. Ancestral camel bones, from a dry period more than two million years ago, have been found in the brown (or younger) gravel on the south side of the Sunset Bench. The nonglaciated Sapphire

*Glacial Lake Missoula was a mammoth backup of water, comparable in size to modern-day Lake Ontario, caused when the Purcell Trench glacier flowed south and plugged the Clark Fork River in the area of today's Pend Oreille Lake, Idaho. The waters, at their highest, rose in the Bitterroot Valley to 4,350 feet. Eventually, the lake waters floated the ice plug, washing it away, and the lake evacuated (in a matter of days, it is thought) like the flushing of a giant toilet bowl—the largest flood in known geological record—leaving dramatic evidence of its force all the way to the Pacific Ocean. The advancing end of the Lobe then formed a new plug.

Range presents a lower profile—softly rounded, more hill-like. It also contributes feeder streams to the main river, though fewer in number and of less in volume than those flowing out of the Bitterroots. At its widest, the valley is ten to twelve miles across, although it's approximately eight where we have taken up residence. The bench on which the barn sits is of more recent making—carved, all the same, by the action of the river—yet no longer within the five-hundred-year floodplain.

The Bitterroot Valley—as we saw it upon our arrival—surrounded east, west, and south by designated wilderness or national forest, offered up a unique rural fringe. The town of Missoula lies just to the north: the population was roughly 43,000 in a county of 78,000.* The peaks of the Bitterroots, in the sunsets of these modern times, stand as a flatiron gateway to the Bitterroot-Salmon-Selway Wilderness—largest remaining intact wilderness in the contiguous forty-eight.†

As for the wildlife inhabiting the rural fringe, there is, of course, the species *Resident bitterrooters* (sometimes quite wild!) and then the myriad of other species. Large herds of elk migrate down onto grassy slopes, in winter at times clear to the river. Bobcat and marten prowl the side canyons by night, red fox and fisher also by day. Porcupine and skunk come waddling across roads, often to be squished under wheels. A few bighorn sheep occasionally slip into a farmer's hayfield;

Town might sound like the wrong term for a municipality the size of Missoula, but in this state, often prized as the "Last Best Place," *city* is not a word in common usage.

†Bitterroot-Salmon-Selway Wilderness is a name I've concocted to denote the areas included in the Selway-Bitterroot Wilderness and the Frank Church River of No Return Wilderness through which the Salmon River runs. Together, these two wilderness areas encompass parts of six national forests: the Bitterroot National Forest, the Clearwater National Forest, the Lolo National Forest, the Nez Perce National Forest, the Salmon National Forest, and the Payette National Forest.

coyotes roam willfully the hillsides and river bottom. The riparian habitats are home to raccoon, beaver, muskrat, otter, mink, weasel, and ermine. Our yellow-bellied marmots abound, taking up residence not only under barns, outbuildings, and woodpiles but in the river's rock riprap. Substantial communities of Columbian ground squirrels that in their homemaking riddle meadows with leg-breaking holes provide ample opportunity for "varmint hunting" (a Montana pastime, advertised as such in tourist literature, and typically accompanied by a six-pack of beer). The jackrabbit, it is said, is mostly gone—not a breeding pair left, hunted out for food, fun, and what is termed nuisance. Mountain cottontail, though, can sometimes still be seen in the drier sagebrush draws. Sticking to the illusory high-and-away are wily lynx and shy mountain goat. Plus a few grizzly, or perhaps merely their ghosts, ranging far back in the mountains . . . while down in town, a proposed federal reintroduction program would soon raise hair, ire, and fierce controversy.

Land linkages to other expanses of wilderness are now considered essential for the larger, farther-ranging mammals—for maintaining viable gene pools against extinction. The Bitterroot Valley, we were to learn, is crucially situated in the paths of these animals. A biological corridor—also called a least cost route (to the safety of the animal)—connecting the Bitterroot-Salmon-Selway with the Glacier–Bob Marshall Wilderness, crosses Highway 93 in the Bitterroot Valley's northern third. (The other corridor connecting these two wildernesses involves an even more formidable road crossing, that of Interstate 90 west of Missoula.) The corridor that connects the Bitterroot-Salmon-Selway with the Greater Yellowstone Wilderness crosses Highway 93 at the base of the nose. Taking a simplistic view of preservation—that is, with only one variable—it is the largest protected parks and wilderness areas that will, over the long term, because of their size, support the greatest variety of species, or the richest biodiversity.* Yet as human societies snug up against the boundaries of these areas, the "protection" tends to erode and the connecting corridors to disappear.

With the first step through the door of a seventy-five-year-old dairy barn, like the hit upside the head with the two-by-four, it came clear to me: we were thinking to make fit for humans quarters that had previously been occupied by cows and goats and chickens, sparrows and pigeons, deer mice, the occasional shrew from the creek bank, and bats. The carriage makers had begun on improvements, sheeting over the floors with four-by-twelve-foot pressboard to cover the gaping holes in urine-rotted timbers—caused by cows standing on the ground floor and, we would later learn from a neighbor, chickens kept in a corner on the second floor. The sheeting also sealed off a series of hay chutes (square holes in the upstairs floor), one above each long-gone manger. The mow (rhymes with *how*), the open, two-and-a-half-story upstairs, with large doors at either end and traditionally meant for hay storage, had been turned into the carriage makers' workshop. In an improbable sheeny show of silver, rolled insulation hung stapled against the old and breezy board-and-board siding and up across the rafters. In all, it formed an impressively high reflective arch. Out of this grand vaulted space dropped two rows of utilitarian fluorescent lighting, stretching the room's length. Additional electrical wiring, strung along the walls inside conduit, offered outlets every twelve feet.

The ground floor had lately been used as storage for

*Biodiversity, short for biological diversity and a rather new term in our vocabulary, has been defined as the collective variety of species that make up the living world.

wagon and buggy parts, with a walled-off room that served as a business office. The day we arrived, Bill Benish was still carrying out wheel hubs and fellies and spokes, ash tongues and shafts, and a dozen of the steam-bent oak bows for covered wagons. We chose the downstairs for our primary living space and, to bring it into the age of Edison, dropped extension cords down the still plentiful pass-throughs in the open studding. The downstairs walls were wainscoted with horizontal rough-sawn pine, with the upper halves sporting bare Sheetrock. Daylight filtered in through small and dirty four-paned windows—five on the long sides and one on either side of the north (or front) door. To anyone entering, six massive posts define the main floor's central passageway while carrying the stout center beams that in turn support the mow's floor joists. The posts over the years had been polished to a sheen from the brush of passing animals. The beams dripped black and white with bird poop. Dangling overhead, in precariously attached chunks, from all the cracks between the mow's original floorboards, was a now dried substance—an amalgam, it would seem, of the chaff sifting down from the mow and the body steam rising off animals. (As I describe this latter, it doesn't sound so awfully bad. The truth? It looked like a ceiling of dingleberries!) With tools adapted from bent nails, wires, and screwdrivers, we picked and scraped for two days until the ceiling came clean above the areas where we planned to cook and eat.

Just inside the front door, a wide staircase to the mow takes off to the left. On past it is a cubbyhole room the carriage men had planned to convert into a bathroom. We pronounced it our mud room (boot, coat, hat, coverall, and tool storage) and then designated the office, next down the line, for a roomy bathroom. After washing windows and sweeping away gauzy cobwebs and scatterings of mouse turds, we laid out our self-inflating mattresses and bedroll opposite the staircase. This was the cool spot for afternoon naps, with the mow reaching for 100°F by noon. Beyond the bathroom, where the area opens up, we positioned two ladder-back chairs and a maple picnic-style table—a 1942 Macy's special that had once belonged to my parents. Across the central passage from the bathroom, we created a kitchen by hanging a utility reflector light from an overhead nail and fashioning counters out of two work benches and a 1950s Formica-topped dinette table, all conveniently bequeathed us by the carriage makers. The rest we set up as camp: two large Igloo coolers, our two-burner propane stove, and, hanging from more overhead nails, my set of cast-iron frying pans and Patrick's three long-handled crepe pans.

Dishwashing we had at first managed open-air style, by lining up buckets and the dish drainer along the edge of the porch. After hiring a backhoe operator, laying water lines in from the well, and installing a hot water heater, washing machine, and bathtub, we moved to doing dishes in the tub—a backbreaking arrangement. But now, with my new sink, we could haul water from the tub in a dishpan and—tra-la!—wash dishes standing up. The dish drainer had itself a home, as did the pots and pans and flatware and dish towels, plus any number of other things I might choose to tuck into the drawers and cupboards.

I leaned back against the barn in a glow of satisfaction. I was in a mood to admire everything: the richness of the marmot's brown-and-yellow coat, a weaving of colors, a hairdresser might call it. One clap of my hands and he disappeared, black snoot first, down a gap in the jumble of wood. At the final sight of His Bulbousness squeezing between the boards, I laughed out loud. Bent on finishing my project, I tossed a good night to the loquacious marmot and the biggest Big Dipper I had ever seen. Then I scooped up my new enamel drawers and strolled inside.

. . .

There is an unspoken right of passage in the Bitterroot, in probably much of the West, having to do with the ordeal of your first winter. If you don't pass the thirty to sixty below windchills in an uninsulated house trailer banked with hay bales, a packer's wall tent, a tepee, or a shanty such as our leaky-sided barn; if you don't somehow suffer a grim, harrowing, bitter existence, survivable by only the toughest-of-nails individuals; if you don't emerge in spring with a hairy story to tell and retell, you forever remain an outsider to the old-timers. It was with flags and banners and the tooting of horns that we passed.

During the sweltering days of late August, when the mercury was riding at 104°F, we had sat down and parceled out our meager savings for projects of immediacy: drinking and washing water; fences and shelters for the horses. A sufficient means for heating the barn was the farthest thing from our minds. (From mine purely because I was melting so, I couldn't imagine ever being cold again; from Patrick's because he takes things as they come, and icicles were not on the afternoon horizon.) A commercial-sized propane heater, installed by the carriage company, hung well above head height in the mow. A little too blithely we imagined cutting a hole in the floor, positioning a square summer fan in the opening, and blowing heat downstairs. When the time came for it, when an Arctic clipper scudding down from Canada sent the ambient outside temperature to twenty-four below (inside, twenty-three below), I stood directly beneath the propane heater and recalled all too keenly my high school physics: heat rises. No balmy whiffle reached my head, let alone the story below me. The howling north wind, whistling effortlessly through gaping cracks in the old barn siding, whisked every calorie of warmth out the peak.

With Patrick's having grown up in and around Sault Sainte Marie, Michigan—the hardscrabble Upper Peninsula country against the Canadian border—for much of the time in an uninsulated house, he had a stash of tricks for winter survival, in addition to an old tin woodstove from his tepee days. We removed one of the small barn windows, nailed up a sheet of gray mortarboard, and, through the hole we carved in its center, ran a stovepipe out twelve feet, laughably for code. We finished it off with a four-foot, right-angled upturn at the end. Bingo! We had heat! We also had a stove that regularly billowed black smoke, and we had a serious weekly project of disassembling and cleaning out the pipes in which creosote collected as swiftly, I thought, as black ice on the road out front spun passing vehicles. From storage, we dragged home more dining chairs to plant in a semicircle around the stove. If I retreated farther than three feet from its glowing girth, all benefit of warmth was lost. One morning we awoke to bombs going off, bottles of Calistoga water left on the floor—frozen and exploding. When not in bed, I lurked close by the stove. Like a rabbit turning on a spit, I scorched first one side, then the other, at once freezing and broiling: just part of the annealing of body, character, and soul in a good first winter. Patrick, it seemed, required no further toughening, and he wasn't nearly as cold.

Being a person of slow pulse and low blood pressure, underactive thyroid and lousy arterial circulation, I was inspired to call Northern Outfitters in Salt Lake City, a company that supplies clothing for arctic expeditions, and order up an ensemble—Federal Express. For the next two months, I wore my gargantuan boots and foam-filled snowsuit, the latter outdoors, indoors, and to bed. This roly-poly getup of insulation, however, did nothing to save me from the outhouse, and no one hereabouts bothered to counsel me until our second winter in the contriving of a freezing-weather seat—something fashioned by sawing a hole in a square of Styrofoam, material that instantly assumes the temperature of one's bum. Mine turned red, then black. Slipping into bed at night looking the picture of the Pillsbury Doughboy robbed me of every trace of sensuality, not to mention all romantic convenience. The steaminess of Patrick's and my relationship slowed to the flow of an icebound creek, muffled tricklings beneath deep layers awaiting the spring thaw.

Our first Christmas was one I'll not forget. During the pre-holiday deep-freeze days, the bathroom pipes on the outside wall, those stubbed in for a sink not yet installed and thus gone unnoticed, froze and cracked. On the afternoon of Christmas Eve, aided by a bright sun and two little electric heaters, the bathroom warmed up enough to unleash the powers of Oceanus and Tethys. I walked in and found a six-foot geyser showering the room. That night, while Santa stuffed stockings around the world, we were kept busy in a similar up-and-down rhythm: stoking the stove, repositioning the heaters, and running the bathtub tap to dislodge slush forming in the trap. I confess now it was only Patrick who was up and down, gallantly tending to things. Though I supplied, I'm certain, invaluable spiritual support from under my hummock of covers. As the sun came up we fell asleep. It was four o'clock in the afternoon when I began cooking our Christmas dinner on the camp stove—a meal of boiled red potatoes with butter, and watermelon pickles. Cooking at such temperatures necessitated wearing mittens, to keep my fingers from freezing to the utensils. After dining we locked up and, in a screaming fit of cabin fever, minus one thought as to what might be playing, drove the twelve miles to the Roxy, the small-town theater in Hamilton. In two-foot-high black letters—plain as all hell—the marquee read MISERY, the title of the Stephen King horror flick.

Bitterroot Valley &
Bitterroot River Watershed
(a simplistic view)

Missoula

MONTANA

IDAHO

Lolo Crk.

Lolo

Carlton Crk.
One Horse Crk.
Sweeney Crk.
Bass Crk.
Kootenai Crk.

Florence

SAPPHIRE

Threemile Crk.

Big Crk.
Sweathouse Crk.
Bear Crk.

Stevensville

Burnt Fork Bitterroot River

Fred Burr Crk.
Sheafman Crk.
Mill Crk.
Blodgett Crk.

Victor

Canyon Crk.
Sawtooth Crk.
Roaring Lion Crk.

Corvallis

Eastside Hwy

BITTERROOT MOUNTAINS

Hamilton

MOUNTAINS

Skalkaho Crk.

Sleeping Child Crk.

Lost Horse Crk.

Rock Crk.

Lake
Como

Darby

Rye Crk.

Tin Cup Crk.

Hwy 93

Sula

East Fork Bitterroot River

Trapper Crk.

43

Nez Perce Fork

West Fork Bitterroot River

to Big Hole

IDAHO

MONTANA

IDAHO

MONTANA

Hwy 93

Hwy 93 to Salmon, ID.

N

An Abridged History of
Bitterroot Settlement

For longer than is conjurable, the heavily timbered Bitterroot watershed, with its sunny grassy exposures and bankside willowy red osier, was part of the home ground of a seasonally nomadic people: the indigenous Salish. Their cultural history dates back ten to twelve thousand years, as evidenced in the place-names that tribal elders and linguists tell us are among the oldest words in the Salish language. What we presently know as Sleeping Child Hot Springs is, in Salish, Snetetšé, or Place of the Sleeping Baby.* Many local place-names are rooted in Salish creation stories woven with geological descriptions of the last ice age. The Bitterroot Valley, tucked within the Northwest's interior procession of high, snow-clad, and formidably rocky mountains, offered the Salish a mild miniclimate. The area bore game, a variety of berries, and the prized bulbs of camas and bitterroot flowers. To hunt buffalo, the Salish traveled south over the Continental Divide into the Big Hole Valley and adjacent valleys. To lay in winter caches of fish, they journeyed west and north to prime spots on the Snake and Columbia Rivers.

*Noted here with permission; *The Salish People and the Lewis and Clark Expedition*, published by the Salish–Pend d'Oreille Culture Committee.

The first group of white men, and one black man, arrived in the valley in 1805. They were Meriwether Lewis and William Clark with their military entourage, the Corps of Discovery, commissioned by President Thomas Jefferson to find a northwest water passage to the Pacific.* After wintering in the Mandan villages of what would later become South Dakota, they were accompanied west by the Shoshone woman Sacagawea, her infant son, and her husband, the French trader Toussaint Charbonneau. The search for the Missouri River's headwaters eventually led the expedition across what we call Montana—up the Jefferson River, the Beaverhead River, and finally to Lemhi Pass, where, topping out at the Continental Divide, they dropped into Indian villages that are today the towns of Tendoy and Salmon, Idaho. Finding the westward-draining Salmon River impassable (it was soon dubbed the River of No Return), they were forced to abandon the idea of continued boat passage to the Pacific. The party instead turned north and, ascending a tortuous pass—perhaps a short distance west of what is now Lost Trail Pass—arrived at the beginnings of another watershed, the Bitterroot's.

After the expedition's passing back through on their return trip from the coast the following summer, the Bitterroot Valley remained fairly untouched by white notions of progress for the next fifty years—or, as one Anglo account describes it: Nothing happened. White settlement of the Bitterroot began in the mid-1800s. By the 1880s, a wild-paced migration had a good start on establishing eight frontier towns. The Northern Pacific transcontinental railroad began to service Missoula in 1883. A spur up the Bitterroot, laid in 1887, brought its first passengers to the boomtown of

---

*The expedition's name, Corps of Discovery, is being seen by many nowadays as containing within it arrogance and the diminution of long-standing cultures in established territories—as though the existence of such sprang into being only with the entrance of Europeans.

Victor. Silver mining, fruit farming, timber, and land specu-
lation became rollicking businesses. As was typical everywhere in the settling of the arid West, water wars soon broke
out—here, over rights to creek allotments. In the years to
follow, various local investment groups constructed small
impoundment dams for irrigation on a score of the river's
western tributaries. Money from as far away as Chicago built
the grand Eastside Canal (known locally as the Big Ditch),
which took water from Como Lake and in an elaborate system of canals conveyed it the length of the valley. Immense
in scope, it was a land development scheme resembling that
of the railroads: adjacent lands were bought up cheaply and
upon completion of the project sold for high dollar—in this
case, picked up for as little as $2.50 an acre and turned over
for as much as $1,000. In 1910, as part of the Chicago-based
interests, the architect Frank Lloyd Wright designed an
upscale hotel, the Bitter Root Inn, for a town of the same
name (platted five and a half miles northeast of today's town
of Stevensville). With the Big Ditch completed, the inn became the north valley sales headquarters for the Bitter Root
District Irrigation Co. and its associated lands.

In an effort to lure settlers to the valley, local merchants
and realtors, the railroad, the Board of County Commissioners, the Chamber of Commerce, the Bitter Root Fruit
Growers' Association, the orchard-land companies as in
McIntosh-Morello Orchards, Inc.—and no entity more so
than the Bitter Root District Irrigation Co.—engaged in
shameless advertising:

The Land of the MacIntosh Red
No worms

No crop failures

All apples—fancy apples.
*—The Board of County Commissioners of Ravalli
County and the Bitter Root Fruit Growers'
Association; an advertisement*

"Where apples are better in color, flavor, and keeping qualities than are any other apples in the world—'the only apple that can be eaten fearlessly in the dark.' "

". . . crop failures are unknown and always will be."
—*Bitter Root District Irrigation Co.; promotional brochure*

Regarding climate: "There are no blizzards, no tornadoes, no violent thunderstorms, no oppressive heat in summer and no stinging blasts in winter."

Regarding roads: "Nature has supplied us with an erosive ballast that keeps them in perfect condition; no dust to soil you, or rock to shake you."
—*Chamber of Commerce literature*

"To those who have never seen Bitter Root apples, they are certainly a revelation. Large, luscious, brilliant, perfect in form and color, not a worm hole or a blemish in a hundred thousand boxes, they are the most remarkable product on earth."
—*From governmental reports about the Bitterroot;*
Bureau of Agriculture, Labor, and Industry, Helena, MT

The BRDI Co. (today it's the BRID Co.) purchased six chauffeured Locomobiles—splendorously long, red, convertible touring cars. Prospective settlers, already arriving by free rail from the East, were greeted with fanfare in Missoula and delivered in style to the new inn. There the lavishness continued in food and drink until they signed on. Those parties who had purchased their land sight unseen before heading west were shown directly to their property, where they were unceremoniously dumped.

The apple crops peaked a decade later, in 1921, the fruit's quality and quantity waning because of nitrogen-depleted soils. Then a series of hard winters—1922, 1923, and 1924—destroyed a substantial portion of the trees. The climate was never right for the large-scale commercial apple enterprises.

The boom was finished. Much of the land reverted to the county for unpaid taxes, and in 1924, as if to remove reminder, the Bitter Root Inn burned. The town of Bitter Root then vanished, save for three of the old houses, still occupied today.

Silver mining also had petered out, earlier, in 1893, with repeal of the government's buying program, the Sherman Silver Purchase Act. Prices crashed overnight, precipitating closures of mines and mills. Yet the Bitterroot had been permanently claimed for progress; nothing underscored that more than the government's relocation (in 1891) of the last band of Salish to a reservation north of Missoula. Small groups from the tribe continued to come south on hunting and gathering forays, but understanding of their nomadic ways and empathy for their displacement were generally lacking among the settlers. The clashes that ensued became increasingly ugly.

Timber, ranching, and farming have prevailed now for more than a century—through periods of boom, bust, storm, and drought. About the time Patrick and I set down in Victor, the heavily resource-based economy was beginning to come seriously undone and a new kind of living was under way. Environmentalists were successfully shutting down timber sales. Tourism was being touted as a panacea for economic depression; personalized invitations to visit Montana were being mailed out from the governor's office (you could send over the addresses of your relatives and friends). Heavyweight land developers with big plans started filtering in. Real estate agents and construction contractors sensed a wave swelling large on the horizon. Our enduring barn looked out on U.S. Highway 93, the north-south rural two-lane that within two years would come under study for a four- and five-lane improvement. Contained in the fine print: a NAFTA corridor connecting Canada to Mexico.

BAREFOOT-HEARTED

Twisted into Corkscrews

Living on This Earth Is No Simple Matter

In setting up housekeeping in our new domicile, we became the first of the species *Homo sapiens* to nest-build and vie for domain under the broad gambrel roof. During the long-light days of summer, we'd made acquaintance with the extended marmot family. As nights chilled down and they took seriously to hibernation, another species lobbied for top contender of our space.

Had someone asked me, before we moved into the barn, to sit down and ponder the worldwide parade of wildlife that humans have displaced, I'd have listed grizzly bears and wolves, caribou and turtles, coyotes perhaps, whales and manatees, certainly all the spectacular African beasts, and a broad range of brilliantly graceful waterfowl. Never mice! In the perennial trigger-finger and backhoe desiccation wrought on the world by humans, some species fare better than others. Some are the fortunate ones, the ones we take to passionately with preservation in mind (albeit, frequently after they're almost gone). Pandas we love. Snakes, skunks, slugs, grubs, mice—though equally sentient beings in the eyes of any great spirit, are to most of us two-leggeds not so cuddly. In our first years in the barn, we were overrun with deer mice. We caught them with traps, old-fashioned ones we bought at the hardware store, Victor brand, two for $1.25.

The war was on. Miniature massacres took place daily, and the traps required attention. Without pang of conscience, I went about my tasks, never once thinking that in staking out a place to live I shouldn't just clear away whatever critters were distasteful to me. Extirpation full ahead: I'd been taught well by my lineage. Here in the northern New World, such behavioral characteristics are traceable directly to my own muttlike bloodlines: Irish, English, French, and Germanic peoples, a smidgen of Dutch, and then the hearty Scottish clan, descended—my mother once read, to her horror—from cannibals. These were the folks in the westward claiming and taming of America who had seized every spot that was to their liking, appropriated unbidden rights to mow down all irritants standing in their way. Pomposity. I was, it appeared, a further shining example.

I found it amazing that we required no cheese for the traps; it took only a bit of fibrous material, invariably a scrap of shredded yarn, brushed with a hint of peanut butter, to snag their teeth. Tucking the lure into the curve of the bait pedal, I set each spring-loaded mechanism, oh so carefully, so as not to trigger a sudden mashing of my thumb. I performed my half of the baiting and disposal chores dutifully—shirking only when it wasn't too obvious. Patrick's balanced outlook on male and female workloads, careers, opportunities was, upon our meeting, part of his great appeal. His unique "equal-everything-equal" philosophy, so suited to my own, most likely harkened back to 1975 when NOW, the National Organization for Women, started chipping away at the traditional family foundations in his hometown in Michigan. A friend corralled him into "filling up a chair" at the initial get-together. When the evening closed on Chippewa

County's new chapter of NOW, it was Patrick who was its secretary. What woman doesn't love the man who will do, if not quite half the cooking, then more than half the dishes! Wash his own clothes! Sew on his own buttons! Yet, naturally, a female counterpart must pull back from throwing over her own set of philosophies just because an instance turns fusty—just because Patrick's current "Your turn today!" applied to grim mice chores. To *my* emptying the traps. I now admit I fell disgracefully short of the mark. But my probable 30 percent felt, at the time, like 85. I was, indeed, plagued by a pervasive sense of ickiness—a dread of having to touch the dead bodies. Still, I took a certain pride in coping better than one woman I met. She lived for a spell in an old farmhouse ravaged by mice, and with every cold carcass, so as not to lay fingers on it, she tossed out a spanking new mousetrap, then dashed to the store and purchased another dozen.

With autumn full on, the mice were burrowing into walls and under floors, stashing supplies for the long, cold months ahead. Their scamperings took them everywhere. This hulk of a structure, red paint faded and peeling, was their legacy. For how many generations? I tried to imagine. Calculating conservatively, the female deer mouse, or *Peromyscus maniculatus*, has three litters per year. With four pups (or pinkies) to a batch, two or three of which are themselves females capable of reproducing within five to six weeks, the numbers amass to 210 generations since the building of the barn. Not taking into account loss by disease, embryo mortality, old age (at two years), predation by owl, fox, coyote, and human hand, and beginning the tally each spring with a judiciously estimated number of five females "in the family way," I came up with a sum that rose exponentially to 90,000 mice!

.   .   .

It was an October afternoon in the old hay mow, long since cleared of the last stem of timothy, and I sat at my computer. Almost a reflex swiveled my gaze from the screen and heeled it floor level to the corner of a red metal filing cabinet, pillar to the sheet of plywood serving as my writing desk. She was in cross-floor sprint, perhaps reconnoitering another cache for seeds. Our roving glances linked, and we fell fixed—each full upon the face of the other.

Yi! Who are you?

Well, who are you?

The strange, instant warmth that flooded my heart—something reserved for sisters—led me to believe this small mammal was a she-mouse. She had come fully into view before skidding to stone. Taken together, her soft eyes, her big, round ears, her crop of fine whiskers arching off sides of a slender nose supplied the perfect complement to a plump gray frame, white at the underbelly, and riding atop scores of minuscule footsteps. Ours was a meeting of aliens, a brush with utterly foreign, even enemy worlds: we might have been cockatoo and snow leopard, horny toad and great blue whale. The air between us held surprise mingling with curiosity—all shot through with wariness, trepidation, defense of territory. We were perhaps more like long-standing, hostile heads of state, momentarily come to the bargaining table.

It was her barn!

It was my barn!

My heart beat with the suddenness of our encounter. It had halted my work as abruptly as someone's throwing an ax through it. I found myself trying desperately not to move, not to scare her. I barely breathed. Our mute, unflinching stares stretched to fill minutes, almost going over to sweetness and friendship, sweetness definitely on my part. Whatever was she thinking? Or feeling? Suddenly the phone rang, seeming to bounce out of its cradle. In a scurry of tiny toes, she spun, streaked back along her route of entry, and was gone.

Just as suddenly the phone ceased ringing, and I sat in silence. Then a thundering guilt of the ages washed down over me like a mountain avalanche. Deep sadness. Uncrossable chasm. The sight of her—the innocence!—inked its permanence on my memory.

I thought of our nights with the trap line set, ten altogether, cleverly baited and stationed in obvious runways throughout the barn. *Whap!* A trap's springing, piercing the cool night air, could bring me fully awake. Snuggled safely beneath quilted layers, curved to the sweet warmth of Patrick, I often listened to the *plap-plap-plap* of some little bugger with a leg caught, dragging the trap across the floor. Then more slowly. *Plap. Plap.* By morning there were corpses, drools of coagulated blood, the crushed skulls and chests of stiff, warmthless bodies lying torqued into grotesque shapes—a head turned half around, pink twigs of legs thrust at odd, immodest angles. In trying to wrench free, some had twisted themselves into corkscrews. Others seemed barely hurt, yet just as dead. Had those last died of fright? Given up at the overwhelming odds? Or had they parted this planet with broken hearts, at the unfairness of it all?

To a mouse spouse, I wondered, would it be like a husband's going out for a carton of milk and never returning? Certainly they do not couple as wedded partners in the sense that we do. Partnerships, of any sort, probably don't exist—promiscuity their way of life. Yet at least one species of mice (the house mouse) we know lives in groups, sharing escape hatches and communal eating and toilet areas—they even groom each other. What, then, does their assemblage think when a spot at the breakfast table comes up empty? The ill-fated ones in our barn died without family (so it appeared), their only partner in death, struggle against the Victor vise. I felt oddly grateful for the ones with smashed skulls: the instantaneousness of it.

The thought of dying alone or of suffering slowly is to most humans unthinkable. How could we be certain that mice, in their own way, were any different? Humans and mice share 97 percent of their deoxyribonucleic acid (DNA), a substance associated with the transmission of genetic information. In the evolutionary chain, it was not long ago that we forked apart. And it had taken only that one unwavering, unfeigned look upon that delicate face, the face of another mortal—a warm-bodied being, small of frame but perhaps not of stature, with digestive tract and reproductive organs much like my own, and for whom I had plans tonight to set the deadly traps—to start my mind paddling back over my own closest experiences with death.

There had been a time when I sat quietly at the bedside of my father and then, eight years later, of my mother, stroking a forehead or an arm, holding a hand. The strong grasp that had once punched and tugged and lifted a world around, for ninety-two years in my mother's case, gradually surrendered and for all practical purposes lay limp. In my hand, hers was no heavier than a leaf that has been pressed between pages of a book. Her skin had taken on the translucent properties of cellophane, affording little camouflage to the port-dark delta of veins still carrying along blood, giving me the sensation I might see my own hand by looking down through hers. My father, at the end of seven months of diagnosed lung cancer, lay quietly for the final five days, in a coma in his own bed, an intravenous catheter in his arm to receive the morphine.

During the days, Mother and friends and I had gathered with him on the big bed. Nights, his wife alone curled to him. It was a scene I'll not forget, that bedroom of twenty-two years: carpet worn into shiny paths, Father's force reduced to slender bends beneath a light bedsheet, his forehead and cheeks gone waxen and white. With facial plumpness vanished, flesh laying close to bone, his aquiline nose became an even longer, thinner, and somewhat ungainly protuberance, accentuated all the more, laced as it was with plastic tubing winding to a green torpedo of oxygen. In the low light of the room, his skin took on an almost phosphorescent glow. For the large-framed, physically meaty, and dynamically inventive, the sometimes irreverent and ribald and explosive man I had known him to be, his last hours were wreathed in an uncanny, ethereal stillness. Just the basics, I thought: skin, bone, light breaths. What a time to know him—in this simplicity—this world without words and assumptions and expectations. His heart slowed and the space between breaths lengthened ever so gradually, until, at the end, his labored inhalations seemed minutes apart.

I never honored my father's last request; I couldn't bring myself to it at the time. Now, years later, I wish that I had—and not coddled my own needs. You had to have known my father to understand his outlandish request as befitting of his humor and his Great Depression–based horror of wasting money. He had said with an oddly drollish sincerity, not as a way of self-deprecation, "Just put me out with the Thursday garbage." When I picked up his box of ashes from the crematorium, I clung to it with a protective fierceness. My father inside a garbage can? Then inside a clanging garbage truck, slathered with slime, foul and reeking stuff on its way to becoming sludge, compacted along with tossed-out Big Mac wrappers and soiled disposable diapers, slick-paper junk mail, plastic popcorn and bubble wrap, moldering leftovers sprung from the backs of refrigerators, scooped-up lumps of stinking cat litter and backyard doggie shit—all buzzing with flies? Not on your life! I wasn't certain what dreadful things might befall a person who violated deathbed wishes, but no matter what I imagined, I couldn't make myself deposit that box, smaller than a shoe box, rattling with the last physical remnants of my father, into that big, cavernous, brown plastic garbage can. Though I did buy him a drink, and I think he would have liked that.

My friend Ronita and I took him for dry martinis and a Maine lobster dinner—Father's two favorite things in the world—at Scoma's on San Francisco Bay. We ordered for him, and then drank and ate for him. "Another for Harold please!" We pointed to the third chair, empty save for a peach-colored Chloe shopping bag with matching tissue paper peaking out the top: Father's box of bone shards masquerading as a just-purchased Victorian negligee.

Some years before their deaths, my parents had made their cremation arrangements. When the time came for my mother, a man from the funeral society arrived with a bareboard gurney. He was drunk and disheveled. He wrapped her body in a sheet of tough, clear plastic, without ceremony, the way you would roll up a rug. Working as if alone in his carpet warehouse, he threw her first one way, then another—getting the job done. I wilted when he whipped the plastic around her head, encasing her white wisps of hair, and snugged it across her face. It lent her that quizzical look of someone's pressing a nose to a windowpane, thumbs in ears, fingers waving, "Nyah, nyah!" But in her case: an immutable good-bye. "She can't BREATHE!" I cried. I should have punched him.

All in all, the serene and natural manner of my parents' deaths had been a gift. Their easings out of this world had been strangely lovely, infused with a miracle quality like a birthing—an ethereal gearing down at the other end of a springing to life. I'd felt terribly blessed, though it was a funny thing to tell anyone. Your father died on Saturday? So sorry, how awful for you. No, no, it was quite nice. Yet I never knew how either parent saw it: they were days past speech, hours past offering signs of recognition. It is said that people in a coma can hear what's taking place around them. I had hoped my presence was felt.

A very different matter of dying was the nightly carnage in our barn. No cross-country flights, no deathbed vigils, no last requests, no memorial dinners out. Had I assumed, on some level, it would be the mouse family's place to provide the hospice comfort? Or was that sort of musing absurd? Elephants are said to weep, geese to mope and mourn. Upon the death of a mate, falcons have been known to wail, while whales are thought to moan. Dian Fossey said an orphaned mountain gorilla sobbed and shed tears. Mice, perhaps, had tiny mouse emotions that took forms we didn't understand yet. One only hopes that since these small beings propagate with so much greater speed than do humans, their grieving periods might be comparably shorter; one hopes they don't have a broad capacity for heartsickness and memory; one hopes they don't require the time between copulation partners that I would, to sing for a long spell the melancholy strains of Tom Paxton, "Getting up early, remembering you."

Mornings we extricated the stilled bodies from the traps, tossing them by the tail over the back fence to become feed for magpies and crows, coyote and fox. Then we reset the springs. Even with our fully baited trap line, at times the mice were everywhere. They nibbled at our locally handmade bar of Beautiful Soap and trotted around in the bathtub. Against white porcelain, tiny black feces and some sort of flea were the blatant signs. Did these mice typically crap on the move, leaving scat every few feet? Or were the small black pellets—reminiscent of in shape, but smaller than, the

Good & Plenty candy of my childhood—more a result of their frantic exertions, repeated leapings at the slippery sides in trying to get out? Was I to think they had been in the tub when there were no signs? What could I catch by soaking in the tub after one of their visits?

Their presence was not limited to our bathroom. In their rampant scavenging, they broke open bags of rice, gouged holes in butter and bread, devoured a sack of the horses' COB (corn, oats, and barley), shredded the blue felt liners to my winter pacs.* The resultant fuzz they molded with our birdseed mix—millet, peanut hearts, canary seed, hulled oats, striped sunflower seeds—to form a colorful compound with which they repacked my boots to the ankle. I began to hear stories. One woman, in remodeling her house, took apart a wall and found it stuffed stud to stud with dog food. A neighbor man found his knee-high mud boots brimming with cat food. Pack rats, wood rats, squirrels, I thought. But our deer mice were proving equally industrious. Some were smarter than others and grew to be wary critters, avoiding our traps for days. Sunflower seeds disappeared by the pound from our bird feeders and began amassing between the box springs and the mattress of our newly acquired bed. The trap line continued daily to yield two to five mice, never a diminishing supply.

In the simplest of terms, everything boils down to territory—that same territory in this world that keeps shrinking, pieces of the global pie today skimpy by hunter-gatherer standards. One particularly gruesome night of territorial display sticks in my mind.

The previous owners of the barn, the carriage makers,

---

*Winter pacs: western slang for any number of brands of clunky rubber-bottomed boots with leather uppers and removable felt or foam liners.

had rebuilt everything from buggies to covered wagons to Yellowstone stagecoaches. To create access to the mow for rolling vehicles, they cut a large double door in the south wall (as well as eight tall windows for light) and then built an outside platform and a long ramp. Horse-drawn vehicles were winched up the ramp, across the small deck, and into the mow. On all but the worst wintry and stormy nights now, Patrick and I roll out our camp bedding and sleep on that platform. Mounted on a railing, virtually over our heads, there sits a yet smaller platform: a homemade bird feeder, fashioned from a slab of fir and rimmed with pine boughs, which I purposefully positioned to complete the scene from my inside writing station. The view from my desk takes in a line of craggy mountain peaks tilted against a wide sky, horse-speckled hayfields, deer roaming the willowy river bottom, and, up close, the season's spectrum of birds— raucous, pecking and squabbling. A novelist friend of mine writes in a box of a room lacking a ray of sunlight, fearful that sights of outside life will distract her. It is a grand view that I require in order to focus small; it's the cooped up part of writing I hate. Mornings on the deck, the birds begin feeding before I open my eyes, tossing hulls and birdseed into my hair.

On the night remembered, a cavalcade of mice sprinted back and forth between the feeder and their hideaways inside the barn, trafficking birdseed and turning the deck a few inches from our heads into a thoroughfare. Eventually, some inner coil of Patrick's being came unsprung—in the wild, boinging manner of newly strung fence wire come loose at a staple. Leaping from the covers, armed with one of his size sixteen boots, he stationed himself by the obscure hole where the wee ones trailed in and out. His wait wasn't long. With boot heel for bludgeon, he smashed four or five and cavalierly raked them off the deck. This must be a male thing, I thought, something one can do after Marine Corps training. I pulled the covers over my head and shrank from the slaughter. I might have divorced him then and there, but this is the same man who is accusatory when I manage to capture flies with sticky paper. The same man who, in a pure-hearted gesture of thoughtfulness, carries a pie tin of water to the family of snakes living in summer's cool beneath the concrete slab off the milk house, allowing them a drink without their having to slither all the way to the creek. He is the man whose eyes tear up upon finding that a bat's died, unable to get loose of the mow; a hummingbird's perished, trapped and dehydrated in a shed; a cat's flattened on the highway, dried into a fur board.

We all have our various boundaries with the things we call Nature: wolves, weeds, spiders. Patrick's, that particular night, did not include precisely those mice.

Some years ago, I lived for a short time quite peaceably with mice. For the duration of a week, we shared a cabin in British Columbia. I had flown into a remote lake. There was no walking in or out—the underbrush would have worn out machetes—and I'd made arrangements for the plane's return. I went there to heal from a great loss, to scream and dance naked on the beach until I was free of pain. At first, the frenetic cabin mice afforded small comfort. But my spirits being in such a state that I blathered to myself in a steady stream of consciousness, I was soon also conversing with the little guys. Not there to judge, enlighten, or solve, they quickly became endearing buddies. Eight or ten cavorted over the countertops and shelves, speed demons and acrobats all, inspecting everything. Available to me as part of the cabin equipment—along with stove, stack of wood, and outhouse—was a "mouse drowner." It was a galvanized pail partially filled with water. Across its top was strung a tin can slathered with peanut butter, designed to spin under the weight of a mouse and fling all that passed over to a certain wet death. (Mice do swim; it's exhaustion from which they die, trying to claw their way up the pail's vertical sides, finally slipping under.)

I didn't use it. On the contrary, the furry pip-squeaks came to dinner—at my place setting on the cabin table. Though I remained the sole feaster, they moved in close, a bevy of them, shiny-eyed, looking like warm-faced friends circled around a campfire. I needed only to have sung out, "Buffalo gal, won't you come out tonight!" and surely they'd have taken up the chorus.

If my cabin mates were busy at high noon, they were busier under cloak of night. Scurrying up and down the bedposts, racing across the bare springs of the bunk overhead, periodically they would pause to peek over my shoulder, seeming to peer and puzzle at the very words on the pages of my book. Their brazen antics became my entertainment, my medicine. Within a few days, I laughed.

The more extreme tussles for territory create displacement, a clearing out of a species (or social, religious, or ethnic group)—in its worst result, extinction. Before barn living, the image I pulled forth when thinking of displacement was that of a bird. Years ago in urban California, I witnessed a lone, disoriented great egret, standing with its wispy white feathers resplendent against brittle brown weeds in the middle of a vacant triangular lot, far from any water, watching rush-hour traffic whiz by on all sides. That lot has since become a three-story office building, rising directly from the sidewalk. Were a housing development to spring up around our barn, the mice would thin down to a few stragglers, not enough to sustain the resident coyotes and great horned owls. Caroming off, the larger species would then vie for space among other coyotes and owls hovering at the edges of human habitation—those places where we live, en-sconced, and incensed by their snagging of a domestic pet.

Who then holds sway on this planet? And whose barn is it? Where do we—the ordinarily all-powerful *Homo sapiens*—draw the line with who shall live? Is it with other humans? With pandas? With grizzlies and wolves? Or with mice? How many of us would agree to protecting flies? Are the planet's biggest-brained and largest-framed species, by virtue of brilliance and bulk, flatly due inalienable rights? Are a certain number of deer mice expendable because they are not on the endangered species list? The Canadian author Farley Mowat in *Never Cry Wolf* saw clearly the interlocking relationship of mouse, wolf, and caribou—upset one and you upset it all. Vision in the wilds is not muddied by freeways and housing tracts. My own line, I'm afraid, is a broken and squiggly one, a doodle down a page. Red ants that bite like hell, I step on; the rest go free. I feel no compunction about swatting flies—sometimes there are just too bloody many of them. Bats, which many people fear and kill, I welcome: they eat moths, beetles, pesty things.

I was coming to know I was not a homestead woman, sturdy lot that they were, ringing the necks of chickens, shooting marauders, and, I would bet, never giving pause to the fate of a mouse. But I also was not—had never been, really—an urban woman of the sort we had as visitors. Two friends on separate occasions leaped onto our guest bed, which is tucked in a corner of the mow, and shrieked, "Kill it!" I inhabited some nether zone—not of the expedient past, not of the hysterical present. What my role might be with the larger animals, the endangered animals, the animals not directly underfoot, was fairly clear to me. I wasn't doing as well with our legions of deer mice. Under the gambrel roof, the paths to coexisting were grown with shin-tangle.

In a Native American legend, retold by John Steptoe in

the children's book *The Story of Jumping Mouse,* a mouse turns into an eagle. The Blackfeet believe their ancestors turn up sometimes as mice. In the eyes of many, I was not just clearing my home ground of mice; I was whacking potential eagles; I was committing mat-, pat-, grandpat-, probably all of those -ricides. Was the she-mouse whose eyes I'd held for that parturient moment my mother?

Living on this earth is no simple matter. I'm sure I have only the smallest notion of the hundreds of obscure ways, every day, I inadvertently squeeze the life out of other species in my jig through what Patrick calls our Consumer-Puke Society. Who is displacing whom? This can be a question of nightmarish twists; it can also be a question of some delicacy. I feel a curious pride that I've owned only three petroleum-propelled vehicles in almost forty years of driving, all bought used, the most expensive costing fifteen hundred dollars. I did not, however, set out with righteous intention. My conservation occurred largely as a side effect of far less noble origin—a beggarly bank account. It feels good to be living now in an old dairy barn, a structure already built and requiring no further use of raw materials. But that also was not a clear consideration in acquisition: Charm and a dirt cheap selling price had governed. I have borne no children, not in accordance with any philosophy so high-minded as planet worship, but purely out of circumstance and selfishness. Somewhat by default, I consider myself "becoming educated." Freedom that comes with membership in a dominant species does not translate to license. And humans are too many—like flies—and wanting too much.

I saw those of us choosing to inhabit the rural fringe—where patio furniture and clipped grass finger into sagebrush, riverbank, and forest—as carrying a greater responsibility than most to foster coexistence with wildness. We were the high-profile group making headlines, setting the tone for "management." There were days when I agonized: were we—the species that has learned to settle with more permanence than most—to go on forever building homes in floodplains and demanding flood control; building homes in forested canyons and demanding fire suppression; raising pets, children, and livestock adjacent to wildlands and demanding eradication of predators from the woods?

Something more than territory, ownership, and overpopulation is at work here. We have perhaps not learned to prize highly enough the developing of empathetic relationships. To this, there will be those who say my adoration for the she-mouse stems strictly from the mush of a woman's heart, or worse, that I have slipped into anthropomorphizing: assigning the human attributes of grieving, heartsickness, and the singing of camp songs to mice. Unforgivable! they will say.

Really?

Pooh-bah! is my answer. Do we so easily forget we are one of the animals? Or that animals other than humans have their own forms of rape, war, murder, and addiction? Why should we think they are terribly different with joy, pain, grief, and dying? With even singing?

The removal from scientific study of anthropomorphism and, one would hope, anthropocentrism (interpreting the world in terms of human values and experiences, with dominant men as the central most significant factor in the universe) we might eventually agree is a good thing. But to eliminate from our minds the possibility that species hold in common vastly more than we now suspect and to eliminate from our hearts the compassion welling when we feel a closeness for Earth's other beings—that is the unforgivable.

Perhaps in knowing more of the intimate details of other species we bring ourselves onto a fuller stage. I am reminded of the teachings of a friend, Mountain Mary, a woman of the wild Rockies and a rehabist working in her wildlife shelter at the edge of the woods. Even a short conversation with her brings to light things I never before knew. Of a kingfisher she is treating for a broken wing, she says, "With his weird little toes and heavy head, he can barely stand up. Without a branch, he would always be tipping over." The muskrat's tail is not limp like a mouse's. "It's a tough *burky* thing," she says, "used for swimming." At a party, her red hair piled high, she reposes in a big leather chair, holding court for festively attired guests, and expounding on the lifestyle of raccoons. Her long fingers seemingly playing at a small harp in her lap, she says, "This is not just for washing food. They relate to their entire world this way, picking it up, turning it over and over." I find Mary someone to believe when she says she hears worms chewing.

Yet in this barn, we continued to set the traps!

I wrestled with a torment of flip-flops, trying to line up my beliefs with my living space. Where were my boundaries? How many of Earth's other beings was I willing to tolerate running across our floors? Our barn abode was somehow not like my cabin in British Columbia, a place to visit for a week—in a crazed state of mind at that—and then leave behind. Yet wasn't I also fooling myself, looking upon mice the way the first westward immigrants saw the herds of buffalo—as an inexhaustible supply? And then, there came the continual confrontations, the importance of what others called "learning the lessons critical to our own survival."

Jim Dodge, another writerly sort living on a rural fringe, wrote an account of his cohabitation with a series of ludicrous wood rats. In comparing his noble acceptance to our killing fields, I slumped into bottomless remorse. A story related by my Blackfeet friend Woody, a Vietnam veteran and member of the American Indian Movement from the 1970s, completed my shaming. One day he opened his desk drawer to two weanling mice. Then he shut the drawer and let them live. "It's tough," he said, with a wry look, "being an Indian some days."

I might have felt altogether pious had I been making good use of the pelts, as did the ancient peoples of the Southwest. In 1924, archaeologists at Lovelock Cave in Nevada discovered a blanket tethered together from the skins of six hundred meadow mice. The skins had been cut into strips, sewn into mouse fur rope, and bound into a blanket with two-thousand-year durability. But I wasn't thus inspired.

Eventually (four years down the road), hantavirus pulmonary syndrome, or HPS, would emerge on the scene and provide logical excuse for our behavior. It was recognized first in New Mexico from a cluster of deaths in the Four Corners area, and later found in twenty more states and other parts of the world. Deer mice are the major carriers. This news hurled our nuisance syndrome into another category, one life-threatening. A disease "small but deadly," the federal Centers for Disease Control and Prevention call it. The early symptoms are flulike: headache, fever, chills, and muscle pain, which progress to nausea and vomiting, then rapidly to shortness of breath, and, in roughly 40 percent of cases, death. Not so many cases actually—most arise in rural areas with high rodent populations, particularly among people handling stored grain—but if you happened to be one, you could easily die in waiting too long to seek help. There is no known cure; the only treatment is by means of hospital support systems. When I looked up the website for the Centers for Disease Control, blinking red letters said, "Rodent-proof your home and workplace. Mice belong outside." Curled up to these words was an animated deer mouse with one wiggling ear and twitching tip of tail. The hantavirus excreted in their urine, droppings, and saliva contaminates dirt and dust, which, when it is disturbed—say during cabin, shed, or barn cleaning—we are apt to breathe. Direct contact with the mice can also cause infection. Prevention is said to be the best strategy. Some suggestions I found on another website included disinfecting carcasses by spraying rodent and trap with a solution of household bleach and letting sit ten minutes before handling; plugging all holes in your house larger than a quarter inch with steel wool.

I laughed, a hysterical little choked-off chord.

As it was, when I thought about the day we would leave the barn, move on to another life, it pleased me to know there was a fair chance no one after us would take up residence here. As yet there was no kitchen, no sink save a five-gallon bucket catching drips beneath my old standing cabinet-sink. There were no finished walls, floors, or ceilings; I hung oil paintings and watercolors on bare gypsum board and taped calendars and favorite postcards straight to insulation. Into cracks around the windows, I stuffed tissue. Rain and snow flowed in around the doors. Draft-free was an alien concept: on a windy day, the great arched, silver-lined mow with its insulation billowing in and out felt more like the chest cavity of a breathing beast. Breaks in the foundation exposed our feet to winter's rip of fifty below windchills; we might just as well have been traversing ice fields as sheets of pressboard. And the flooring historically recorded everything we and the carriage company had ever spilled. In any direction I looked, a sizable project loomed, requiring money or time. When we departed, the whole place could easily slide back to the mice, true interlopers gone.

Hugging that thought eased my heart. Still, I stared at the corner of the red metal filing cabinet, as if through wild magic my she-mouse might reappear. Yes, it had been her merry old barn. I was wanting to talk with her. Wanting *her* to be one who didn't get caught. I thought of gathering up all the traps. For a moment, my mind taunted me; I saw the spring-loaded bar, lethal and impartial, snapping hard on her neck, a final pool of bright blood oozing delicately from the corner of her mouth. No, no! I wouldn't let it happen. How could we be killing these dear little creatures? They had personalities, hearts, and hopes. They had families! We weren't even eating them, just eliminating a nuisance factor.

Then I got a grip. Hey! It was a chance encounter. Yes, a rotten matter of territory. Sure, she had family, and her brothers and sisters, aunts and uncles, her five hundred grandchildren all would be just as adorably cute. We'd be inundated! Before the barn's appearance on this spot, before humans bringing in birdseed and grain for livestock, in all probability the deer mice population topped out at ten to fifteen per acre—not the present tenement density. This was not a displacement. This was a fabricated lunch counter that we had adopted for a home. Any notion of a balanced distribution of species was completely out of whack. My resolve suddenly congealed into granite. *No breaks for the little guys!* Barn life, it seemed, was turning me into a Republican.

I had failed in this case as a resident of the rural fringe, failed to be what I had hoped for the world to be. Yet the grander picture was this: mice are not frogs and not grizzlies, in that I am inclined to worry about the greater implications of their potential extinction. Though no less important, mice are the adaptable ones able to propagate almost anywhere. And more of the picture was this: the proud mush of my heart had grown another lobe on my conscience. I was now programmed differently. I saw value in unraveling the complexities of imbalance—a largely human-induced imbalance. And I saw a cross-species largesse as the beginning point to learning.

.   .   .

In our second year in the barn, Patrick and I acquired cats. The first came to us thin and bedraggled; then we brought home another, and another. More than willingly they took over the chores of extermination. That left us once removed, not such bad guys again. My shame at the pompousness of our killing faded into the past. No longer was I a murderess. It was just the food chain now. You could almost feel sorry for us: the cats brought us leftovers, tips of noses and snips of tails, a vole's head with the body eaten away; they puked up half-masticated meat, the fur still attached, the entire mess riddled with worms. We became *cat caregivers*—a respected position once again in the total scheme of things. We mopped up gak, doctored abscesses, threw pills down throats, combed out mats, untangled burrs.

A warm, purring mound of fluff on the lap. Two or three on the bed. I was fulfilling my new benign role, taking to basking in it, not thinking about massacred mice anymore. Until one morning . . . on the doormat there lay the exquisite yellow-tipped feathers of an American goldfinch, *Carduelis tristis*.

A local naturalist tells me domestic cats are responsible worldwide for the extinction of fifteen species of birds.

Take Me,
Take My Flies

A Weedy Species

If, inside my refrigerator I were to find, along with the crisp fresh vegetables, the jars of chutneys and jams, Nancy's yogurt, marinating venison, imported Romano, leftover black bean chili and salsa, a beefy black fly, flopped on its back, feet jutting skyward in cartoon-chicken rigor mortis, I'd flip out—that would be the end of life as I have known it. Of this, I'm certain. How, exactly, it would play out I'm not as sure. My brains might boil and head split open. Or, all reason seized by blind frenzy, I might swing the cast-iron frying pans until the four are broken and the barn topples in splinters. Everyone has a threshold of tolerance. This is mine: No flies in the refrigerator.

It's good, I'm thinking, to clearly know your limits, as I wave away a zooming fly that is taking a circle toward the light at the back of the box. Missed it! I try scooping it out, chasing it with the cup of my hand while screaming (screaming helps), "You can't stay in there, damn it. GET OUT!" I'm shuffling bottles and jars. Whisk. Whoosh. No pay dirt, but the little bugger is getting lethargic in the cold and takes a final dive behind the maple syrup and a box of film. I grab a tissue, move the syrup tin, and snag him. I am thinking it is a *him*, why is that?

. . .

A barn by nature is expected to have flies. I had thought nothing of it when, in taking respite from our hectic settling-in projects, we'd stretched out for afternoon snoozes in the cool of the downstairs and a couple sassy houseflies had come along and pestered us. Fiendish in their ways, they let us drop just toward unconsciousness before coming to tickle an ear, cheek, lip, or eyelid, buzz up a nostril, prance across a hand. Determined to foil their antics, Patrick dug out his mosquito netting, a Michigan woodsman's item of necessity, which he'd fashioned some years back curiously out of bridal veiling. (It was on sale.) He shook it out and pinned it to a nail overhead. White netting flounced down around us like the folds of a huge, immodest circular skirt, weighted in place by the rope he'd carefully stitched into its hem. After-noons when we crawled in, I couldn't help imagining I was in Africa, that within the hour we would be up and hunting lions with Robert and Meryl, or shooting rapids with Kate and Bogie. Yet more to the point, from then on, beneath the wedding veil we were at our leisure to sink into restful naps, or torment-free romps.

Everything then with our lives, insect-wise, went along swimmingly until the time the aspens began to shimmer in bright yellows and the night temperatures dipped be-low freezing. The shift in season was the bell toll for a different species of fly, though at the time we knew only that the number of flies in the barn suddenly increased a hun-dredfold. To be more accurate, a thousandfold—this our introduction to what we later came to know as the infamous Bitterroot Fly Season. All up and down the valley, shiny little bulbous black bodies cover the sunny south sides of build-ings, looking like blankets of squirming raisins. More than once within the space of a few days, I mistook one for just that in my oatmeal. They swam in my tea, they plopped in my soup. They dove into the tight curls of my hair and became ensnared. Buzzing frenzies ensued. I was driven half mad.

Patrick, on the other hand, through what I could only guess was some peculiar genetic or ancestral trait, avoided (almost altogether) seeing them. All the while in the evenings, flies died in droves—not all of them, mind you, but plainly *hundreds*—and lay scattered over the floors, food counters, clothes, desks, the dining table.

Meet the cluster fly, *Pollenia rudis*, an insect slightly larger and darker than a housefly, identified by the short, crinkly, golden hairs among larger hairy bristles on its thorax. The larvae, or maggots, develop as parasites of earthworms, four different species living near the soil's surface. After chewing for a couple weeks, the larvae tunnel out of the earthworms' carcasses and pupate in the soil. Then they fly off to mate and lay their fertilized eggs where other earthworm hosts will wiggle upon them. At the coming of winter, through with eating and breeding, they seek protective cover, seeming to prefer the siding of houses, where they crawl into cracks and huddle in large clusters. Hence the name. By one report they are "quite innocuous," meaning they are not filth flies feeding on feces, rotting garbage, or moldering carrion and thus not worrisome as links between pathogens—such as poliomyelitis, infectious hepatitis, cholera, amoebic dysentery—and people. Yet one study of their European counterparts records them as visiting horse manure in the months of July and September. And, God knows, with draft horses, we had enough of that around here. But, then, I knew nothing of any of this in those early years.

What I did know was the little black buzzing machines— or *cluster-fuckers*, to adopt a favorite expression of Patrick's (though he typically employs the term in its verb form, applying it to people, for, say, celebrity mobbings or holiday sale scenes)—acted like kamikaze pilots on bungee cords. They crashed headlong into walls, posts, doors, the book you were reading, only to rebound and boing into your face. Concussions appeared not to faze them in the slightest. I came to think they wore rubber bumper hats. Furthermore, they seemed to arrange themselves in squadrons: a bunch would soar around every night in the barn and fall out of the air goners, while others hung back in the woodwork assembling the sequential assaults. In any case, there was never a shortage of daily reinforcements to replace those expired.

During this time, a side of Patrick emerged that I had never seen before. The background fly noise that was the constant accompaniment of our days—a buzzing up-and-down-the-windows racket like a million mosquitoes on amphetamines—he professed not to mind. Flies that plummeted into his food, he quietly with the tip of his spoon set aside. Those prostrate all over the floor, he paid positively no heed. And my obvious disquietude in the face of this invasion went, if not completely unnoticed, then without an ounce of sympathy. No ardent wedding veil rescue here! In my dearest's walking about, he squished the stilled bodies until the floor was coated in paths of glossy fly-guts patina. Now, a dead fly can easily be picked up, or sucked up. Not so once it has been squished. When I would seek to mention that perhaps he might look where he was going, point out in my probably not so perfectly tactful manner the thoughtlessness—not toward the dead flies but toward the person who seemed the only one hereabouts with a plan to pick them up—of his tromping upon them, his squeezed out responses were of an offhand, otherwise-occupied nature: "Those little things?" and versions thereof. At the end of the day, I was left warding off the strong inner feeling I was some kind of overly fastidious neurotic. It was in dispensing with just this feeling, a month into the onslaught, that I came to take a sin-born tumble.

There are no excuses for what I did next, though I'm still grasping at the straw of "extenuating circumstances." It was with a severely flawed wisdom, spurred by a burning desire not to lose this relationship, that I concocted a plan. Though with the mice I had sort of managed, I could not live with these flies, I knew, and therefore could not live in this barn—which would bollix up our great settling down plans. Wagon train bonding notwithstanding, the tall Irishman at this point was still mostly an enigma to me. And our relationship, in the communication department, was indeed struggling. Some days it lurched forward a few strides; other days it teetered on the brink of dissolution. Neither of us, it was becoming quite evident, had a talent for productive verbal exchange. We were two only children, reared without siblings, and sorely deficient—a therapist told us—in any kinds of skills of negotiation. I'd been taught to shout my anger, rather than break things. Yet shouting at Patrick only triggered his primal fighting instincts, which led to his breaking the things I hadn't. Our deficiencies in negotiation we more than made up for by being virtuosos of blaming, defensive posturing, argument escalating, ultimatum flinging. "Oh yeah? Well then, I'm gone." One incident in particular remains a chapter in my memory.

It was on a day when we were still touring, camped in a lovely meadow with the horses and wagon, and we started butting opinions on some little thing, lost to me now. Strangely, we each possessed the knack for generating a set of assumptions about the other that we then would respond to rather than to the person who stood opposite. Soon, I had had it. I threw down a feed bucket and starting hoofing it to the nearby dirt road with no other thought than to walk myself into a different life. In my resolute marching, I was not aware of Patrick until he came abreast of me. His face screwed into a black rage, he bellowed, "I'm leaving!" *Oh no you're not.* "I'm the one leaving!" I hollered it. His long legs were carrying him along at a brisker pace than mine. I broke into a jog. He did as well. Then we were running.

Whenever I recall this story, it seems to me we might have at this point burst into falling-down laughing at ourselves, but we didn't that day. We couldn't.

What we did have acting in our favor was a passionate love affair and a sense we *belonged* together, plus an underlying desire and commitment, however tenuous at first, to work things out. Whenever our travel schedule produced an opening, we immersed ourselves in marathon therapy—or tool building as we saw it. Other newly formed couples bought dishwashers and SUVs, we bought psychodynamic counseling. We would fly off and engage in eight or ten days of intense two-hour sorting sessions, then leap back into life on the road. Standing in the place of marriage vows, we had made this pledge: "Should we arrive at our Gordian knot, we promise to take one trip to the therapist we trust." She taught us to replace our penchant for threatening each other with taking permanent hikes (dropping bombs it was called) with an agreement: When pissed off, we would take plainly stated cooling-off walks, with a reassuring "I'll be back in an hour." She gave us rules for turn-talking, or one person's listening, and listening only, until the other said, "Okay, I'm finished." There would be no more interrupting, screaming, escalating. "I did not! You just love to twist everything *all around!*"

Ever so slowly, we inched toward an ability to listen to each other—the goal being doing so without correcting or defending. Meanwhile, wherever we went, we packed in the twelve-step meetings, those that focused on codependent relationships and adult children of addictive heritage—familial and cultural. In these sessions, we learned to "stay on our own sides of the street," we learned whose business was whose, and we became enlightened as to our tactics of manipulating and controlling. Trust, however, was a long time in coming. At its fragile beginnings, it only follows successes; to sustain itself over bumps, history is required. Little did I know it was going to take seven or eight years before our communication would begin to spring from a more instinctive well.

And yet, my taking up with Patrick was the first match for me that showed signs of being grounded in movement toward healthy coupling. We had two trainloads of baggage, but we were meeting all of it at the station. There was much for me to learn. All of my adult life, I'd been looking out for myself. I had lived in a kind of aloneness, not without friends, or roommates at times, or romantic liaisons, but relying for my future on essentially nothing beyond the body and brains I inhabited. I was not what you would call schooled in the essentials for long-term partnership. If Patrick and I were not going to live in this barn, I had neither the vision nor the trust that we would do anything but go our separate ways.

It was from that old alone place—of feeling I could depend upon only my own wherewithal to mold a desired outcome—that I decided to bug-bomb the barn.

I planned this knowing Patrick was dead set against pesticides. He was, I knew, a man of many convictions. He had given up eating commercially raised meat twenty years before meeting me, to escape ingesting antibiotics and growth hormones. (He's not a vegetarian per se; he will sit down to a plate of wild game or organically raised turkey.) Prescription drugs he'd never touched, unless he was near to dying. He had never smoked. And only once in his life had he drunk a cup of coffee. It was after tramping for a long, cold, rainy day through Michigan's Porcupine Mountains. Soaked and hungry, he'd come on a camp and a man boiling something in a pot over a fire. "Can I have a cup of *that?*" he burst in, not caring if it were dishwater. Coffee, it was. To this day he remembers having an interminably long conversation with the man, though about just what he doesn't recall. As for me, I wasn't completely in the dark about pesticides. From my San Joaquin Valley days and my marchings with the Farm Workers Union, I clearly understood the dangers when it came to a farmworker's exposure. Yet I hailed from a warm climate where fleas propagated overnight into voracious hordes, and if you kept indoor pets, it was necessary about once a year to flea-bomb your house.

Patrick is being silly, of course. And utterly unreasonable! He couldn't really expect anyone to live in a place full of flies. This was, after all, an old dairy barn; he had remarked on it himself, that assuredly over the years it had absorbed a load of pesticides. But sensing there was no room for discussion on the matter, I chose a weekend when he was off at a horseshoeing clinic, four hundred miles away. Certain I was doing the right thing, taking the only possible course under the circumstances, I bought five bombs, two for the downstairs and three for the high-ceilinged mow. The latter I positioned on the tops of stepladders I had kept from my drywall taping days.

Rising at four o'clock the next morning to get a jump on the sun, I readied the place as best I could, throwing cheap plastic painters' tarps over dishes, utensils, towels, bedding, clothing. The food and coolers I dragged to the milk house. "Shake well," I read on the side of a can. Following the rest of the instructions, I broke off a tab on each sprayer apparatus—to lock the valves open for automatic discharge—and then, starting upstairs, I ran from one to the next, snapping down the trigger buttons. The clouds began to spew forth with a hissing sound, altogether more menacing than I'd remembered. I hurried to get out, pulling the front door tight behind me and securing the padlock. For the next two hours, the time span suggested in the directions to allow for extermination, I sat in a Victor cafe, eating breakfast, nursing cups of coffee, reading the morning papers.

Upon my return, I discovered a sight more loathsome than any I could have imagined. The porch and the ground adjacent to the barn—to a distance of three feet out and a general depth of two inches—were black with dead flies. I promptly leaned over into the weeds and retched up my hash browns and eggs.

There was, however, more to my stomach unrest than dead flies. Through a little window of hindsight, my sensibly reasoned-out plan began to feel more like a foul, self-centered rationalization, and I was now shuddering like a ship battered on big seas, ready to go down. It was not so much a moral revelation by bolt of lightning that hit me but a slow-burgeoning terror of discovery. What if someone were to come by just now? What would I do? What if someone had *already* come by while I was gone? We knew few people here yet, but this country had a neighborliness to it. Folks just dropped by any old time, and there were plenty who still took this to be the carriage company. Should a car suddenly turn down the driveway, I would have to pray the occupants would never think to mention this striking carpet of croaked flies to my beloved, or, worse yet, I might have to take someone I barely knew into my confidence, against that same beloved. In plain truth, my morning's actions were a betrayal. Going farther in the same direction, I saw, was not an option: setting off bombs was one thing, flat-out lying was another. Still, it was not purely the malevolent deceit of it all. My system simply couldn't handle having someone floating around out there, God knew who and where, holding such a secret. Oh, the curious ramifications of dirty deeds, how they swell in complexity with the unforeseen. My anxiety level soaring, I snatched up the broom.

I thought to clear off the porch quickly so that I might stand upon it to greet anyone arriving. Dried grasses helped camouflage the evidence down the barn's long sides. As I flicked the broom along, brushing the little bodies off the deck's edge and into paper bags, which by some fortunate turn of providence I had a stack of in my truck, I continued to be astounded by the numbers. How many flies must there be in the world? I had once heard that China managed to totally eliminate flies by handing out swatters to everyone and decreeing a war. Well not so here! Also, the sweeping in itself wasn't easy. Fly carcasses became matted in the broomcorn like oatmeal glommed in a pan scrubbie. And there was a softness to the heaped masses that created the feel of sweeping slushy snow.

Next was to open the front door and see what the inside presented. I turned the key and wrenched off the padlock, holding my breath, preparing to find flies a foot deep. An amazing surprise! Though there were dead flies everywhere, it was not a solid covering. My first feeling of relief since I arrived home quickly vanished, however, as I ran through the choking air to throw open doors and windows, and a picture started to piece itself together in my head. As the poison clouds had risen to fill the barn, the flies had apparently struggled en masse to wiggle their way out any crack they could find. The dead ones scattered around on the floor had been those last in line, poor things—not that a one of them had had a bit of a chance. The image came to me again in a kind of Disney-like animation: the barn's walls bulging, the big structure heaving and shuddering, showers of black specks arcing out. Except that this was a frightening scene of destruction. And at my hand. This thought, though it was only flies, weighed heavily on me. For a moment. Then it

was smothered by a down-deep regaling, my feeling highly
pleased that these beasts, once I figured a way to dispose of
them, would be out of my life! The fact that there had been
so many, so many that we might have cozied up to all winter,
lined up on the side that I'd done the right thing, or if not the
right thing, then an action I was glad I had taken.

Feeling safer with the porch presentable, I leaned into the
rest of my job, tugging around the big Shop-Vac, our only
vacuum. Four hours later, I had worked my way upstairs and
across the mow. I switched off the motor and stepped out to
check the state of our sleeping deck, and a squabbling of
birds rose to my ears. I scooted down the back stairs and
peeked around the corner. Down the side of the barn, I saw
fourteen magpies, all squawking, crow-hopping, flapping,
wholly intent on scavenging bellyfuls of dead flies. Yikes!
Pesticide whooshing up the food chain! There it went, and I
the witness. The vagaries of my life, all laid bare before me.
I had grown to be a forthright person (on the whole), not so
much through grand purities in thought and deed but more
out of fears of reprisal and punishment and anticipation of
this phenomenon I was now experiencing full in the face: instant karma.

Patrick arrived home.

He threw open the door, sang out his favorite parody—
"Honey, I'm home!"—and plopped his duffel bags on the
floor. I ran to meet him, receiving a feet-off-the-floor hug.
For my part, I put on my no-real-news-everything's-peachy
look. It was soon quite evident that, just as he hadn't noticed
our plague's presence, he took no note of its absence. But the
flies weren't completely absent. Every day twenty or thirty
entered the barn, and instead of their usual act of dropping
stone dead each night, they convulsed on the floor in elaborate death dances—the chemical residue attacking their ner-
vous systems?—entailing five-minute-long spastic buzzings.

On their backs, wings vibrating like propellers, they spun in circles of ever-shrinking diameters, until finally expiring. Invariably, they chose a spot for this right beside Patrick's chair. The change in fly behavior seemed blatant to me, seemed a billboard written with PESTICIDE! PESTICIDE! LOOK WHAT YOUR DEAREST DARLING DID! Stomach clenched once again, I looked upon each spiraling death throe as my potential undoing.

The kicker to all this was, in two weeks' time, the barn was chock-full of flies again. Operating, at this point, under the realization that I could not emotionally (let alone healthwise) withstand setting off a round of bombs every few weeks, an old adage, edited a bit for my situation, came into play: "Cavalcades of flies are the mother of invention!"

From the hardware store, I brought home five dozen of an item labeled FLY CATCHER, EL MOSQUERO, THE WORLD'S LEADER IN NON-POISONOUS PEST CONTROL PRODUCTS. A Victor brand offering again. The packaging promised: "No baiting." "No poisons." "No vapors." "No mess." Just pull the little red string, and out popped a handy thumbtack, already attached to the end of a fly paper. I unwound the long, sticky strips, counterclockwise as indicated, from their small cardboard tubes, and hung three in each window. They seemed lost in the tall windows of the mow, but I hung three in each anyway. The slug-guts coloring of the gluey paper rang with familiarity from my childhood; I remembered the strips dangling in the houses of old people. The less than savory appearance I might put up with, I supposed, if they worked. But, soon enough, I learned they caught very few flies—in view of how many I needed to catch. And there was this further fault I saw as more serious. If I were the least bit casual in my movements, they reached for my hair like octopuses coated in library paste. Incidents of this sort were not mere inconveniences: they were nearer lethal and, on occasion, involved ripping out chunks of hair.

Regrouping. I launched into a program of vacuuming, sucking flies off the windows, where they seemed inclined to gather. I noticed they followed the sun like flowers' faces in a garden; it was the east-side windows in the mornings, the west-side in the afternoons. To keep up with their numbers, I toted the unwieldy Shop-Vac up and down the stairs four times a day. In this way, I was able to capture most of the daily crop before evening's cadaver hail, which had the added benefit of giving me a jump on floor cleaning. The flies around the dining table, nonetheless, continued to be a bother of high distaste. But even more irritating was being stretched out evenings on the bed, relaxing into our nightly reading time, and having three or four flies play a version of fly handball inside the lampshade: *bap, bap-bap-bap, bap-bap.* My goal—a goal rarely attained—became to catch the last buzzing bastard before bedtime.

My vacuuming scheme proved about 80 percent effective and with some small auxiliary program would have worked fine to this day—had I no other plans for my life. "Suck duty" occupied too many hours. With the thought to streamline my labors, I invested in a superpowered Dustbuster. On its trial run, I drained it of juice by noon. Its small compartment filled up quickly, and I felt compelled to walk at least to the other side of the barnyard before emptying it, as the majority of the captives *flew* away. Strangely, though, my purchase of the Dustbuster brought Patrick to consciousness, if only tangentially, with fly combat: He announced to everyone who stopped by, "Watch out for Kathleen, she's packing her sidearm!" What was even odder was that I actually took pride in his seeming praise!

Still of the mind that the situation called for supplementary strategies, I set my creativity to bubbling again.

Left with virtually empty hours while the Dustbuster was recharging for the evening shift, I discovered I could open the small barn windows downstairs and the flies dawdling upon them would take off. To accomplish this, I had to sneak up to them and complete the maneuver in an oxymoronic halcyon rush, or prematurely to my purpose they flew off around the room. Surely once outdoors they merely re-lighted on the barn siding. I don't know how long it took for them to crawl back through the cracks and fall in behind the reinforcements, but I liked to think they were out of my hair, literally, for an evening. The mow's tall windows do not open, so I kept the Shop-Vac upstairs. In a few minutes its elephantine hose could inhale four hundred flies. Between vacuumings, I would snug on the crevice tool, the slit open-ing of which I had sealed with duct tape; this thwarted the escape of any flies crawling back out the hose. Over these weeks I found it best not to ponder what might be hatching inside the Shop-Vac. What with sucking up flies daily, it was impossible to schedule the emptying of it for a time when they had all quit kicking but were not yet making maggots. I tried to err on the side of letting loose a few live ones.

That winter was a cold one, and so busy was I keeping warm and chasing flies—not to mention cleaning stovepipes and setting mousetraps—I hardly registered when it was January. Along about the second week, the flies completely vanished, or perhaps I just caught the last one cloistered in the barn. Whatever the case, we were not troubled by them again until the following October.

Our second fall, being older and wiser, we ingeniously planned to be better prepared for the Arctic clippers of win-ter and to get ourselves out of stovepipe chores. We hired a mason, a genius with all manner of brick and stone. His name is Guy. Together we took up the floor in the southwest corner, poured a slab, built a chimney. We mixed the concrete mortar in a wheelbarrow, and, stacking the squarish gray blocks and the oval sections of clay liner, ran them up through the mow floor and on through the roof until the chimney top cleared the level of the ridge. Thirty-nine feet. Then we bought a used barrel woodstove, which to my joy had a glass front. Setting it on a platform of cinder blocks and fitting it with two right-angle bends of stovepipe readied us for blizzards. Well, better readied us. Finally, to give ourselves a break, we arranged with Neville's, one of the valley's many log home builders, to buy their discarded ends, cut to length for the stove. All that remained was to chop ten cords of wood.

The first time the temperature dipped, I laid in kindling and three big chunks from the wall of wood we'd stacked to window height behind the rocking chair. Feeling the warmth from that first crackling fire, I thought, How heavenly! Watching the cheery flames lick the logs into red embers, I thought, How romantic!

And how I had forgotten: Cluster flies thought the same.

With the first blast from the new woodstove, flies streamed out of the walls. I was soon wedded again to my vacuuming regime, sucking up the 80 percent. But this year, I had more of my wits about me and I sought to corral the final 20. Observing that hundreds of flies collected in the peak of the mow, energetically zinging around in the hot air at the south end above the propane heater, particularly after dark, when the windows no longer afforded warmth, I designed a contraption. From the junk lumber pile, I pulled a piece of slab wood still edged with bark, a seven-foot length of two-by-twelve. At the hardware store, I bought a cleat, a handful of nails, a rope, and two dozen of the ringlet flypapers again (they must be good for something). I fashioned the plank gizmo to hang on edge, horizontally, and set to attaching the rope and driving nails all along its length. Then I unfurled and fastened one of the curly slug-guts strips to each nail. Employing the old hayfork block that still runs freely along a beam at the peak, I hoisted away and sent my contrivance, a virtual wall of stickiness, sailing up to its new home. A couple half hitches thrown around the cleat I'd mounted on the wall and—voilà!

While waiting for the evening's swarm of flies to start batting around bonkers in the peak, I strode about with my chest puffed out, tickled as all hell. My gadget was a glorious thing to behold—that is, for a person in my living predicament—and I showed it off to Patrick and he was duly impressed. It hung there for four years. I actually forgot about it, until we were expecting some fairly prissy visitors and I had to haul the unsightly thing down and pitched it in the trash. In all that time, it had caught sixty-four flies.

Two things occurred our third fall that ultimately delivered me from the majority of my hours on fly patrol. One day it just plain hit me that the flies, besides being drawn to heat, were attracted to light—ergo, the bap-bapping around in the light over the dining table and inside the shade of the bed lamp. No wonder they clambered at the windows, which offered heat *and* light. Suddenly I understood better why they liked the tip-top of the mow. In the evenings, with the fluorescent lights turned on, the silver-backed insulation up there reflected as bright as daylight. And I noticed that, when I turned the lights off in my office corner and headed downstairs for dinner, the flies in the peak gradually followed, seeking other light.

I started mapping out another fly catcher. We had an extra three-foot-long fluorescent light, and I hung it on the opposite side of the mow from my desk, at chest level. Nightly while occupied downstairs with dinner, I left that light on and all the others off. Just as I thought, the peak flies gravitated to it, and soon their lifeless bodies, in the strange evening die-offs, littered the floor beneath it. Often many were still buzzing around by the time I came up for an evening stint of work, but to my delight they tarried by the fluorescent light, perhaps because it was brighter than my desk lamp. I dubbed my new contrivance Ye Grand Ole Fly Trap. My vacuuming shrunk to one small area of the mow, and that on a once-a-week basis.

Not long after this, at the hardware store, I came across a product named Fly Scoops (the SureFire Fly Trap), three to a box: eight-inch-long rectangular shells of white plastic with instructions to stick them to the bottoms of windows. Their top edges are designed to cock out from the glass about an inch. Inside you drop a stiff paper insert that comes slathered with a thick coating of sticky glue—so sticky it's sometimes tough to peel off the wax paper covering—but then you sit down and put your feet up, nothing more to do! An amazing notion. Except during the height of fly season—and then I was having to reline the traps daily. Still and all, this stole only one hour from my day. I stuck the scoops to the small windows downstairs. I stuck them to the large windows upstairs. I stuck them all along the sides of Ye Grand Ole Fly Trap. For some reason there was always a finite number to the daily onslaught of flies; that is, no more emerged after about five o'clock. Miraculously, these scoop traps caught almost every fly by sundown. In their paroxysms of zinging from window top to window bottom, the flies dove right into the stickum. What's more, the traps faced outward, blocking from view the unsightly deathbeds. The barn had a new, fresh look. I had a life! To SureFire, I owe my relationship, my writing life, the possibility of dinner parties. For the stubborn dozen or so flies that still circulated at dinner hour,

I suspended three of the scoops from the milky plastic bowl of a lampshade overhead (another hand-me-down from the carriage company). Then I made a deal with Patrick: No overhead lights in the mow during "croak hour."

One minor hitch, *minor* to my mind. During the Bitterroot's milder winters, interspersed with sixty-degree days when cluster flies renew themselves outdoors by some means—wild mating? new hatches?—fly season will stretch on past January clear into April, and I can spend four hundred dollars(!) on Fly Scoops. As I said, of piddling concern.

Because we lived in an old barn, I suppose, and not a real house, I had assumed we were the only people with fly problems. Cluster flies, as it turns out, are a stand-up species, not discriminating as to race, religion, or economic status. And they plainly are not simply lowlifes. Some of their larger numbers are to be found in the Bitterroot's priciest log mansions.

Patrick and I had acquired a house ourselves. When the old two-story farmhouse and its one acre came up for sale, we bought it—in effect, putting a bit of the old dairy back together. To cover the monthly mortgage payments, we were forced into becoming landlords. We hadn't rushed to pack up and move in ourselves because, for one thing, we had no desire to live there, and beyond that nobody would be stupid enough to *pay* to live in the barn. In readying the place for rent, I realized we had purchased another Bitterroot haven for cluster flies. And this led me directly to thinking no one would be stupid enough to rent a farmhouse full of flies. The rental ad was in the paper. I would be showing the place any time.

In the morning sun, I sat on a stump in front of the barn, reading the paper and awaiting the arrival of the dreaded exterminator, the Bug Man. I'd called him the previous afternoon to explore the idea of spraying a more benign substance than fog bombs. It sounded mostly organic, except for 10 percent, or so, he said was "secret." I was no dummy: *Secret* meant poison. But in my mind, this was "next door," and this was "business." What else could we do? File bankruptcy? Yet my insides were knotted into another pest-control turmoil, which was manifesting itself in my bemoaning my role as land baron, longing for all my years as the righteous tenant, the indignant downtrodden. Now I'd become the object of my scorn.

"I have an opening at eight-thirty tomorrow morning," the Bug Man had said brightly on the phone. He was booked the following day and henceforth, it seemed. Without planning to, I had snagged an appointment. As Patrick and I were going to bed, I broke the news about the morning's engagement, feeling a bit sheepish about not having discussed it first. It had been a rotten last few days all around: We were working on an August extension on taxes; Patrick was racked with an upper-respiratory flu; my back was out, and, unable to tolerate the confines of a sleeping bag, I had taken to sprawling across our big bed trying to loosen strung muscles. Thus for two nights we had not slept together. When sick, Patrick can behave like a tormented bear, but before heading for bed on the deck he did no more than mumble a few words about being surprised he had taken my announcement so well. The same refrain was running through my mind. But in the morning, he wasn't speaking. Twenty minutes after the Bug Man should have arrived, Patrick found me on the stump. Face flushed red, eyes welling, he said, "If it's come to this, if you go ahead with spraying, we can talk about my leaving here."

I hated to think what might have happened if the Bug Man had been on time. I also hated to think about what I had once done that he did not know I'd done. I was finally realizing the depth of Patrick's convictions. My secret would be going with me to the grave. (I had no notion I would ever put pen to the full extent of this story, no notion it couldn't be told except in its most complete, truth-bared measure.)

We gave the choice of spraying to our tenants, and none so far have opted for it.

One year, a longtime friend and cohort from 1970s wild-river-saving politics drove up from California. Her household goods followed via Mayflower, and she settled into the farmhouse. It was a move she had wanted to make for some time; by chance, it coincided with an extra-early Bitterroot Fly Season. It was our sixth annual go-round with the insects; their mobs had never arrived this early, and I'd been caught off guard. More pinched than usual, in our perpetual land-rich state of pennilessness, we were awaiting my fall royalty check to order the season's supply of scoops.

One evening, Carol joined us for dinner. We were all pleasantly catching up on the years when a cluster fly belly flopped onto her plate and spread-eagled into the oil of the pasta. With polite indifference, she piled bits of sun-dried tomato over it and went on eating by skirting around the little mausoleum. I was struck by how she'd handled this. Ms. Cool! Had I gone to someone's house and this happened to me, my gag reflex would have fetched up my last few swallows, which is also my reaction to finding a hair in my food, even when I know it's my own.

With Patrick, it requires a great deal more than a fly or a hair to offend his sense of what's appetizing. I can frankly say there has been only one time I've seen him looking nauseated (even when he gets flu, it is a respiratory or lower-intestinal kind, never the puke-up type). We were out restauranting, at a place that's now gone; we were working on predinner salads consisting of a slice of tomato, a couple slices of cucumber, a few strings of red onion, and leaves of romaine, when Patrick found himself chewing longer than necessary for anything on his plate. He ground away at it nonetheless, with his inbred diligence, until I finally saw him pick something off the end of his tongue. A false fingernail! Replete with pink nail polish! It was easy for me to laugh, it wasn't in *my* mouth. Seeing his body lurch forward, with an involuntary puffing of cheeks, was such novel entertainment in itself, for a moment I didn't comply with sympathy.

The following evening found me cooking again. When it is straight-up pasta-oil-and-garlic (I live with the Pastaman, he can eat pasta seven nights running) or simply boiled potatoes with sliced tomatoes, Patrick will cook; anything veering toward added ingredients or embellishment is up to me. (I should not leave unsaid that it's in laboring over elaborate treats that he truly shines, impressing company with his puffed Finnish *krupsua* or his New York cheesecake, the latter a Lindy's recipe with pastry crust, thrice-baked.) Before getting started, I busted flies for half an hour, yet with such a reluctance for the chore—I was sorely missing my Fly Scoops—I didn't capture them all. After setting out the makings for salsa—tomato, red onion, jalapeño pepper, cilantro—I began chopping. With the windows dark, flies homed in on the lights. I opened two cans of black beans, after rinsing dumped them into a pot, and, with a little water, set them on a burner. *Thwap-thwap.* Above, four flies rebounded in the light shade. Black beans and flies are indistinguishable when lumped together. I grabbed a lid for the pot. To the salsa, I added cumin, cayenne, olive oil, a squeeze of lime. All the while I worked, I kept my sights scanning like searchlights over the countertops and floor. Into heating cast-iron skillets, I dropped tortillas topped with a slice of cheese each and plunked on lids—this time mostly to keep in the heat and melt the cheese.

On the table, I set the salsa and then smaller dishes of black olives, red lettuce strips, and avocado slices. Half a dozen flies in the milky bowl overhead caromed around with the zing of pool balls from a hard-hit opening break. Cluster flies seemed to pour on the speed for their final hour of life and then plummet like aerial battery toys run out of juice. Ten or twelve more, just waiting their turn, clung nearby to the ceiling beams. I moved the bowls to a corner of the table, out of range of falling bodies. Back in the kitchen, there were four corpses to pluck off the floor.

"God, I don't like this," I whined.

Patrick, at that moment, walked in and sat down at the table, his usual reading place, and picked his *Anvil* magazine out of the pile of mail. "Anything I can do?" he asked.

Seeing him thus positioned and with his offer, I was momentarily heartened. "Oh good!" I said. "You can be on fly patrol."

"Oh, I'll be on tight fly patrol," he avowed.

"Yeah, I'll bet!" I said half under my breath.

With a big slotted spoon, I flung a portion of black beans—imagining them all turned to flies—on top of his tortillas and cheese. I threw the plate down in front of him. "Here's a lovely fly taco, my sweet!" Fetching my own plate, I sat down across from him and slid the bowls of fixings to the middle of the table. Then I flipped, with the ease of dialing radio channels, into common courteous conversation.

"I didn't want to set these in the middle when we weren't watching for dropping flies." At which I noticed a large fly on his shoulder. "There's a big fat bugger on your shoulder." He swiveled his head and looked the bug in the eye. He swiveled back, and his gaze locked on me. "Pretend it's a parrot," he said.

We ate in silence. Then I started on two more tacos. Waiting for the cheese to melt, I spied three flies beneath the dish drainer. They'd expired in just the past few minutes. Two lay helplessly on their backs, legs spastic in final jiggles; the third was nose-down in a splash of water. I snatched up the toilet paper roll (we were out of Kleenex, too expensive this month), ripped off two squares, scooped up the three black-guards, and flung them in the garbage. *I doooo hate this!*

I dropped another plate with black beans before him. Picking up the yogurt tub that sat near me (I'm the only one who likes yogurt on tacos), I peeled off the lid, intending to dab on a blob for anchoring my olives. My spoon cut into the creamy whiteness just as a fly slammed into it. "Gross!" I yelled. Patrick leaped up to rescue me from dementia. He was going to take the tub to the kitchen and dispose of the fly. But it was too late.

Before he was halfway around the table, I sharply straightened up. "That's all right," I said, sweetly through my teeth, "I'll just work around it." *I'll leave it for your breakfast!* (It's on granola and pancakes that Patrick puts yogurt.)

I shot him a stony glare. One to which he would usually respond with "That's the best glare I've seen all day!" But not this time. My mood was too scary. Jumping to change the subject, he asked if I remembered *Westward Whoa*, a book I'd given him a couple years back, the account of a cross-country quest retracing the journey of Lewis and Clark. Well, it seemed its author, W. Hodding Carter, was building a Viking boat and planned to sail it from Greenland to the United States next summer.

"He's sailing a Viking boat alone?"

"Oh, no."

"No? Maybe you should go apply."

All the fun drained from his face. I'd broken the mood, crossed some line, pricked the balloon of insane banter that's a midwesterner's way of getting through hard times, that "never let the bastards get you down!" attitude. Quickly, I looked for a backpaddle. "Isn't that something you'd like to do?" I quizzed, as though that was all I had meant.

"Do you remember a movie called *Caveman*?" I heard him ask.

"Nope." I had grabbed up a pen and begun scribbling around the edges of an envelope.

Patrick spouted on about two cavemen camped in the desert. One was Ringo Starr. He'd awakened in the morning, as it went, to see a fly as big as a football sitting on his friend's face. "He swatted it," Patrick said. Out of the corner of my eye, I saw Patrick's hand at the end of his long arm make a sweep from near ceiling down to the table. Bam! "And a mass of green gush spread across his face!"

I am fifty-two years old, and I am listening to this? during dinner? My mother would never have found herself in a verbal exchange of this sort, not on any occasion. Perhaps this is the conversation of two people who did too many drugs in their youth? Except that *I* didn't. Much.

"GROSS!" My hands shot up, as if I were warding off a hit in the head with a volleyball.

"What are you writing over there?" In a bounce, he was at my side and I was flipping the envelope over.

"Never you mind," I said. *You wait until I have this on paper.* (Call it a writer's instinct.)

Then I was being tickled and buzzed, the way you play "the circling bee is going to get you" with an infant.

Not amused, I left him the dishes and headed upstairs. The mow was dark except for my desk light and, of course, the corner fly catcher (minus its scoops). In half an hour, I heard Patrick coming my way. But my mind was occupied and his shufflings became lost to me in the cavern.

Soon he sprang into the circle of light—a clown!—at center stage, *bbzzzzzzzing* again, this time wearing his Clarabell wig with the fake orange curls encircling the bald rubber crown.

"Whadda we got here, Pooks?"

"Not much yet." I was on page three. I clicked on the scroller and rolled the screen out of sight. Swatting the top of my head where I thought a fly had landed, I scratched the spot.

Patrick mimicked me and said, "Where's that *fun* girl I used to know?"

My mind was in a racing ponder of the role I play in this. *How is it that I'm living in this fly-ridden barn? Not a one of my friends would ever do this. Surely I've become inured beyond belief. This can't be just love. I'm a sick person.* Patrick was suddenly whipping my swivel chair toward him. He was twinkling, his cheeks cherublike apples above a stinkingly cute grin. He was on one knee. He grabbed me. "Kiss me, you fool!"

The next morning, when I staggered sleepy-eyed to the bathroom, I saw him sitting at his spot at the table, scissors in hand, cutting up paper. He looked like a second-grader making paper dolls. I asked what he was doing.

"Something," he sang.

When I exited the bathroom, I saw he had fashioned long strips of white paper from a large (to be recycled) envelope and taped them to the milky bowl. They hung in the manner of a beaded lampshade. Down the length of each with bold black marker pen he had printed BBZZZZZZZZZZZZ. A laugh escaped my lips.

Then he was again a circling fly and grabbing at parts of my body.

"No, wait! You *have* to stop this buzzing. *I can't stand it.*"

"Okay," he said. "I suppose we can't use the F-word either." My mind was not tracking. What in hell had *fuck* got to do with anything? At the exasperatingly puzzled look on my face, he whispered, "Fly."

I fell hopelessly into his arms.

My check arrived. The boxes of Fly Scoops arrived. Our lives swung back to normal, or what I considered a cope-able condition. I was content again with the number of hours devoted to insect attention; plus, I was assimilating a bit of my old guilt (episodes like the taco dinner had the effect of grinding the edges off it).

Then, a few weeks later, another fly dilemma—again one of an ethical nature—rose right out of the dust.

My South African friend Rikki, a self-taught artisan in tin-smithing and a woman with whom I have a deep sisterly bond, came over to make Christmas gnomes, an activity for which I try to reserve a day in early December.

A few years before I departed California, I had flung my over-the-top Christmas buying habits onto the operating table and performed major surgery. Except to a couple of people who felt like family, I'd said, "No more presents." We'll write letters. We'll take long walks. We'll gather for potlucks. It's been no hardship in the barn to take that one step further and omit a tree; I don't think Patrick could tolerate one, in the traditional vein. He's a person who reels at living in the opulence of a house, the opulence of a rough barn, and would prefer not owning furniture. When it comes to shopping for anything beyond food, essentials, and outdoor sporting equipment, he has that word: *consumer-puking*. The Christmas season is naturally the height of CP. A decorated tree, surprisingly, is not something I've mourned. I slave instead over a pine-bough door swag, each year wiring on the same big red ribbon and long cones from a California sugar

pine. Then I line the windowsills with *julenisse*, little gnomes—
a Norwegian tradition adopted from a friend.

Today the table was spread with work materials: a glue
gun, brushes, little bottles of paint, scissors. For the bodies, I
had set out empty thread spools and acorns and pecans and
filberts. For fashioning clothing, we had swatches of old flannel shirts, snips of leather, buttons and beads, hoarded
lengths of fancy ribbon; for creating hair and beards, there
were tree mosses and animal hair.

A cup of tea and we were just getting started when Rikki
chanced to glance upward and take in my scoop traps attached to the milky bowl. "Kathleen," she said with her
drawn out *e*'s, "are they just stuck on there until they die?"

She was staring at what I knew were twenty newly
snagged flies, as I had freshened the liners that morning in
anticipation of her visit. They were all squirmy and wiggly-
legged, but, I was thankful, no longer buzzing. (There is
evidently something to be said here for pesticides: the duration of agony is shorter. Though who is to know if it's
less painful.) Her face contorted into reproachful horror: I
thought she might leave, except that she had no means to do
so apart from setting out on foot in the snow—her husband
had dropped her off for the day.

"Sort of," I said.

"Do you remember Digger?" she asked, her voice echoing
from a kind of hollow place. Digger was the dog of mutual
friends. I nodded yes, and she proceeded with a story of how
the dog had gone missing, two days, four days—they'd
thought he must be dead. Then a pickup wheeled into their
yard with a nearby rancher driving and Digger sitting pertly
in the cab. He had been caught in a coyote trap. With a
glance up at the flies, Rikki leveled her eyes on me and said,
"He'd been standing there with his foot clamped in that
thing for five days!"

I felt compelled to offer a few defending remarks. "Just on a guess, we have two thousand flies in here every week. Cohabiting with that number gets a little disgusting." Our exchange fell quiet for a spell, and my mind was drawn back along the years to other incidents of similar inference, even outright accusation. "Bugs have a right to live; what are you, God?" And there was the peer pressure I'd felt—by example—from purists, people who happened to be dear to me. Here in the Bitterroot, my friend Bill, an organic landscape gardener and musician, claims that he never minds a mosquito's bite, for it is only the pregnant females that do so, and he's honored to have his blood dispersed into the gene pool that will carry forward their species. After my ponderings on the she-mouse, I could actually fathom that someday we might appreciate that a fly could have hopes and sorrows. But sitting here at the table, my brakes to a particle of further understanding jammed on hard. Silently I was thinking: If these pesky shits are dumb enough to come in here and drive me crazy, then they're going to die. *Hmmm? Wasn't that exactly what we'd said while exterminating the wolf?* And furthermore, damn it, by whatever nontoxic means I can drum up. Hadn't I gone a long way already in avoiding pesticides? How much change could be expected of one person? I felt myself spinning into a philosophical vortex, about to drown like a mouse in the drowner pail, clawing for purchase on anything that might save me from soul-searching, internal craziness.

It was two years before my rescue arrived. It emerged in the form of a panel discussion I attended at the University of Montana. David Quammen, author of *The Song of the Dodo: Island Biogeography in an Age of Extinctions* (though he's perhaps more widely known by his column "Natural Acts" that ran for eleven years in *Outside* magazine), was one of the panelists. On this evening he must have contributed with a range of engaging information, but I absorbed only what my searching-for-answers tentacles lighted upon: his discourse on *weedy* species. Mammals and fish and birds and insects, it seems, can be as weedy as plants. The weedy ones are those capable of reproducing with zeal and easily setting up camp in any number of different habitats. They are experts at resisting onslaught from other species or rapacious creatures themselves. They excel in depleted environments, of which these days we are producing a plentitude. And, most often, they are clever enough or otherwise well-suited to living in close proximity to humans. "Weedy species, we don't have to worry about," Quammen said.

Over the following months, I was to learn more about weedy species, as well as "introduced species," "invasive species," "displaced species," "accelerated extinctions of species," and a phenomenon termed "cascading effects." Ever since the first microscopic batch of amoebae plunged the planet into the world of reproduction with their lusty cell dividing in the muck, the earth's collective number of species has periodically undergone die-offs, or mass extinctions. It is generally accepted now among biologists that the earth is in its sixth colossal wave of extinctions. From a survey commissioned by New York's American Museum of Natural History and reported on by the *Washington Post* staff writer Joby Warrick (April 21, 1998), nearly seven out of ten biologists agreed that a mass extinction is under way. This happens when some force, or gradual change over time, alters the normal way of going—alters the rate of extinctions as they are counterbalanced by the evolution of new species. The extinction background rate, as it is called—during an uneventful, catastrophe-wise, million years—amounts to about one in every major grouping of species. The fifth mass extinction, the one most familiar to us because it took the dinosaurs, transpired at the end of the Cretaceous period, 65 million years ago. The present acceleration of extinctions, before it is finished, is expected to claim as many species as went down with the fifth: a whopping global 76 percent. Yet it was a little half sentence of Joby Warrick's that hit me hardest: ". . . and an equal number [of biologists] predicted that up to one-fifth of all living species could disappear within thirty years." *And how long will it take the earth to evolve again into a state of rich biodiversity?* Perhaps 10 million years.

What is toughest to wrap my mind around is that the onset of the current acceleration clearly coincides with the emergence on Earth of human life. It is an acceleration occurring not as a result of cataclysmic volcanic eruption, lithospheric plate shifting, or meteor collision, but directly at the hand of humanity. *We* are the force. This acceleration might best be called the Great *Homo sapiens* Upset of Introduced Species. Beginning with the earliest peoples' forays and migrations, about the time that Neolithic cultures launched the first seaworthy crafts and began to paddle between islands and continents, we have carried with us species indigenous to one region and deposited them as exotics in another. Sometimes inadvertently, with stowaways in food and boats and clothing, but just as often by plain purposeful design, we have long been about the business of rearranging the planet.

Factors contributing now to speeding along the acceleration constitute an exhausting list: *more and more of the introduced or exotic species proving invasive,* that is, outcompeting or otherwise eliminating native species, an occurrence that is ever on the increase with our modern-day shipping and air travel; *conversion of habitat,* such things as urban sprawl, rainforest demolition, disruption of life on the ocean floor; *fragmentation of habitat,* wildlands shrinking into small, islandlike areas of wilderness and parks; *alteration of the biosphere,* or ozone depletion, greenhouse effect, climatic changes; *advances in tech-*

nology, a tipping too far in a damaging direction. Not to mention *pollution* of air and water and soil. Plus we can expect all of the above to be exacerbated by projected heavy increases in human population and consumption rates.

Directly hooked to the acceleration of extinctions is the occurrence of cascading effects that is in swing, to larger and lesser extents, all over the place—from among remote, back-country communities of plants and animals to the bacteria right at our feet. The term *cascading effects* brings to mind a sentence John Muir is known for having uttered: "When we try to pick something by itself, we find it hitched to everything else in the universe." By way of example, here follows a cascading effect. I have invented this one; it is a case of "let's suppose."

In an isolated coastal valley hemmed in by steep towering mountains, we find the air filled with flitting iridescent yellow birds, the ground carpeted with scarlet trumpeter flowers (which, of course, trumpet upon opening), and an old woman living in a wee tumbledown house. The nectar residing deep inside the trumpeter blossom that has an S-kink at its base, can be reached only by the yellow iridescent bird that is equipped with a flexible, wiry bill with a bitty bulb on the end; the bulb serves to guide a path through the curves without the bill's piercing the flower. The birds for two thousand years have drunk the trumpeters' nectar and in so doing pollinated the flowers. (Point of interest: The name for this relationship is *symbiotic*, each species benefiting the other.) Then one day a backpacker is dropped off on the beach, with a plan to scale the mountains; he has just come from rafting a river in Africa, and, snuggled deep in a pocket of his jacket, he unknowingly carries a fat green beetle, a female ready to pop out 150 baby fat green beetles. Sitting down in the middle of the sunny valley to eat his lunch, our backpacker tosses his jacket on a log, and out crawls the fat green beetle. Safe now from the tortoise spider that persistently scarfed it up in Africa, the fat green beetle in this little valley proliferates. Traveling as a large extended family, two thousand are soon settling into an expansive raspberry patch, and for two years they proceed to feast on the berries and bushes—until the plants are no more. The iridescent yellow bird, I neglected to mention, had always nested in the raspberry bushes, because there it was safe from a notorious indigenous egg-sucking snake that hates thorns. With the raspberry bushes gone and the iridescent yellow birds nesting in the willows, all the birds' eggs disappear down the egg-sucking snakes. Within five years the last pair of adult birds dies of old age. The snakes, a weedy-ish species, go easily back to their old diet of rodents and turtle eggs. The beetles, likewise, move on quite contentedly to eating little bits of any number of other things. The fields of trumpeter flowers without their pollinators die off, and the old woman, dispirited by the loss of trumpeter music and bouquets for her kitchen table, throws herself in the ocean.

So, what do we have here? The trail of the backpacker— he who started this cascade—is cold. The raspberries are extinct, the iridescent yellow bird extinct, the trumpeter flower extinct, the old woman drowned. Now the granddaughters of the old woman have inherited her house and, married as they are to brothers who own a cruise-ship line ready to anchor offshore, have plans to bulldoze Grandma's house and build a tourist mall, where they will sell handbags made from the skins of egg-sucking snakes along with varnished, fat green beetle pendant jewelry. (The relationships remaining now, just for added interest, are in a sense *parasitic*: one species living off another, or in this case two others, with no benefit to the latter.) The scientist will cringe at my scenario, but the reader will get the drift.

Continuing my education, I read a cover story in an issue

of *Harper's* magazine that bore the title "Planet of Weeds: Tallying the Losses of Earth's Animals and Plants." The author again was Quammen, with more on weedy species. "They are scrappers, generalists, opportunists. They tend to thrive in human-dominated terrain because in crucial ways they resemble *Homo sapiens:* aggressive, versatile, prolific, and ready to travel." In the weedy category are city pigeons, several species of rats, the mongoose, fire ants, zebra mussels, kudzu, various cockroaches, crows. Add deer mice to the list; they like to propagate right under Patrick's and my noses and can survive on everything from birdseed and the horses' COB to butter and bread and Beautiful Soap. Thinking further back, surely plains prickly pear—the very species I once spent weeks feeling unsettled about disturbing in the paths around our wagon—is weedy. The cluster fly looks profoundly weedy, or at least until the planet goes entirely over to urban and asphalt, and all the earthworms perish.

The way things are going with extinctions, in five or six human generations—what's that, 150 years, or less?—the earth will be a considerably different place, a place, according to Quammen, of threadbare landscapes leached of diversity, a meaner, far less comfortable place, and a more homogeneous place, reduced to a collection of weedy species. Yet in stark contrast to my thinking of the past twenty-five years—that we are a species bent on mangling our planet to the point of its not sustaining much, not sustaining us; that we will be witnessing our own demise—Quammen points out that *Homo sapiens* is a weedy species, indeed the weediest of all. We have the capability of propagating in every climate. We flit across countries and oceans with increasingly blinding speed. We stockpile weaponry for use on anything and everything and in amounts beyond description. We are rapacious as hell, pushing, twisting, straightening, burning and drowning and burying, dredging up, ripping apart, gluing together *this*, then *that*, all to the end of recomposing every little aspect of our living more to our liking. We will be around.

In view of my newfound knowledge of weedy species, I was only sorry that the flies I was catching had already laid their eggs! And for those thoughtful philosophies and practices of treasured friends? With regard to cluster flies and fleas and a few other things, I pointedly gave them the dropkick.

High-Flying
Pest Control

A Love Story

It was one of those long-drawn July evenings north of the forty-fifth parallel. The sky waxed a deep, seamless electric blue, fiery streaks of tangerine fading last in the notch of Big Creek Canyon—centerpiece to the string of mountains that in this hour of light often seem a child's black construction paper cutout hugging the entire western curve of the earth. Two heavenly bodies faintly began to twinkle, then flamed to a steady neon. They were the planets Venus and Mercury. Arm in arm, Patrick and I stood in the barnyard gaping at the splendor. When heaven's hues drained to a monochrome, we shuffled inside and headed for bed. Our Simmons Maxipedic sat in a corner that was once a cow stanchion, opposite the staircase to the mow. (I had bought two beds since we landed here; a queen for us to use on rainy nights, a double for company. And it was indeed I who bought them—beds show up nowhere on Patrick's "Things Necessary" list!)

Spring this year had been a wet one, and the combination with a simmering summer made for a fierce crop of mosquitoes. I had an important appointment scheduled in the coming week and had chosen to sleep indoors for a few days to save my face from a fate of Cyclops, Rudolph, or lumpy prizefighter. Mosquitoes do not bite Patrick; he will say, like a wiggling finger in the armpit, "Because God loves me!" If that truly is the case, then I am doomed to reside—for all eternity—in the big ecclesiastical doghouse.

It is the female mosquito that bites, requiring the nourishment of a good protein meal before laying her eggs. Damsels of the common North American species *Culex pipiens* seem to take exceptional pleasure in driving their "piercing organ" into my body parts, any exposed from the bedding, including the part in my hair. The females of most species of mosquitoes have an arsenal of apparatus jutting out from between their eyeballs: two long antennae; two longer (or sometimes much shorter) sensory organs called palpi; and the wicked proboscis, which is, curiously, the lady's labium. This last is an organ of unusually complex design: a flexible sheath that houses—this is not something I like to think about while lying in the dark being munched on—six elongated utensils. "There are two pairs of slender cutting organs, the mandibles and maxillae, and two additional organs called the hypopharynx and the labium-epipharynx." Or so say King et al. in "The Mosquitoes of the Southeastern United States" (1944), reprinted in literature I garnered from the university's county extension office.* The two pharynx gadgets mentioned, when fitted together, form the tube through which blood is drawn. In this case mine. I was not, however, proudly or willingly letting it go, as my friend Bill would have been. Blood was being sucked from me, Dracula-style.

But tonight I would be safe, and Patrick had acquiesced to sleeping indoors with me. For the occasion, I donned a long white cotton nightgown replete with Ginger Rogers–esque voluminous hemline, billowing sleeves, and old-fashioned

---

*Chapter 18 of the *Handbook of Pest Control*, Arnold Mallis the editor.

tatted yoke. Patrick tugged on but a T-shirt. We stretched out—lying entwined, each by one leg, with a blue-and-white-striped sheet gently resting over us—to read.

My eyes didn't want to focus on the page. I was savoring a rare moment of utter unconflicted languish, all levels of my being limp as boiled linguine. *This is the life!* Warm waves of luxuriousness were rippling down my limbs, when an almost imperceptible *whoosh* disturbed the still air over the bed. Then *thump!* Something? something? had zoomed down the staircase, passed over top of us, and whacked into the wall to my right. Or had I imagined it? I leaned over and, peering down, beheld on the rag rug a small brown creature. Furry. "E-yi!" I let out, scooting backward across the bed. "It's a bat!" My eyes, though, remained glued to it, lest it go somewhere and I know not where. Its fur was a soft sable color, while its face and ears appeared recently dipped in black paint, as did its feet and wings. Only momentarily dazed, it reached for the wall—the wainscoting planks of rough-sawn fir—and furiously began to climb.

Patrick swung his feet over the side and, in one fluid motion, as though he had been training for this moment his entire life, slipped into his rubber thongs, donned leather work gloves, and circled the bed to where he could gently trap the wriggling little critter between his cupped palms.

"Come on," he said, "let's take him upstairs. Let him go where he can get a good start."

Obeying as though under command, I rose to follow. We mounted the stairs in syncopated cadence. I, the barefoot princess flouncing along behind, found myself perfectly eye level with Patrick's sweetly working buns. So far, this resonated with all the possibilities of superb adventure! Making our way in the dark by memory, we nipped around our makeshift closets and the guest bed, threaded through the maze of covered wagon and two other horse-drawn vehicles, ducked the clothesline, and arrived at the far end of the mow. I jumped to throw open the big door to the deck, and Patrick stepped past me. Gingerly he worked the crawly bundle off his glove and onto the two-by-four railing. We watched it inch erratically in a circle, clinging belly against wood, and then abruptly fly off in a big downward swoop toward the river bottom.

This small brown bat is actually a big brown bat or, by the Linnaean system of nomenclature, *Eptesicus fucus*. With a body weight of three-fifths of an ounce and a forearm measurement* of not more than two inches, it falls in the midrange of bat sizes worldwide. The largest, the fruit-eating flying fox of Southeast Asia, has a wingspan of six feet. The tiny hog-nosed, or bumblebee, bat of Thailand, measuring a little over an inch in head–body length and weighing seven-hundredths of an ounce—the equivalent of a hefty vitamin pill!—is the smallest. It is, in addition, the smallest *mammal* in the world. Of the planet's roughly five thousand species of mammals (those warm-blooded animals giving birth to live young for whom they produce milk), bats make up nearly a fifth. They're found in all parts of the world, save the extreme polar regions. Chiroptera, the name of their order, derives from the Greek *cheir* for "hand" and *pteron* for "wing." The order breaks into two suborders: Megachiroptera, the generally larger bats of the Old World tropics that feed on nectar, fruit, and pollen; and Microchiroptera, the smaller insect-eating and echolocating bats, dispersed worldwide. Chiroptera, uniquely, are the one group of mammals to have developed true flight.

To our present knowledge, bats date back to the Eocene epoch, or some 50 million years. Prior to that, evolution is

*The bat biologist's method of sizing.

thought to have been working its magic on a small nocturnal, shrewlike mammal, developing its arms and hands, immensely elongating its fingers—as framework for wings. A webbing took form, at first between the fingers, perhaps for catching insects with more aplomb, or for gliding like flying squirrels between trees. Today we see this membrane as strung from the finger bones back to the body's trunk and hind legs. Only the thumb remains a short digit, free of the membrane and, in most species, tipped with a claw. The wing muscles, attaching at the breast and the back—unlike a bird's, which attach all at the breast—generate the thrust and lift for flight.

Bats' small and delicate bones do not preserve well as fossils, and evidence of webbing is rarer still. Yet we might guess that to a bat of the Eocene, its membrane would seem New Age miracle material: a thin, double-layered skin imbued with blood vessels, tiny muscles, and elastic fibers, and having the ability to repair small tears in itself with remarkable speed. Of the same makeup is the interfemoral membrane, stretching from leg to leg and in some manner encompassing the tail (except in the species having no tail). In the family of Free-tailed Bats, as one might suspect from the name, a thick, free tail extends beyond the membrane. But the big browns—whose family name springs from physical features at the other end of their bodies, Plain-nosed Bats—have less than spectacular tails, ending abruptly at the edge of the membrane. Such partnership—of arms, hands, fingers, legs, tail, and membrane—often lends bats an ungainly, broken look. That of a buckled half umbrella. When they manage to put all their unusual apparatus to work, the result is a flight that's been likened to an overarm rowing motion. I like to think of it as a swimmer's butterfly stroke, only in the air. It is a distinctive motion—different from a bird's. In Old French, the word *ratapignata* for bat translates as "fluttering flight."

The big brown bats occupy a vast range, extending from southern Canada to northern South America. By day, they will tuck themselves away in any number of odd places—beneath bridges, under eaves, inside hollows of trees and giant saguaro cacti, in storm drains, in the nests of cliff swallows, inside walls, behind shutters, on porches, beneath rocks. Attics, belfries, and old barns like ours are their penthouses, especially when they colonize. The group in our rafters is a nursery colony. The adult females are joined each spring by the yearling females, and their numbers increase annually.* Big brown females of western North America have a litter size of one, and one litter per year, as do most bat species. (Just to keep things from being simple, the big browns of the eastern part of the continent generally give birth to two babies.) Our first year, three bats greeted us in the night, flapping quietly over the deck and our bedroll. Six years later, there were seventy-five.

Though in the barn we were indeed eradicating mice, and one of us was beating off flies, with the bats, we were more accepting. Up in the roof, they were a welcome lot. They ate things: beetles, moths, mosquitoes. Particularly mosquitoes, I thought.

The barn's gambrel roof design offers a bat colony spacious living, though it took me a time, even with my background in building, to figure out just where. Looking at it from the outside, the roof is a two-plane affair: a gentle slope coming off the peak and then a steep drop, angling out but slightly with a little kick at the bottom. Inside, *three* ceiling planes are visible in the mow: the two seen outside and a third of medium steepness between them, for structural bracing. The silver insulation, starting at the floor, flows up the walls, follows the steep planes upward, cuts across the web-

*Males of the species are thought to live singly most of the year or in small colonies of their own.

bings and then along the slopes to the peak. In its run, it creates—above where it's stapled to the webbing—two triangular hollows the length of the barn. Perfect roosts for cavity-dwelling bats.

The colony's preference has been to take up residence at the south end of the west-side cavity, where it is by far the warmest. Landing high on the end wall beneath the roof's overhang—above, yet just out of direct line of, our bedding—they clamber in and out at precisely the point where the two roof planes meet and the chimney punches through the roof. Additional features honed by evolution, a flattened skull configuration and a thin-profiled body (no keel on the breastbone like a bird), allow these bats to squeeze through a small spacing in the skip sheathing to where the cavity opens up to them. Here they hang in their typical upside-down manner, effortlessly, by the claws on their toes— something a bat can do from the moment of birth. This last, Patrick and I must imagine, as to us it is not viewable.

What we do view clearly is bat guano. It rains down the one-inch gap behind the chimney (a space required for compliance with fire code) and bounces like jujubes across the floor. The largest part is caught at mow level, but a noticeable amount sifts down to the ground floor. Over time, I've become an expert—though only enlarging an area of study that's been mine for some years—on the subtle differences of poop! In the barn, namely that of mice and bats. Just ask me—I'm forever vacuuming up the latter's. Mice droppings appear dullish black, while the turds of bats are smoother in texture and shiny. Our third year here, the silver insulation adjacent to the chimney began visibly to sag under its load of guano and threatened to tear loose. This time the vacuum couldn't help us; we rented scaffolding and nailed up four sheets of plywood.

Also slipping down the gap behind the chimney, periodically, will be an adult bat. Out of confusion or curiosity—who really knows?—it crawls down and finds itself in the mow. The winged mother's eyes are good; toss out that old saying "blind as a bat." She is capable of steering a course by sight through familiar landscapes and also, it is thought, over extended distances, using large landmarks such as mountains and valleys, or even the sun and stars. In total darkness, however, and particularly for purposes of hunting her staple diet of flying insects, she sees instead with her ears. Employing a sophisticated sound system called echolocation, she sends out high-frequency calls, interprets the echoes she receives, and pieces together a finely tuned "sound picture." In searching for an exit from the barn, she may take a turn down the staircase and cruise our living quarters, adeptly negotiating the stout pillars and low ceiling hung with dried herbs, baskets, cast-iron frying pans, and my long braids of enormous garlic heads. One tour seems usually to be enough, and she heads back to the mow to land at one end high in the peak, roughly twenty-two feet above the floor. After a few minutes of what I suppose to be rest and contemplation, she swoops down through the middle of the room and up to the peak at the other end. This swooping is repeated over and over. Were a person standing in the center of the floor, he (I can't bring myself, in this instance, to use the stereotypical pronoun *she*) might take the notion that the bat is on the attack, dive-bombing his head. But this is not the case. The bat's maneuvering in such close quarters is in actuality a splendid display of the basic dynamics of flight. Lacking jet engines, a bat gains air speed most easily by diving. As it gains altitude and reaches the other end of the room, its speed slows into a stall, at which point it must turn and dive again, or light on the wall. Hence the swooping. I've witnessed in our years here only two bats rediscovering the chimney and disappearing back into the roof. To assist an entrapped bat in her effort to get free, we open the big doors, flick off the lights, and head downstairs. One *must* head downstairs, as bats, at least ours, fall into the watched-pot-will-never-boil category. On occasion, I've sat motionless upstairs for half an hour or more waiting to see a bat zoom out the doorway—to be certain it is gone before closing things up. The bat will instead flap around colliding with the ceiling and never, it seems, fly low enough to find the door. If I vacate the mow, within ten minutes the bat has done likewise.

Settled back into bed, I had read barely two more sentences of Jon A. Jackson's hot-off-the-press *Dead Folks* when a second bat hit the wall and flapped to the rug. On our rerun upstairs, we found a third dazed on the floor and a fourth, less fortunate, consumed—save for its wings—by one of our cats. Once again we were in bed when the fifth bat bounced hard off the wall and landed smack on my thigh, only the thinness of my gown separating us. The shriek I sent forth coupled with the lightning brush I gave it with the back of my hand—one indefinably welded reflex—reeled it into space. Again, Patrick to the rescue.

After we sent the fifth and then the sixth on their ways, Patrick read another few pages of *Cadillac Jukebox*, James Lee Burke's latest (at the time) crime drama, then reached over and clicked off his light. "Good night, my Passionate Petunia!" He planted a kiss on my neck. "The next six are yours."

"What?!"

This news jolted me worse than any landings of the bats, and just as I was about to wrap myself around his length and slip into dreams. "But, but . . . ?" *But I like it the way it is!* I screamed in my head. You my bare-bummed prince and me in white lace, gliding up and down the staircase.

Not a terribly feminist attitude, croaked a voice from deeper within.

It was just for tonight, I sniffled.

But Patrick was instantly asleep.

Well, shit! At this point, I was more put out by the possibility of having to gear up for an all-night ordeal than concerned about how I might actually go about picking up a live bat, leather gloves even so. But not being one to pout, particularly in darkness, where a bulging bottom lip loses all effect, I headed straight to *pissed.* We were apparently observing again "equal-everything-equal." But, unless I was mistaken, there was one bulky weight missing from my side of the tippy scale; it had to do with the real bombardiers, the tinier black ones with, as I so readily recalled, crinkly golden hairs on their thoraxes. Delivering a little pit bull growl, I defiantly snuggled down against the cooling night, not to register until morning that the Fortunes of Fate—and the bats—had allowed me temporary reprieve from a confrontation with my terrors.

That bats might enjoy some warmth in their roost is not inconceivable to me since I can't get through a Montana winter without ten cords of wood. We know that at least some of our colony, rather than heading to caves or mine shafts, choose to winter over in the barn. On warm February days, I sometimes hear their chittering. Places of optimum condition for a winter stay offer bats safety from predators, limited light, and an ambient temperature not too cold and not too hot. Bats are true hibernators, with a lowered body temperature, a slowed heart rate, and slower yet breathing—pauses of as much as a minute have been recorded. Because of this, they fall into a unique category of animals.

When the mercury drops, a snake will become cold and inactive. Animals that are "cold-blooded" cannot raise their body temperature much above the ambient level, whereas those that are "warm-blooded"—as in mammals and birds—

can, with enough fuel, regulate their temperature nearly at a constant. To take this a little further, humans are homeothermic; in other words, we keep (and need to keep) our internal thermostats—give or take an influenza fever or touch of hypothermia—within a few degrees. Bats and other true hibernators are heterothermic, or capable of wide swings in body temperature. And being able to severely depress their metabolic processes, bats can survive extended periods of inactivity without intake of food, during which time they convert stored body fat into energy. The quality of their winter hideaways takes on greater significance when you think about the huge heat-radiating surface of bats' membranes, which causes them heavier heat losses than those of other mammals of their size. Yet the big browns can tolerate somewhat colder environments than other bats. They have been known to survive at several degrees below freezing without awakening from a deep winter torpor.

Our barn doesn't appear the ideal place for wintering bats. We crank the woodstove up during the hours we're awake and let it go, for the most part, when we're asleep. We sometimes leave for a week or a month and at those times tear down and drain our minimal plumbing in anticipation of indoor temperatures dropping well below freezing. At best, we will turn on the bathroom wall heater, which we installed for our fourth winter, set it on low, and close the door. The bats receive no benefit from the insulation; they live above it. Outside temperatures can plummet to thirty below; an afternoon sun can warm the cavity to fifty degrees. This yo-yoing of temperatures, I would think, would drive the bats into frequent energy-depleting arousals and relocations—up and down the cavity, huddling together, moving apart. Yet when springtime rolls around, we don't seem to have lost bats over it.

. . .

Conditions in the barn are actually decidedly more suitable to mosquitoes, the wee *Culex pipiens*. We know the little biting monsters winter over with us, somewhere in or under the barn; every so often we will see one floating around, trying to zero in. It's rather a novelty—and the only time I'm charmed by this species—being bitten by a mosquito when it's twenty below outside. Most of the *Culex* varieties hibernate during the winter not as larvae but as adult females. In Mallis's book again, Russell et al. found mosquitoes (granted of a different species from our *pipiens*, but apparently not so very different) hibernating in basements in Siberia, where temperatures ranged from 48.2° to −0.4°F. Field researchers would frequently see them frozen to walls and ceilings. After gradually thawing and reviving, they were capable of laying eggs!* And what of the males in Siberia? Nothing is mentioned, though the pages go on in detail about egg laying and reproduction.

The first brood of a female mosquito will number anywhere from fifty to five hundred eggs. After that, in subsequent ovipositions (depositings of eggs), the number diminishes somewhat. Gordon A. Harrison,† speculating on an average of two hundred eggs per brood, half of which would become females, and then taking into consideration that a mosquito is capable of developing to maturity in less than two weeks, calculated that five generations would produce 20 million mosquitoes. Then he posed the exact question that came to my mind: "If we could get twenty million from only one female, what could thousands of females give rise to?" By further simple calculation (mine), this five-generation explosion requires a time frame of only two and a

*Taken from *Practical Malariology*, Paul Russell et al., 1963.
†From his book *Mosquitoes, Malaria, and Man*, 1978—excerpted again by Mallis.

half months. Though in this climate, that would be pushing it for duration. On our sleeping deck, we generally experience hordes of mosquitoes for two to three weeks, during the time of hottest days and warmest nights.

The bite. A female mosquito's gut, Harrison says, generally contains anywhere from one to more than four cubic millimeters of blood. She may, nonetheless, suck twice that much for nourishment for herself and her eggs, and, in fact, virgin females have reportedly taken in fifteen times their own weight in blood. It's during their feeding that mosquitoes pass into their victims foreign proteins contained in their saliva that cause the familiar swelling and itching, and in some people allergic reactions. In Montana we're not too worried about mosquitoes carrying encephalitis or malaria—not yet, that is. A little more global warming and who knows.

The female mosquito has another special organ, the spermatheca. It stores sperm. Once bred, a fecund *Culex* mama carries enough sperm to fertilize eggs throughout her life. Thus her suitor's importance is short-lived. The male mosquito, by all appearances, has a fairly forgotten and dull life. Furthermore, poor fellow, he spends his childhood—his approximately one premating day—with his sex organs on backwards. Material, I'm thinking, for a new page in the Kama Sutra! Except that, during that day, mating for him is impossible. Just in the nick of time, in readying for day two and his big date, the rear segments of his abdomen rotate—yes, rotate—180 degrees. "The dorsal surface comes to lie ventrally and vice versa; back becomes front and front becomes back."*

Oddly enough, for the bats' survival, a summer's heat is just as precious a commodity as a winter's steady coolness.

*Mallis has taken this one from J. D. Gillett's *The Mosquito*, 1972.

Thinking of it in terms of survival of the species as a whole, the idea each year is to get the offspring weaned and reared soon enough for the mothers and youngsters to pack on the fat (much in the manner of bears) that is needed in this mountain climate to see them through almost six months of hibernation. Ergo, female bats have evolved into masters of the challenges of pregnancy and child care.

The big browns begin their annual sojourn into motherhood by settling into their chosen maternity roost in the spring; I hear them in the barn (with either their arrival or their arousal from torpor) and occasionally see one flying out at dusk, starting in April. Within their bodies they carry the sperm from autumn and, perhaps, winter-in-the-roost copulations. The spear-headed sperm cells get all lined up and nosed into a layer of uterine mucus, poised for the starting shot, then find they must play the waiting game until spring. Biologists call this delayed fertilization. In the interim, while the sperm are kept in storage, they're nurtured by gland cells in the female, described by John E. Hill and James D. Smith as possessing "many microscopic, finger-like projections (microvilli) that contact and embrace the head of the sperm cell."* Sounds like foreplay erotica to me! And now is where the heat comes in. To set in motion fertilization and implantation of the egg, warm weather is needed—interpret good feeding, or insect activity—in combination with a cozy roost.

Once the ovum is in place, next is to speed along the gestation process. *Plus chaud! Plus chaud!* "More heat!" (A phrase Patrick picked up from a Quebecois farrier tending his coal forge.) The length of gestation is greatly dependent upon the weather. Furthermore, as noted in *The World of Bats*,† Felix

*In their book, *Bats: A Natural History*, 1984.

†A collaboration by the author Klaus Richarz and the wildlife photographer Alfred Limbrunner, originally published in German; English translation by William Charlton.

Heidinger proposes that pregnant females *actively* influence embryonic development. In his study of a mouse-eared bat colony, Heidinger noticed that, when their food was good and their energy levels high, the soon-to-be moms bunched together in the roost, pushing their body temperatures as high as possible, speeding along fetal development. Weather though recoups the upper hand should it turn too foul for the bats to feed. Forced then to conserve energy, they must move apart and drop into a semitorpor, lowering their body temperatures to ambient conditions. With each trip into this sleep lethargy, the growth of a carried embryo will slacken.

Finally comes Bi-Ba's Week at the Romany Forge: Birthing Baby Bats in the Barn. The event is noticeable to those of us outside the cavity only by a slight increase in chatter. To bring a bald pink infant into the world, the female bat hangs spiderlike, by thumbs and feet, forming her membranes into a basket. Or, sometimes, she turns upside-down (right side up to us) and hangs by her thumb claws, letting the baby plop into the apron of her interfemoral membrane. In any case, the newborn immediately climbs to one of its mother's breast nipples and there hangs on with the tenacity of a barnacle by means of, incredible as it may sound, nursing teeth. An observation written up in the *Journal of Zoology* (March 1994) told of one female bat acting as midwife to another. The biologist Thomas H. Kunz of Boston University, while engaged in a study of bats' milk, happened to witness a mother of the fruit bat species *rodrigues* having a difficult time with a breech birth. The midwifing bat came alongside, hung instructively by her thumbs, and emulated contractions and straining. In addition, during the exceptionally lengthy three-hour birthing, the midwife cradled the mother in her wings and licked and fanned her to keep her cool.

For a mother bat's production of milk to remain vigorous and rich, she requires, once again, a plentitude of insects and a warm roost. The barn's new moms at this stage come wheeling in and out over our heads all night, feeding their newborns and feeding themselves. Patrick and I have never kept an all-night watch, lying on our backs with our eyes propped open, but we do stir frequently to the thunder of the horses ripping around, to a Bengal tiger scream from the swamp—"What the hell was that?"—to the Victor fire horn going off. And always we monitor the bats' activity. At some hours, there is such a hectic interchange of moms, scrambling in and out, they could do with a traffic controller. But their efforts are all to the good: baby bats when fed well and kept warm (90°F or more) grow rapidly and are ready to flex their wings in preparation for flight within a few weeks.

Beyond pregnancy and motherhood, the taxing energy drains for bats are long nightly flights to feeding grounds, long migrations to winter hibernation sites (186 miles has been recorded), and repeated arousals from winter torpor. A bat's chances for survival are markedly increased when its expenditures of energy are minimized. Our barn, in most respects, is an ideal roost. Its location offers a smorgasbord of bat delights, in immediate and diverse buggy areas: marshland, meandering creek, grassy meadow, open woodland, and waters of the main river—all within a quarter mile. For the bats wintering in the barn, it means no commute. Hence, in combination, the nearby prime feeding grounds, the first-class nursery accommodations, and the handy winter shelter—dubious as it might seem to my mind— probably account for the colony's increasing size.

To get the annual count, I take up a post at the southeast corner of the barn and wait patiently for dusk, when I can begin picking out their dark forms emerging against the waning western light. Bats taking off from roosts of complete darkness, like our cavity, appear capable of testing the twilight, or doing what is called light sampling, at the mouth of their cave or exit hole. They don't head out until presumably registering an agreeable amount of darkness. This has apparently more to do with the intensity of light than with the time of sunset; on overcast evenings, they may depart from the roost earlier. When the moment arrives, a colony numbering in the millions and viewed from a distance may be taken for a thick column of smoke on the rise. From our barn, because the exit hole is small, bats pop out in countable ones, twos, and threes. I imagine them all lined up behind the opening, jostling for position like kids in line for ice cream cones. Then suddenly they are off, small silhouettes of erratic fluttering, in silence, careening across the great arc of southern sky and imparting to the fall of evening an unlikely serenity, something as inaudible as the sun's coming up; something I like to depend on.

In predawn's quiet, the bats come slipping back into the barn. About that same still time, before society's masses are up and clanging away, my mind—without an awareness of being alert—sometimes can string together *things* with a creative clarity that's almost frightening. The world's collective inspiration, I always think, must reach its peaks during snatches of mental rest. Yet the term *leisure* generally puts me in mind of old English novels or paintings of Victorian women in high-necked dresses, with parasols, idly poling—can't they row?—wooden boats around lakes of water lilies, butterflies flitting by. I would last about half an hour at such dallying before my mind latched on to some brilliantly obsessive task, some equally absorbing challenge, or I just slipped off my outer layers and went swimming. But with morning's preconscious leisure-of-the-noggin, there is a difference. No boats, no lilies, no parasols—my mind is free to lope with vision. As an entity completely unto itself, seemingly without sponsorship at all, it will work diligently, say, scribbling in ticker tape across my inner forehead the next paragraph of a current writing project. Sentences, all edited and punctuated, await only my awakening and grabbing a pen.

The morning after our night of bats in the bed, my last dreams segued into just this kind of uncluttered cogitating on exactly that episode. The bats that had zoomed down our staircase sharpened into focus on my screen not as dumb bats. Their raining had not been prompted by an over-crowding up in the rafters and their being given the boot. It had not been caused by the cavity's overheating on a long sizzling afternoon and their gasping to get out. So many of them sailing into our living quarters all in one night may have been startling new ground to us, but, on their part, it was clearly not a random occurrence. The colony's pregnant females had delivered their young (the one pup to a mother), we had guessed from the increased activity and onset of daintier chittering, at the end of June; now, in the fourth week of July, it was time for fledgling flight lessons. These, then, were baby bats on their maiden flights—the executions of which they are none too good at. One estimate has it that 60 percent of baby bats die in their first year, for various rea-sons, probably largely because of not putting on enough fat before winter, but certainly not to the exclusion of their first few flapping excursions and slamming into something. A tree. A barn. The wall beside someone's bed. Those juveniles of the previous night had mistakenly taken the chute down the back of the chimney and landed with a *plunk* on the mow floor; they apparently weren't any better at rowing than my Victorian, lily-pond-poling boatwomen. In struggling with their predicament, most had crawled around long enough to discover the stairwell, which offered them easy opportunity to get airborne again.

With this all puzzled out, my eyes opened to the day and

my mind to one fully conscious thought: There was no reason to think flight school wouldn't be in session every night
for a week!

Later that afternoon, I was working away at my desk in the
mow beneath a pitched racket emanating from the colony.
We were having a heat wave. The temperature where I sat
was pushing 95°F. The cavity's temperature I could only
guess was well over 100°. In addition to highly animated
chatter, the roost was a commotion of flutterings and flap-
pings that I might have attributed to the juveniles' wing cal-
isthenics save for the heat, which had me thinking it was
more their attempts to cool themselves by fanning. On hot
days, bats have been known to move from an attic roost
down through walls and even into basements. Big browns,
though they are more tolerant than other species of colder
conditions, are less happy with heat extremes, reportedly vacating roosts when temperatures rise much above 94°F.
Nevertheless, on days hotter than this one, I hear them—a
hyper chorus of chittering and chaos—still up in the cavity.

A bat's vocalizations are like no other sound I've heard—a
sort of rhythmic crinkling of cellophane, gone electronic. I
say "I" because Patrick cannot hear their utterances. It's a fre-
quency not available to him, something he attributes to
years of shooting off firearms, working near the roar of jet
engines (one winter as a cargo handler for MarkAir), and then,
of course, Jimi Hendrix's having left his mark. From a children's radio show, *The Pea Green Boat*, we learned that women
are more likely to hear bat calls than men. Yet the majority of
bat sounds are ultrasonic, or far too high for any human to
decipher. And bats have calls for everything: echolocating
feeding buzzes as they home in on a delectable insect, alarm
and territorial calls, food advertisements (possibly), mating
calls, mother and infant goo-gooings. Big browns, however,
regularly have calls audible below twenty kilohertz, or the
upper end of normal human hearing.

In our first years in the barn, I had gone about blithely as-suming that the chitterings of our bats were, on the whole, sounds of contentment: sleepy-eyed wake-up yawns and a kind of almost cheerful singing. But the big browns, I even-tually was informed, are a species of churlish temperament. Now I pride myself on deciphering the nuances of their ex-changes. There are the July afternoon high hysterics in the oven. The more even timbre of general announcements: "Hey, caddis fly hatch on the river tonight." And the peevish insults, thrown along with the prod of an elbow: "Move over, you mud brown oaf, I need a little air!"

My first full night on duty with the baby bats—"The next six are yours!"—and I wasn't sure how I was going to fare. Patrick had rolled out his bedding on the deck, and I'd slid between the sheets downstairs. Though normally we would do anything to sleep in each other's arms, my dear one was desperate for the night air and, as always, ready to be done with the "miserable black hole of death," as he calls stale air, dust, currents of electricity, refrigerator hum. I had known all day what the evening might hold for me yet had given no more than cursory thought to why, precisely, I was creeped out by the idea of picking up a bat. Once I was in bed, night closed in, spooky as a dark, dense forest, and a pall of anxi-ety settled over me.

Now in many parts of the world, and particularly in our civi-lized northern New World culture, bats, down through the ages, have come to embody a raft of superstitions and fears. Creatures of the night, evil and macabre, bats are the blood-sucking, bad cousins of Halloween's witches and ghouls. Mention "bats" in public and most people grimace and shud-der. There are grown men terrified of bats; my pharmacist of a time belly-crawled into his bedroom with a .22 rifle and drilled holes in his new log home in trying to kill a little bat.

On film, even the smallest bats typically are captured in fearsome portrait: openmouthed, baring full sets of pointy teeth. (Most of the Microchiroptera fly with their mouths open, echolocating.)

It is only in traveling to different cultures, kingdoms, clans, and households—from the primitive to the far from primitive—that we find bats blooming as the antitheses of sinister. There are those who view them as the luckiest of all animals to have around and capable (when dead and nailed over a door) of driving bad luck from a home. Bat images have shown up as deities, as totems, in coats of arms, in family crests. To the Chinese, they are symbols of good luck and happiness; their winged likenesses, often stylized, appear thematically in Chinese art. Bats bedeck Chinese jewelry, fabrics, pottery. In another part of the world, the Ninth Bombardment Squadron of the British Royal Air Force takes a bat and this motto for its badge: *Per noctem volamus,* meaning "By night we fly."

The applications for bats as ingredients in ancient magic trace back to antiquity. Their hairless membranes inspired inclusion in depilatories, while their body fur indicated inherent powers to cure baldness. By means of bat remedy, or elaborate bat ritual, you could make yourself see better, make someone you didn't like go blind; put yourself to sleep, keep yourself awake; relieve the symptoms of gout, asthma, sciatica, paralysis; ease childbirth. Lotions, potions, unguents, amulets have all been fashioned from bat parts and excreta: urine, dung, blood, tongue, gall, heart, brain, the ashes of burned membranes—whatever was deemed appropriate to the purpose. In Glover Morrill Allen's wonderful compilation "Some Strange Uses for Bats,"* I found some dillies: To aid dim vision (this one he takes from Warren R. Dawson's 1925

*Chapter 3 in his book *Bats,* 1939.

finding in an "old Syriac book"), pound the heads of young bats or swallows, mix with honey, and smear on the eyelids. To ease gout, Allen quotes: "Galenus advises three bats boiled in rainwater, to which add an ounce of flaxseed, three raw eggs, a cup of oil, dung of an ox, an ounce of wax—mix well and apply to the afflicted part." And for rheumatism, Allen gives us this from Conrad Gesner (1555): "Take twelve bats, St. Johnswort, rancid butter, aristolochia, and castor, and boil together until it becomes an ointment." Finally, a prescription for love (another from Dawson, this a translation from a Greco-Egyptian papyrus, now in my words): A woman can attract the man she desires by molding a little dog charm out of uncooked flour or unrefined wax and inserting in the charm's right eye the right eye of a bat, taken while alive, but making sure to let the creature go (poor bat!). Allen surmises: it is the characteristic "watchfulness" of the bat and the "faithfulness" of the dog that produce the intended magic. I surmise: I don't know any woman who could do this. Not to worry, guys!

Into none of these slots, however—of religion, superstition, idolization, loathing—did I fit. I was not likely to drink a bat balm as a cure for anything, but I also was not a screamer, unless one of the little dears unexpectedly landed on my thigh. It wasn't bats I feared. It wasn't bloodsucking vampires I feared. (Vampire bats live in the tropics, taking a little blood generally from cows. Humans, for nourishment, traditionally take the *whole* cow!) Furthermore, it wasn't rabies. Rabies is definitely something to be concerned about, but so, too, is driving the highway out front. Along these lines, Merlin Tuttle's rant captured by Diane Ackerman was published in *The New Yorker* magazine. Here follow two sentences: "Less than a dozen people in all the U.S. and Canada are believed to have died of *any* bat-related disease in the past four decades!"

and "We don't get excited about the fact that more people die of food poisoning at church picnics annually than have died *in all history* from contact with bats." Tuttle is the founder of Bat Conservation International, and in his long effort to save and promote understanding of bats, he may have handled more bats than any other human being.

Rather than engendering fear within me, bats have long held out a fascination. During the ten-year stretch of my life that I was camped most summer nights on riverbanks, I played a bat game with myself. At some point each evening, I would glance up and notice that the swallows flitting over the water, hawking insects, had turned into bats—a changing of the guard, so to speak, from diurnal to nocturnal. It became my objective to nail down precisely which one was the last swallow and which the first bat. I sought to witness the enchanting instant of such a change. But with the incessant nature of camp chores, it has been, to this day, a case of "Damn! Missed it again."

Thus, on the larger issue of creepiness, bats and I have always been okay. I don't fear bats per se. I do, nonetheless, retain, probably lingering from childhood, a few idiosyncratic, lopsided fears. They are true heebie-jeebies, deriving from certain motions: flappy things in my face, crawly things inside my clothes, wiggly things in my palm. Once when I was driving down the Ventura Freeway in the San Fernando Valley, a king-sized moth flew up from under the car seat and fluttered in my face as though it thought my eyes and nose and mouth were windows it could get out. I responded in an apoplectic fit of batting it away. That this happened in the early 1960s and at daybreak Sunday morning, with not another soul on the road, was what saved me when I inadvertently cranked the wheel and sped diagonally across four lanes.

·   ·   ·

Preparing myself for my impending evening of ordeal involved a kind of all-body gritting of teeth. I was in no mood for sorting out any deep origins of my phobias. I readied the leather gloves on my nightstand and, seeking to stave off uneasiness, immersed myself in *Dead Folks* again. Jackson's kingpin-of-the-Detroit-mob character, Humphrey DiEbola, who had been feeling grossly overweight, yet not wanting to become too small a man, had whittled his 315 pounds down to 250 on an eating regime laced with fiery chili peppers. Chef Pepe, in the kitchen now, coring the bright orange habaneros, is soon having a hotter time than expected bending the maid Caroline over the butcher block, flipping up her skimpy skirt, and, in his fervor, transferring to their moist coupling parts the capsaicin still on his hands. "After a few minutes, she gasped. 'It's hot! Why is it so h——' "

Hup!—there it was, the electronic cellophane. Right at the top of the stairs. *Here we go!* Tugging on the gloves, sucking in a big breath, I pushed myself to buck up. Then suddenly a cat made a dash up the stairs, and this canceled any timidity on my part. No dithering, I flew from bed to stair top, stampeded the cat, and snatched up the bat so fast there wasn't room for a contrary thought.

I marched across the mow, raised the bar lever with my elbow, and with a toe encouraged the door into its wide swing. "I've got a bat," I announced. "I'm letting it go."

"Mmm." The bare-bummed prince was asleep.

I deposited my little parcel on the railing, and stood watching. Its only snarl had come in response to my nudging it off my glove—no way for it to comprehend being rescued. Churlish species perhaps, but this particular youngster seemed friendly, with a comely look to its face.

Patrick breathed heavily. It was only fitting, as I thought about it, that I should revel in this rite of passage all on my own.

Ten minutes later, the next inexperienced pilot hit the wall by the bed. I scooped it up and carried it out to the front porch, where, with a two-handed, underhand throw that started between bent knees, I gave it a huge heave-ho! and it took off flying over Patrick's shoeing shed.

I was just dropping off to sleep when I thought I heard a gentle *flap-flap*, but shining a flashlight around the walls I saw nothing. Early the next morning, Patrick was rustling in the kitchen, whirring the mechanical eggbeater, when I suddenly awoke and rose up on one elbow with the notion something was up. "Expecting company, were you?" He was pointing to the window above my head. I turned and beheld a bat in full wing expansion clinging to the lace curtain. I bounded out of bed! Actually, to get a camera. And probably scared it. It deftly disentangled itself and flew back to the kitchen, where it lodged on a small ledge above the jars of spices. By now I had on the gloves, and, standing next to Patrick, I urged it into my grasp.

"Come on!" I said to my Equal-Equal Man, tossing him the tilted chin and sideways grin of a watch-how-good-I-am-at-this carriage. "Let's take it outside."

Stretching as high as I could, I let it grab onto a weathered board on the barn's shady west side. Too much daylight for it to fly home—it squeezed instead, upside-down, halfway under the board.

"The little guy needs a drink," I said, thinking back to our first years in the barn, when Patrick had found two dead bats on different mornings in the mow and pronounced them expired from dehydration. (Though I, at the time, was sure they died of exhaustion.)

"The little guy wants to *sleep*," he said.

Oooh, but of course! How short is my memory. This is the state of the universe with us: no matter the event, we experience it from acutely different perspectives. *What does he know about sleep? I am the Maven of Snoozing.* Patrick can operate hand-somely on four and five hours a night, for days. Sleep is highly overrated, he will say, you can sleep when you're dead. We were, though, approaching the point where it was no longer so critical to the survival of our egos and control-ling natures to argue one another into the dirt.

Rummaging around, I found an eyedropper. The bat's eye-lids were clamped shut. Patrick stood at my shoulder: "Yup, he wants to sleep." (The bat had become a "he," Patrick un-doubtedly identifying, thanks to having suffered too many of my sleepless nights of tossing and turning and intermit-tently posing questions like "Are you awake?") I raised the dropper to the bat's mouth and watched him lap up two drops. Turning my head, I offered Patrick a broad, tight-lipped grin.

He returned with: "Best glare I've seen all day!"

Satisfied with the hydrating, I dressed and rushed off to pick up mealworms from Mountain Mary and came home with a cottage-cheese carton, from which I selected a small but juicy-looking specimen. With a tweezers I stuck the end of the worm into the bat's mouth, and he immediately dropped it. Just then Patrick stepped around the corner.

"You're waking him up *a-gain?*"

"Uh-huh, he needs to eat. Then he can sleep."

I offered another to the little guy's now open mouth. Pos-sibly he *was* just plain incensed at being disturbed, but I was not sure his widemouthed gape wasn't a death throe and thus was pleased when his teeth closed down on it. I went off to find some cardboard to tack up for afternoon shade, and when I returned the mealworm was gone. Not on the ground. Presumably eaten!

The bat stayed tucked in his shady nook until dusk, and then flew off. Another success story.

·   ·   ·

With one day yet to go before my important appointment, I was missing snuggling with Patrick.

I didn't suppose the female bats were missing the males in their lives on any nightly basis, or with any particular throbbings of heart. Their sex drives would not engage until their nursery charges matured to self-sufficiency later in the summer. (Nursing would continue on through a grace period after the youngsters started to fly.) The mating behavior of big brown bats, in any event, remains mostly conjecture. Although the sum total of what we know about bats is probably more than that about mice—outside of laboratories, that is—and certainly more than that about cluster flies, the specific intimacies of the big browns are a subject of nature not yet studied. From other bat species a few things are known, as well as one striking fact that surely applies also to big browns: males have startlingly long penises! When the male mounts the female from behind—in the typical animal-lacking-the-influence-of-missionaries posture, except that they are hanging upside-down—he must have an organ equal to the job of reaching around the tail and interfemoral membrane. And mammals, I was finding out, achieve erection in complicated ways.

One day, I am having a cup of tea with a friend in her kitchen. (She's a jaded and irreverent sort, but equally shy, and doesn't want to be mentioned by name.)

"What are you writing about now?" she asks.

"Bats," I say.

"Eee-u!" Her nose wrinkles up and her shoulders jerk.

"No, no, this is pretty good stuff. I'm reading about penises! Bats happen to have exceptionally long poke-hers."

"Yeah?" I have her attention now—a subject apparently dearer to her heart than bats. She sets down her teacup.

By way of explanation, I give her a short description of bat anatomy—membranes, tails. "And mammals have various equipment for getting hard-ons. Hards-on? Anyway, with some, it's a fibroelastic penis that remains semierect. You know, like dogs."

"And some have bones!" She's motioning me into the living room. "That," she says, pointing at what looks to me like an oddly shaped ivory tusk, almost two feet long, hanging by a strip of rawhide choked around one end, "is a walrus's penis bone."

"You're kidding! Hanging right here on your wall? How'd you get a thing like that?"

"An old boyfriend. He hunted in Alaska. It's called an oosik." She takes it down and offers it for my inspection. It is polished to a sheen; there is a slight curve to its length; it is thicker and heavier on one end.

"A walrus's penis bone." I am weak with awe. The substance of it is dense, with heft similar to that of my three-pound workout weight. It is an item you are naturally compelled to run your hands up and down, at least I am. The slimmer end fits my grasp perfectly. I wield its weight around in a big arc, thinking it would make a good club. (Later Patrick will inform me, from his MarkAir stint, that everyone in Barrow, Alaska, has a walrus's oosik; the native Iñupiats scour the beaches for them, to sell. But the word "oosik," come to find out, in talking to Jana, the Iñupiat woman I am given to when I call the North Slope Borough in Barrow to inquire about a native dictionary—the politest way I can think of to ask a complete stranger, long-distance, for the spelling in her language of *penis*—is the anglicized version of the Iñupiat word for a human penis, or *usuk*, pronounced "oo-sook." A walrus's penis bone is *usuaq*, pronounced "oo-soo-awk.")

My friend is fingering through her bookcase. "Raccoons have penis bones," she says, "little ones. I have this catalog. You can order them." She pulls out a thin pamphlet and flips to its picture—a wee, decidedly J-shaped bone that inspires pondering as to quite how it might be used—and then to the order form: Raccoon Penis Bone, Texas Tickler, $4.98.

"Jeez! Actually, I heard somewhere that grizzlies have penis bones, and, now that I think about it, some of the species of bats—bacula they're called. But nothing so impressive I'm sure"—I'm still turning the *usuaq* over in my hands— "and only as ossified tips on their *corpora cavernosa.*"

My friend was once a nurse; she knows *corpora cavernosa*, the paired cylinders of spongy vascular tissue in men's penises (in fact, in the penises of all higher primates, bats included), that spring erect with engorgement of blood during sexual excitement.

"But that's just the beginning!" I cry. She tops off my tea. "There's something called the *corpus spongiosum*, erectile tissue that surrounds their urethras. But this is the best: *accessory cavernous tissue*. Erections with accessories! Well, born-with accessories," I quickly add, remembering shops in San Francisco's North Beach. "This stuff invades the foreskin, but only after penetration so it bonds their intercourse. Some bats can virtually lock into humping and then drop together into winter torpor."

"God," she frowns. "You'd never get anything done!"

"I thought it was kind of sweet."

"Hmm," we hum in unison.

Sipping our tea, we stare out the window, each suddenly lost in private recollecting.

The gigantic flying foxes of India have a ludicrously high old time in mating. And their behavior is not, if I might say, too far afield from that of various humans I've known. To begin with, they are a promiscuous lot, as observed by the German zoologist Gerhard Neuweiler,* from his study of a colony

*As noted in *The World of Bats*, Richarz and Limbrunner again.

numbering one thousand and roosting in banyan trees in Madras. The females being what Neuweiler calls (in translation) "passive" and "brusque," the males will "sniff as they approach the females and try to lick them in the genital region. This licking makes the females less unfriendly and more accommodating." Nonetheless, as the males maneuver toward mounting to breed, the females send up "shrill defensive cries." Should attempts at intromission fail (often three successive couplings are necessary for an ejaculation) or should the cornered female try to escape the roost, then it is the male's turn for loud protesting cries—behavior, Neuweiler says, that's been seen as intimidation to make the female more receptive to renewed efforts at mating. *What is that line? "There'll be days like this, my mama said!"* At the peak of their breeding season, the cries of one male can stimulate all the other males into synchronously mounting any handy female, and the roost becomes for the ensuing hour a "deafening screeching and copulating mass."

But male bats are plainly not all cads of the wham-bam-thank-you-ma'am ilk. With some, it's courtship singing, "honeymoon" roosts, waftings of scintillating pheromones, and dazzling "erectile head-crests" that remind one of 1940s chapeau frippery.

I definitely thought of our barn's bats as an integral part of my love life: their consumption of mosquitoes paved the way for more nights sleeping with my Pastaman. Every bat I saved meant, in my mind, several million mosquitoes that wouldn't be gnawing on me.

For another night I stood at the ready for rescues, but no more babies crash-landed. The following night, my appointment kept, I prepared to rejoin Patrick on the deck. I coated not my body with love potions but my face with an oily citronella product, an organic bug spray. Its protective action would last not all night . . . but long enough.

I drifted asleep feeling Patrick's arm snug me in against his belly. In my ear, he whispered, "Good night, my Citronella Cutie."

Several years later, after reading three of his books on bats, I placed a call to the venerable chiropterologist Dr. M. Brock Fenton, known as the "batman" of York University in Toronto. I had in mind to learn something about the peculiarities of our bats. In the course of our conversation, I happened to mention I particularly adored these bats because we slept outdoors and they ate so many mosquitoes.

"They don't eat mosquitoes." He said it with an edge, as though it were a correction he was forced to make often.

"They don't?" I was stunned. "Not at all?" Surely they ate *some* mosquitoes. I'd read, all my life it seemed, of the hundreds of mosquitoes a bat eats in one night, the hundreds of pounds in a year.

"Not at all," he said.

"Not any bats?" I wasn't giving up. Perhaps, I thought, little browns were also roosting in the cavity. They did this sometimes, species roosting together. "What about *little* browns?"

"None." (Again!) "It's rare that a bat will eat a mosquito." By accident, he seemed to be saying, while flying with their mouths open!

There went my love story.

A few nights after Dr. Fenton's reparative tutelage, an adult bat slipped into the mow while I was working. She took one high turn around the room and landed back on the chimney. Spread-eagled, clutching with her thumb and toe claws, feet angled out behind in the manner of a lizard's, she inched

sideways around the rough gray cinder block. I was reminded of a rock climber's technique—body splayed flat,
feet and hands spread for working cracks and crevices. And
oh, those feet! They seemed to me miniatures of black
human hands.

Instantly, I knew it was not the colony's eating habits that
earned them their place in my barn. It was their nature and
behavior, the beings of the bats themselves—and maybe a
little bit their bacula!—that had so captivated my affections.

For all time.

Bouquet of Musk

With Chocolates

Years ago in California, in the dead of a summer night, I turned into one of those thousands of alarmed people who dial 911 for some loopy reason and then go down in the annals of police dispatches alongside criers of emergencies such as "The dog's head's stuck in the banister!" "Whaddo I do with a flat tire?" "My plumbing's backing up!" My particular whimper, of course, was an actual crisis.

I had awakened to my cat's scratching on the window screen, her way of asking to be let in. In a sleep-stupor, I'd stumbled through the kitchen to the one door of my half-basement apartment. Back in bed, drifting off again, I heard noisy lapping from the toilet bowl, something my all-too-proper cat would never do. Next came the clatter of cat dishes from the kitchen, every sound hitting me now as though wired to a loudspeaker. *I must have left the door open. A dog must have come in.* I switched on the bed lamp, and my feet hit the floor not twenty-four inches from the hind end of a skunk. That it was strikingly glossy in its blackness and whiteness was, however oddly, my first thought—I never before having appraised a live skunk at this range. The sleek intruder waddled off toward the living room. My couch held an array of clean and neatly stacked clothes to be tucked into a duffel bag for an early-morning flight. In a panic I grabbed up the receiver, dialed the ingrained three numbers, and to a dispatcher wailed, "There's a skunk in my house!" It is not possible to climb into the closeness of an airplane, and a system of canned air, smelling of skunk. I'd be bludgeoned and thrown off.

I was living at the time on an *urban* fringe, the third house from the end of a cul-de-sac in the town of San Anselmo. Wildlife didn't last long in the human crush of settlement. The fates of invaders ranged from one, being run over, to two, being quickly exterminated. Not that I hadn't witnessed a six-point buck racing in a tight end's zigzag pattern down the inside lane of the town's divided four-lane, a road flanked to sidewalk's edge by a furniture store, a Chinese restaurant, a framing shop, a natural foods grocery, a bar, a movie theater, and a package-and-mail-it business. Not that I hadn't seen my stately great egret poised in the dried weeds of the vacant lot, bewildered, bearings lost, two miles from water. Not that great horned owls didn't hoot in the night and my cat didn't occasionally guide home a raccoon. Yet the overall marquee message for wildlife, in a large bold font, read:

STAY OUT OF TOWN
KEEP TO THE NICE HILLSIDES

At first this might seem a fair allocation—except humans make the rules, and the rules included our automatically spilling onto the open acres to hike, bike, jog, picnic. The town barriers to wildlife, by contrast, tend to remain abrupt, and this particular night I was wishing they were more abrupt.

The dispatcher for 911 referred me to the Humane Society. I called, and a kindly man told me if I turned on all the lights the skunk would probably leave without squirting. My landlady, Suellen, was good enough to climb out of bed, trundle down the path from upstairs, and cock open my door from the outside. The skunk marched out into the night. Flight and vacation went off as scheduled.

Now, many years hence, and several years into barn life, my outlook on allocations and dividing lines has changed—matured, I like to think. Here, but for a few boards, my Irish sweetie and I are cohabiting with wild skunks. Occasional scufflings and purrings indicate their quarters are under the floor in the southwest corner, beneath our woodstove. The old barn stands tall on the skyline of palatial lodgings for a skunk. The half dozen holes in the foundation—the marmots' work—offer them entrances and exits, the creek is a short jaunt away for a good drink, and the ground beneath our bird feeders provides a handy supply of black sunflower seeds. Though Patrick and I took lessons in trapping and relocating skunks from our rehabist friend Mountain Mary, who has some other-than-earthly ability to grab a skunk without getting sprayed, it is undoubtedly our indolence at putting our homework into practice that screws in the hook for the big neon vacancy sign.

"Five wee ones and a mother!" I was protruding to the waist out one of the eastside barn windows early on a July afternoon; it was half past three—not a normal hour to encounter nocturnal animals abroad. For a week, we had seen four—the mom and three youngsters—slinking around just after dusk, their white markings gleaming like dem-bones skeletons. Lately their foraging schedule had changed to six o'clock, and then to quarter to four. Again I counted the furry bundles motoring through the grass. "Seven skunks!" I amended. They didn't mind my talking to myself, didn't even look up. But Patrick's sudden stepping around the corner of the milk house caused a fright, and they jostled like subway riders, in a dive for their hole.

"Come see!" I hollered, pointing downward. Patrick jogged in and removed another window. We leaned out, chatting, while watching from above—as though awaiting a Macy's Thanksgiving Day Parade.

"Mom's getting tired of this nursing routine," I said.

"Get these brats emancipated!"

Here they came again, scrambling out the hole, directly beneath Patrick's window. First the three familiar young chunks. Then another three—rather smaller siblings, now that I was seeing them one by one, and unsure of themselves. Were the second three, we wondered, adopted orphans?

Female skunks—sometimes as many as twenty—typically den up together over the winter in an effort to conserve body heat. Ever since our third year here, we have been host to two or three winter residents. Skunks are classified in the Mustelidae or weasel family, along with martens and fishers, ferrets and minks, otters, badgers, and wolverines. Ours are the striped species, or *Mephitis mephitis*, with a range confined to North America. In warmer climates, they stay active all year. Skunks are not true hibernators—their body temperature, heartbeat, and metabolism never appreciably slow down—but in Montana winters they tend to lay low, loaf and snooze a lot, and then at intervals stretch their legs to nab an easy meal or grab a drink. The patterns of their activity are fairly regular around the barn, as evidenced by the path they etch in the snow, under the fence and down to the creek. Only an extended deep freeze keeps them from venturing out.

Then, sometime before May, the population drops to one: female skunks prefer solitude for birthings. How they drew lots we didn't know, but the rest packed up and left. Heavens be thanked! (Though each mother might pop out only the expected four to eight kits, she carried the potential for six-teen. Three times sixteen, I didn't even want to think about.) The young are born anywhere from late April into June. They arrive in the world blind and, it is thought, with a pay-load of musk primed and awaiting only the development of their squirt muscles. Newborns are about the size of mice—a half ounce—their bodies hairless, or nearly so, yet they al-ready sport the family tartan. Pinkish skin indicates where the white fur will grow: a pencil blaze down the face and a wider stripe beginning at the nape and forking down the back. Often there are frostings in the tail. Markings may vary greatly throughout the species, but there is always a strong biological family resemblance. The three smaller siblings bore markings similar to Mom's. If they were adopted, was it from a sister? And how were the arrangements made?

With the entrance hole steep-sided, the peewee ones were having a time of it, one's foot on another's head—only to in-eptly bump together, tumble back in, and begin again. They gave the impression this was their first day's squint at the big world. The mother skunk was discernibly larger than the fleshiest of her litter and easily distinguished by the brown-ish base hair in her tail. She was also the boss. Coming out of the hole last, intent on her own lunch, she collared in her teeth one of the pesky babies in her way and, by the nape of the neck, stuffed it back down the hole.

The family sojourn delivered them first to skunk play-ground, a four-foot-wide swath of thigh-high pasture grass that had grown too fast, too tall, for our push mower and still stood alongside the barn uncut. The skunks had beaten down a maze of tunnels through it. Ten feet farther along, opposite my window, was the sidewalk cafe: a mound of black sunflower seeds, six feet in diameter.

Apparently thirsty, in addition to being hungry, the older

crew were soon off to the creek, Mom leading the way. They crossed the desolate open stretch of mowed grass, weaved through a tall stand of weeds, and peeled over the bank. The first little offspring behind walked with his nose fairly up his mother's ass. Coupled like boxcars, they moved in unison around the bends—whether for security or in an attempt to nurse I could only guess. Completing the train, the other two followed nose to butt.

Left to their own devices, the smaller trio romped and wrestled in the grass maze with the abandon of kittens. It was a game of hide-and-seek. Where-did-you-go? Oops-there-you-are! Hisses and soprano snarls and chatters were clearly audible in the not-more-than-five-foot rise to our observation posts. Soon they advanced from kids' play to binge eating and then the strategies of war games. This entailed a side-to-side rocking motion followed by stamping of feet and false charging. The more vigorous lunges and nippings of flank sparked brief whirling balls of fur. Already they were practicing the defensive maneuver for which they are infamous, employing it to best advantage when commandeering small patches of mound territory. No need to halt voracious seed cracking to wave tails like ostrich plumes, swing rears round, and emit delicate puffs of musk. Patrick and I rolled our eyes and chuckled. Nothing to pinch a nose over.

The word *skunk* derives from the Abenaki word *seganku*, in the Algonquian linguistic family. The Indian usage of the term may be more forgiving of the animal's eccentricities than English has been. There are tribal cultures that hold the skunk in sacred esteem for its sexual magic—its power to attract and repel—learning from its teachings to foster a wise balancing of energy. The English synonym is *polecat*, a word turned to phrase in old western movies: "You dirty polecat!" A low, contemptible person. To be *skunked*, in the verb form, means to be beaten in cards, games, or contests so badly as to have failed to score. Wholesale we snatch up the skunk noun as flogging stick, in indiscriminate maligning and character assassination, in metaphor for mean-spirited bullying. The animal's odor we class with rotting carrion and sewer smells. In 1997, the world-renowned skunk specialist Jerry Dragoo began to make the case for an elevation of the skunk's status. Dragoo is a rehabist busy with relocating myriad unwanted skunks. For his personal pleasure, he keeps six armed wild skunks as house pets. As a postdoctoral fellow at the University of New Mexico, he studies skunks in the genetics laboratory. Through DNA analysis, he has established overwhelming premise for reclassification of skunks into a distinct family: Mephitidae, which would include striped, spotted, and hog-nosed skunks, as well as the stink badger.

In Peterson's *Field Guide to the Mammals* the striped skunk's description reads thus: "Head and body 13–18 in.; tail 7–10 in., wt. 6–14 lb. Often seen dead along highway." In northern climates, when we observe the first skunks of the year dead on the road—their powerful smell whipping into wheel wells and up our noses—they are, in all likelihood, males who have begun to move about. Spring fever seizes Montana's male skunk before some of us have packed away the Christmas lights. In pursuit of a mate, a male will travel several miles in one night—no mean feat for a waddler. Anatomically the "skunk walk" is the old gunslinger gait, thumbs in front pockets, all together now: right limbs, left limbs. Hard to imagine, they also have at their command a bounding canter and a gallop. The *Canadian Field-Naturalist*, May 1936, carried a report by D. A. MacLulish clocking striped skunks in his headlights at speeds of six, eight, and nine miles an hour!

The mating season rituals of our barn skunks span six

weeks, from the latter weeks of January into the first half of March, which departs considerably from information in any book. As the suitors begin arriving, our lower lodgings— an area Patrick's dubbed Our Apartments—come alive with thumpings, bumpings, and high-pitched yattering and screeching. Each episode—once or twice weekly on average but sometimes three days in a row—is accompanied by horrific blasts of skunk musk. Wild trysting takes place at all hours of the night and, with the exception of the winter nesting corner, from one end of the building to the other. Integral parts of their coitus, it seems, include a vociferous, annoyed scrapping and spraying. Patrick and I from the start have conjured singular sexist images. The crabby female protesteth: "Not now! I'm sleepy." Then mine: At the very point of male ecstasy, in the throes of wild, kingly thrusting, he lets loose in all directions, sending his genetic payload into the female and splattering everything to the rear with musk—as much as to shout, "Let it be known I have scored!"

Upon a bit of library study and consultation with experts, I found that theories perhaps more scientific than ours indicate females send forth their musk as a homing device to help the males locate them. The scrapping and snarling, at its fiercer levels, might instead be males fighting over a female or arise from a female's driving off still persistently interested gents once she's successfully bred. As for the musk, males typically do not fire off during duels, and neither sex is known for letting loose as a copulation ritual. What's more, skunks don't like getting musk on themselves. What then is going on beneath our floor?

Skunks are a species "very understudied," says Serge Larivière, who is a stew of eccentricities himself: a man of French heritage, living in Tennessee, working as a research scientist for Ducks Unlimited, who did his Ph.D. on skunks at the University of Saskatchewan in Saskatoon. Dr. Larivière, at the time of my speaking to him, was co-preparing a series of studies. The hypothesis he planned to test was that one dominant adult male, after having duked it out in the fall, will lodge in the females' den over the winter, poised for when they come into estrus. Skunk harem heaven! The skunks then that we find smushed on the road in late winter and early spring would more precisely be juveniles or bumbling adult males, individuals not having had much luck in the fall that are again biologically on the prowl. And knocking on the barn door! Still and all, much of our skunks' behavior remains a mystery.

A certain "skunkiness" in and around the barn—fleeting wafts here and there—is something Patrick and I have come to delight in most of the year. The tempered odor is quite livable. If we don't catch a whiff now and again, we begin to miss the little beasts. Where are the skunks? we say. I haven't seen one lately, have you? I hope they haven't moved on.

During the six-week mating season, however, the skunk spirits go all out to test our mettle; musk released with regularity permeates every moment of our existence. The Latin name, *Mephitis mephitis*, derives from the word *foul*. Double foul! Ernest Thompson Seton, the American naturalist and author of a series of books on wildlife in the early 1900s, describes skunk musk as a "mixture of strong ammonia, essence of garlic, burning sulphur, a volume of sewer gas, a vitriol spray, a dash of perfume musk, all mixed together and intensified a thousand times."* Though the glop itself is contained beneath our flooring, it vaporizes and, in the manner that helium fills a balloon, all but pressurizes the whole interior, its strength lessening only as it dissipates from its source, and over time.

I'm happy to say we have escaped, so far, the misfortune of

---

*From the series *Lives of Game Animals*, Volume 2.

being directly sprayed. Our skunks are friendly, shy, gentle little souls, and when they see us coming do no more than tumble down their hole. If a skunk can run away, it generally will. If not, it may perk up its tail and, trying to appear larger to an enemy, fluff out its hair. It may stamp its front feet and arch its back like a Halloween cat. Sometimes it will hiss. At any point, if you talk lovingly—"Pretty skunk!" "Nice skunky!" "Don't spray, you little shit!"—it's the tone that counts, and step ever-so-slowly backward, no fast moves, you may save yourself. However, Dragoo tells me a skunk won't always give these warnings. "Skunks are individuals, and they have their bad days, just like us." They are fully capable of bending into a U-shape and, while looking right at you, nailing you. "Watch out"—he laughs—"when you see them coming at you from both ends."

The musk itself is an oily, yellowish liquid of a fluorescent nature. It's expelled in a stream containing globs that are similar, Mountain Mary says, to snot. Others have called them curds. It may well have been the skunk that served as the prototype for the modern-day squirt bottle, with the stream setting and the atomized cloud. The latter Jerry Dragoo calls the shotgun blast, a skunk's perfect finesse when on the run from coyotes. The stream he christens the .357 Magnum. A skunk's two musk glands, each as big as the end of a thumb, reside on either side of its rectum. Surrounded by powerful muscles and equipped with a set of retractable nipples, the gland apparatus enables a firing of ten to fifteen feet with surprising accuracy. Having been blasted in the face, Dragoo says the substance causes a burning temporary blindness, but no lasting damage. And the taste? I ask. Conveniently, for his line of work, he has no sense of smell, and in turn a greatly diminished sense of taste (a condition known as hyposmia). Others report the flavor resembles that of gasoline.

At the vapor's freshest and strongest in the barn, we are

under assault by toxin. The military could use this stuff for chemical warfare. And in fact, according to William Wood, professor of chemistry at Humboldt State University in Arcata, California, skunk musk contains the properties of tear gas. It is a gas of the *lachrymatory* (tear-producing) and *asphyxiating* type. Breathing becomes difficult; retching feels a second away. Consider this: a mile circle of skunk odor radiating off a freshly flattened highway kill, all gathered together and corked in the barn.

Deeply asleep one February night, oblivious to any passionate mephitine foreplay, I awoke when a brutally dense vapor socked me in the nose. The odor spread in a great gaseous swell, expanding and rising, as though no barriers to it existed, until filling the barn to the ridgepole. Sleeping where I was, the most intense front edge of the system broke over me like a toxic tsunami.

Patrick and I, at the time, happened to be in the final stages of a respiratory virus, he a few days ahead of me. Though we had contracted the same bug, our selected manners of treatment were diametrically opposite, and we'd been sleeping separately for a week. Believing fresh air for the lungs was the cure, he'd been rolling out his bag on the deck in the snow. Certain that my recovery required rest, staying warm, and pushing gallons of liquid (the latter requiring my lurching around at night), I'd been bunking indoors. Shortly before dawn, I heard the bar-and-lever clang of Patrick's throwing open the door to the mow. Then his stumbling down the stairs.

"Waugh! Are you alive in here?"

"Barely," I groaned, the covers pulled over my head.

"I opened the door and this stuff *poured* over me. The cats wouldn't even come in. It was like *pawing* my way into a curdled miasma," he said. "Pepe Le Pew Passion Pit! You'd better call Steffini." Steffini is a young, entrepreneurial house-cleaner, and she was due at noon.

A small aside. Two years after we settled into the barn, Patrick's willingness to take on half the home choring, that is, the indoor housecleaning part—something that had so endeared him to me—slowly dissolved until quite mysteriously I had taken it all on, along with a good case of resentment at what I suspected was a blunt plot of dupery. Never had I planned on a life of housework! (In all fairness, I must report that Patrick—with his long-armed swing and lifetime of practice—assumed the chore of chopping our wood, which, had I chosen splitting the ten cords, would have swallowed up every minute of my time until the following June.) But I also went kind of crazy when the place was askew and knee-deep in dust balls. It was Steffini who came to our rescue. When we were flush, she cleaned every week; this year it was every other Friday. Hers and mine is a relationship not precisely representative of a reemerging class society and its hired help: I pay her twenty-five dollars and she stays three hours, the first one and a half of which we visit. Then she mops and vacuums like a dervish, while I work ahead of her straightening and dusting. When she leaves, the downstairs sparkles—as much as an old barn stained with bird poop can.

Today the place needed a healthy going-over, and I'd been looking forward to Steffini's coming. When Patrick happily slipped out for a prearranged early breakfast with a farrier chum, I rose before I normally would have and took a gander at the outdoor temperature: thirty-seven degrees. Perhaps I could stand it. I removed the two south windows, east and west, and dragged a big box fan down from the mow, where we employ it for the summer. I threw open the front door, plunked the fan in the doorway facing the barnyard, and twisted its one simple knob to High. With this arrangement I hoped to draw fresh air in through the windows. Then I stoked up the stove and put on water for coffee. In twenty minutes nothing had changed. Except I was feeling queasy. Ready to try a different approach, I reversed the fan so it blew crisp air *into* the barn. I tugged on a coat and started making breakfast. Half an hour later there appeared still to be no improvement, while I had managed to cool the barn considerably. Defeated, I clicked off the fan, closed up everything, and reached for the phone. Steffini was a trouper with little whiffles of skunk, but she had let me know once, quite pointedly, her whole car reeked of it.

"You'd probably rather not come today," I said. "The skunks have been mating."

She agreed, and we set another date. I said, "See ya." She said, "Don't forget not to go anywhere!" Meaning: Remember that skunk odor has properties similar to campfire smoke and permeates hair and clothing.

Skunk musk was just about running my life. Its all-consuming presence had the effect of driving me to probe deeper into the mysteries of life. How do noses work? Why are some things stinky to one person and not to another?

In the ancient philosopher Plato's slim categories for odor—pleasant and unpleasant—the polecat's would have fallen into the second. Aristotle next separated the sensations occurring in the mouth from those in the nose, suggesting for our sniffers six divisions: sweet, sour, succulent, pungent, harsh, and fetid. By the definitions of these words, skunk odor might fall into each of the last three. Two thousand years later, in 1752, the Swedish naturalist Carl Linnaeus—classifier of all classifiers (who gave us the binomial system whereby each species of plant and animal has a Latin or Greek genus name followed by a specific name)—

set forth his own standard of seven odors: aromatic, fragrant, ambrosial (musky), alliaceous (garlicky), hircine (goaty), repulsive, and nauseous. This gets not only complex but a bit sticky now. *Aromatic* is defined as powerfully scented or fragrant; *fragrant* as sweet-smelling or ambrosial; *ambrosial* as worthy of the gods, or as paradise or the divine. *Musk* is the term for skunk spray; many mammals have *musk* glands; *musk* refers to a whole range of strong-smelling secretions; and *musk*, the chocolate-colored substance derived from the glands of the Asian male musk deer, forms the basis of many perfumes. *Alliaceousness* is a condition of living with Patrick, who tosses three slivered heads (yes, heads, not cloves) into the pasta and calls it "a hint of garlic!" He pouts should I suggest two for company. You could say we lust after the smell of garlic, consider it ambrosial. *Repulsive* is not a description of a skunk's spray—toxic, perhaps, but not repulsive. *Hircine* is something we reserve for Our Apartments' marmots. While *nauseous*, in my book, is a jackpot! Yet skunk in its milder doses we would assign to the first division of Aristotle: sweet.

Noses, by report, are boundlessly different: men's, women's, races', species', individuals'. Since Linnaeus's day, olfactology has evolved into a multifaceted science: apocrine secretions, sex pheromones, allomones, anosmia, hyposmia, and the notes, chords, and symphonies of perfumery. Industries and economies teeter on olfaction. But set aside now all manner of newly burst blossom, crushed pine needle, bruised sage, gentle sea breeze, a lover's precious sweat. What interest me are loathsome odors: how much of their revulsion and repulsion power stems from the apparatus of our physiological receptors, and how much from culture. "Both contribute significantly to our experience of smell," says Dr. Charles Wysocki, a neuroscientist studying individual variations in the perception of odors at Philadelphia's Monell Chemical

Senses Center. By way of example, he tells me over the phone he hated lemons as a child after bringing a bottle of lemon concentrate to his nose, "because it smelled like skunk." A few years later, when he came to appreciate lemonade, he also took a liking to skunk musk and is now captivated by it.

What is thought of as fragrant or bewitching differs not only among individuals but cultures. Some African peoples smear their bodies with cow dung to express fertility; others covet the aroma of onions as an alluring perfume. Over the years, I've grown to feel almost nauseous in close quarters with a woman wearing any kind of commercially bottled perfume. I wear none myself anymore, preferring the smell of rain, woods, fields, the barn, my body. Constance Classen, David Howes, and Anthony Synnott in their book *Aroma: The Cultural History of Smell* write: "The perception of smell . . . consists not only of the sensation of the odours themselves, but of the experiences and emotions associated with them." I was evidently associating skunk musk with a place of sweet romance, in league with my unusual man. Even so, at our most choking moments, we would swear to trap and relocate our under-floor neighbors. Because of what?—laziness? more pressing things to do once toxic levels dissipated? sheer fascination?—the follow-through never materialized.

A strange enthrallment with musk is not ours alone. The odor of skunk has been considered far nicer stuff than the musk of fox, mink, or weasel. (All carnivores have scent glands. In mustelids, they are enlarged and in skunks hugely enlarged.) In his book *Squirrels and Other Fur-bearers*, published in 1909, John Burroughs penned of skunk musk: "It is a rank [by the older definition *vigorous* and *luxuriant*], living smell, and has none of the sickening qualities of disease or putrefaction. Indeed, I think a good smeller will enjoy its most refined intensity. It approaches the sublime, and makes the nose tingle. It is tonic and bracing, and I can readily believe has rare medicinal qualities." A distinction needs to be made between the strong and toxic doses Seton describes and the milder aromas of Burroughs. With that in mind, I can't help wondering to what extent our culture might change if children, at the gentle drifting in of a little skunkiness, heard "ah!" and not "pew!" from their elders.

I straightened up all the newspapers and dusted a bit in view of Steffini's absence, but I was having trouble yet spooning down my granola. Upon Patrick's return from his breakfast out, he tossed me—in his typical straight-man humor—a reminder. "You're ready, of course, for our big annual literary and chocolate evening."

Every year, close to Valentine's Day, the local library schedules a Sweet Taste of Literature fund-raiser. Supporters bake umpteen varieties of gooey, double and triple chocolate delights. The goodies, together with a bevy of local authors signing their books, provide the lure for new and repledging patrons. It is an event we never miss, a time to visit with people we seldom encounter the rest of the year, and we are both avid supporters of libraries, Patrick fiercely so. He believes in them as a public service for citizen edification, places of knowledge open and free to everyone, and needless to say spent many of his penniless, rambling days in the quiet rooms of our nation's libraries. Holed up comfortably, he became the well-read man. On occasions now when he is missing, late for an engagement, I worry not about another woman but rather about *which* library to call. As for me—my very presence on this earth stems from the archives of the New York Public Library. My mother held the position of main reference librarian in the early 1940s, and it was there she met my father, who was teaching himself calculus. Father's uncle Johnny was the library's janitor, which meant

Pop was readily able to peruse sections not open to the public. For all I know, I was conceived in the back stacks.

"Chocolate and *skunk*, oh God!" I wailed.

"Great combo!" That's my Michigan man, always catching the upbeat.

With housecleaning postponed, I decided a trip to Missoula was in order. I had a few pressing errands, but it was also my notion to test out ratings on the state of my odoriferousness. There were times when reality could only be gauged in reflection from others. A week after a good blinding and gagging release, I have thrown open the door to my bosom friend and walking companion Katya, artist, writer, and strikingly gorgeous Norwegian. "My God, how can you live like this?" she howls. I would be suffering from *olfactory fatigue*, the scientific term for a nose worn out on a smell. "Come on in," I'd say, with the sweep of an arm. "Just twenty minutes and it's a flower shop." I couldn't understand it, she always declined. Today I imagined a personal stink meter with a needle swinging in an arc from zero to fifty—socially acceptable to you-rank-gagging-idiot-get-away.

Fact and Fiction was my first stop, where I needed to pick up a book I'd ordered. I stood across the counter chatting with the owner, Barbara Theroux, a congenial bookseller hanging on in the face of Missoula's fast-disappearing independents. In the movement of digging for my checkbook and pen, I released from the Polarfleece jacket I wore an invisible malodorous cloud that wafted upward around my head. I could almost see the gas expanding. A glance around the store told me I was the sole customer. This wasn't going to be like farting in the theater line. Handing her the check, I decided to own it. "Smelling skunk yet?"

"Yes! I just got it!" she said, her animated look indicating its strength. Ha, I thought, a twenty-five or thirty at least—fifty being someone wearing a direct squirt.

I told her it was airborne-ing off my clothes, that skunks were mating beneath our floor, and I had this literary social coming up. She laughed. "Material for a writer!" I joked. She laughed again.

The Great Bear Foundation was my next stop, a visit with Dr. Charles Jonkel, a wildlife biologist whose specialty is bears. There my unusual perfume prompted a stream of reminiscences. Jonkel told me he had grown up on a dairy farm in Wisconsin and gone to school smelling of cows, except when he was hunting skunks, and then that smell obliterated everything. The boys had liked him well enough, but the girls had bolted away. "Probably kept me out of trouble longer than most," he said.

With telltale fondness, Jonkel went on to describe a stump he once found in the woods where skunks slept away the winter. Conveniently among the roots were gaps where he could kneel down and poke his head in and observe. "They were all in a pile," he said, "six or eight of them, wriggling a little, purring softly, staying warm together. Except for the one on top that kept crawling down and burrowing back in at the bottom. Just like a crowd of people!" He uses the pile-of-skunks image a lot now, he says. "As a metaphor—for everyone's elbowing their way to the best spot."

On the trip home, I pondered the protocol of showing up at a social function reeking of skunk. More than one friend would think I should stay home. "Fussy folk" Patrick called them. I toyed with the idea of calling ahead, trying to reach Patty Jo, the librarian. Offer fair warning. I put the notion to Patrick when I got home. "We just go," he blurted. "It's not like we've done something wrong." I read that as a Patrick-ism and quietly set about—at the least—washing my hair just prior to our leaving. As I raced around wet-headed getting dressed, the very wetness, in my great sweeps up and down the stairs, seemed to collect molecules of odor like a sponge whisking up dust. The scope of hopelessness broadened as I donned my winter coat, a garment that has been my partner for thirty-five years. It's the coffee-colored, imitation-alpaca lining of a World War II army trench coat. Early on, I had turned the seams and trimmed it in colorful braid, then a few years back stitched on leather elbow patches. This grand garb has served as my skiing coat, my camping coat, and now in Montana my only good cold-weather apparel. In its time it had sucked up the smoke of hundreds of campfires, though this evening I walked out the door a bear smelling of skunk.

Slogging through a block of sidewalk slush, we arrived at the old storefront on Main Street, the new library addition, which was empty yet of books and for the fund-raiser set up with tables and flowers and candles. Through the plate-glass window, I was already searching for a friendly face—or rather, the face of someone understanding of skunks. I combed the room for the cropped shock of strawberry hair that would be Janine Benyus, a passionate science writer, author of *Beastly Behaviors: A Zoo Lover's Companion* and several wildlife books. She'd recently published her groundbreaking work *Biomimicry: Innovation Inspired by Nature*. Her section headings read like a salvatory revolution. "Running a Business like a Redwood Forest." "Weaving Fibers like a Spider." "Gathering Energy like a Leaf." "Computing like a Cell." Interviewing biomimic scientists around the world, she had delivered up a treatise, based on sound economics and viable ecological practices. In the first chapter, I'd found the following statement: "The most irrevocable of these [ecological] laws says that a species cannot occupy a niche that appropriates all resources—there has to be some sharing. Any species that ignores this law winds up destroying its community to support its own expansion. . . . Nature rewards cooperation." This I read after several years of living in close proximity with our mephitine families. Janine had put the illuminating words to our stumbling instincts to live and let live with skunks. I felt certain that, if nothing else tonight, with her I could loiter in a corner.

But Janine, I was soon to learn, was out on lecture tour. It was Jon Jackson, our local master of the crime drama, who strode across the floor to greet us. Jon stands at medium height and broadening a smidgen from his gourmand tendencies; he cohosts *The Food Guys*, a Sunday morning radio show on Montana Public Radio, and writes the commentary "Eating" for *Big Sky Journal*. This evening, for signing his latest novel, *Go by Go*, set in Butte, Montana, he'd come attired in a Ralph Lauren–ish polo shirt, topped with a snappy sport jacket, and over his winter-pale pate, a green loden fedora. As we hugged, I quickly queried, "Smelling skunk?" I wanted it dead in the open, not leaving anyone to think Patrick and I were neglectful of our personal hygiene and just walked around like this not knowing it.

"No," he shot back, followed immediately with "I do now!"

From there the library soiree unfolded, with the grace of an evening primrose really, but on waftings of musk, everyone swapping skunk stories and recipes for odor removal. I soon maneuvered to the libation table, where Patty Jo, in an old-fashioned ankle-length dress, was filling paper cups with sparkling cider and champagne. She is a petite woman with aristocratic cheekbones. Her long, dark tresses, now lively with gray, are center-parted and swept up in symmetrical waves clasped with antique flower barrettes, while the length is braided and piled regally across her crown. Perhaps the most amazing aspect of her librarianship is that the North Valley Library has a *virtual* card catalog—no little cabinet with long drawers full of manila cards, no Dewey decimal on computer. Patty Jo files everything in her head. As I sidled up, she said not a word about my aroma. When I offered a bit of explanation for my condition, she uttered a small "oh!" and threw me an odd, sidelong glance.

With the shindig moving into its last hour, people were still coming and going. Bart Ladd, a large-animal veterinarian, blew through the door wearing his green slicker bib overalls and looking about as chagrined as I felt. He had just come from pulling the first calves of the year. Afraid the chocolate evening would be over if he took time to drive home and change, he'd washed off the slop, mud, and blood as best he could. He was not about to miss this event with his wife, Diann Ladd, one of the Discovery Writers, six women who had recently published the book *Lewis and Clark in the Bitterroot*. Diann had drawn the illustrations. Another of the Discovery Writers, Jean Clary, I knew as my hairdresser's mother. She sat in a group around a table, and a few moments after I approached, she exclaimed to all, "Patty Jo was right! There *is* a skunk around here." Our librarian had apparently been smelling skunk for three days. And here I could have tricked the whole attendance by just appearing to search for the real item.

Instead, Patrick and I—between bites of chocolate pecan turtles and slices of velvet chocolate cheesecake, walnut brownies, Belgian chocolate tortes, pineapple chunks and strawberries drenched in white chocolate, hunky chocolate chip cookies, and double chocolate rum truffles—worked our way from group to group, talking mostly skunk. A little black-and-white family once quartered under Jon's house but was persuaded to search out new real estate when he placed his son's boom box in the crawl space, set it on continuous play, popped in the tape of a heavy metal band, and then promptly fled for the weekend. Bart attested to his personal experience with the inadequacy of a shoot-the-skunk-under-the-porch approach. After unleashing its load, it had crawled up under the house and died where he couldn't retrieve it. "It's self-explanatory, once you do it," he said. "You live with the smell forever!"

The winning concoction for odor erasure was offered up by several library patrons and confirmed by Patrick, an item retrieved from his never-ending storehouse of peculiar scraps of knowledge: a solution of hydrogen peroxide and baking soda. Was it a cup to a teaspoon? A quart to a pinch? No one remembered.

To neutralize skunk spray, according to Professor William Wood, the chemicals must be changed to a different type of molecule. The tomato juice so often suggested merely ends up smelling like tomatoes con musk. Gwen Dragoo, a biologist in her own right, but as Jerry's wife an expert on this subject, washes skunky clothes with a diluted solution of bleach. Wood recommends one cup of liquid laundry bleach per gallon of water. For cleaning up pets that have been squirted, it's a version of the library party's winning formula plus a little liquid detergent, but there are some cautions, all discussed on Wood's website, http://www.humboldt.edu/~wfw2/deodorize.shtml.

Although it was not an evening filled with scintillating repartee, the main topic was indeed a fresh one, and, coupled with the range of facial expressions I had witnessed over the past forty-eight hours, it was enough to set me pondering again. Upon what eccentric mule had I ridden in—that I came to relish skunky stuff?

Odors, it is commonly known, trigger memory. The steam that rises off blistering asphalt when pelted by a summer shower can deliver me back over forty years to the streets of a small shore town in New Jersey. The earthy fecundity released by digging in damp garden humus on a crisp fall day wings me straight to the opposite coast, the pumpkin fields of Half Moon Bay. Without passing through thought, an odor can cause an all-encompassing image to appear to us, not just projected on a flat frontal screen but as though we were dropped into a three-dimensional scene. Yet for me, the odor of skunk fails to produce any Star Trek transport. My childhood stuffed animals offer no further clue; they were pastel Easter bunnies my great-aunt annually brought from Gimbel's, where she worked, and a green calico pig. Exactly where and when I took a liking to skunks is not clear to me. But this I know: I am building odor memory in this barn and will, for the rest of my life wherever I go, careen instantly back here with any soupçon of skunk.

Now for a weightier question: What good is a skunk? Bliss, I am here to tell you, is a skunk eating earwigs, beetles, and mice under my barn. Or grasshoppers, one of their favorites, that in hordes come chomping through the shrubbery and flowers. At someone else's place it might be grubs, lizards, crickets, baby rats. In the night, when the yellow jacket cools down, the skunk digs up and devours its communal nest. A skunk will scarf up duck eggs, it is true, but also the eggs of the snapping turtle that likewise gobbles duck eggs—perhaps it is a wash. Skunks, like almost everything else, are connected up the food chain as well as down: the juveniles end up as steak tartare for coyote, fox, bobcat, eagle, great horned owl. (Striped skunks are a weedy species. They prosper in a wide variety of habitats from the alleys in towns to the wilds at ten thousand feet, and they produce caboodles of kits. But they also sustain a high annual mortality rate—about 40 percent, due in greater part, in these times, to unsuccessful forays across busy roads.) On further behalf of the species' worth, I offer up a favorite kitchen tip: Dr. C. Hart, author of *Mammals of the Adirondacks*, 1886, wrote that the flesh of the skunk is "white, tender, and sweet, and . . . delicious eating." More delicate than chicken! To this he attested after eating skunk "boiled, broiled, roasted, fried, and fricasseed." As for the little stinkers' entertainment value? Patrick and I will affirm it.

I take no small comfort in knowing a few other seemingly sane mortals live with skunks. First there are the rehabists Mountain Mary and Jerry Dragoo, who think *seganku* the finest of neighbors and roommates. Their advice: Talk sweet and watch for the warnings, life is ever a risk.

Then there's my friend Alecia, with skunks living under her barn. At night when she makes the rounds, feeding her menagerie of gimpy horses, chickens, eight adopted dogs, seven adopted cats, she tosses a cupful of cat food down the skunk hole. "It's a form of extortion," she admits, "to keep them down at the barn and not coming around the house and spraying the dogs." Yet it's with distinct longing that she talks about a childhood in Alabama as her reason for tolerance of skunks today. "There *are* no skunks anymore, none, and no animals, not in the way there were when I was young. We loved to go to the ponds to see the tracks all around the edges and make up stories about who'd been visiting. Now the banks of the creeks where I swam as a child have all been strip-mined. They're cesspools of muck. If you step in, the stench is overpowering."

The most improbable skunk lovers are my friends Joanne and Bjorn, who live in Tiburon, California, in a conceivably more-than-million-dollar house (going on ten years in a Montana barn, my mind doesn't compute these figures anymore). Skunks have always lived beneath their outdoor staircase. It is a unique soak I receive, luxuriating in their backyard hot tub. Multifragrances drifting from a stately throng of eucalyptus trees and a lovingly cared for English flower garden mix and mingle on a gentle zephyr, seasoned like a giant gourmet salad with salty bay air. All this, accompanied not by the sweet strains of a string quartet but by the wide-winged draft of an owl swooping low and the wobbling by on the redwood decking of an amicable little black-and-white fact.

Upon one thing we all agree: Why eliminate our skunks when another one or two will likely come along? The ones camped with us now know us. They're comfortable with us. They don't squirt us. We kind of love them.

When the young son of a friend comes visiting us now, catches a whiff of skunk, and yelps, "Shoot 'em!" I am dumbstruck. For the coming year, I'm determined to move onto yet trickier ground: eliminate all skunk-related derogatory words, as in *reek, stink, stench*. And any apology. I'm feeling inspired to throw a skunk-honoring party, pick a date at the height of mating season for a sort of pithy initiation rite, invite a few sturdy souls, and, following Jerry Dragoo's lead, propel the species's status to a higher plateau. Each one of us then, as we depart the evening, will, without exhaustive laboring effort or Internet, in an old-fashioned way—à la Janine Benyus and the biomimic scientists—carry forth the spirit of *seganku*, saturated as it will be in the fibers of our clothes and hair.

In the meantime, I await the coming of February for a different reason, with a wild personal anticipation. Diane Ackerman in her book *A Natural History of the Senses* asked: Can smells influence us biologically? "Absolutely," she answered. "Musk produces a hormonal change in the woman who smells it." Heap upon that, if you will, Valentine's Day, chocolate aphrodisiacs, and hours of involuntary exposure to vicarious humping, and February always registers a noticeable, creative rise in the Irishman's and my bedroll activities!

5

The Berry
or the Bear

Backyards,
Front Yards

It was a cool and moonless, starry night in August. Four
o'clock in the morning. We were soundly asleep in our flannel sacking on the deck when an unbridled clamor in the
creek bottom startled me awake. The racket brought back a
Jessica Harper children's song:

> *Crash bang, crash bang boom!*
> *Something's going on in Nora's room.*
> *Sounds like the bear is dancing with the moose.*
> *They like to dance when they're on the loose.*

"Hear that?" I whispered, twice squeezing Patrick's shoulder, tucked under my chin.

"You mean those gentle little footfalls?" He too was
stretching awake. Yesterday our neighbors, Kathy and Arden, had seen a moose and a grown black bear nibbling
through their place, the 170-acre strip lying between us and
the main river.

I peered hard into the pitchy night, wishing indisputably
to determine: bear-beast or moose-beast? My straining was
to no avail, the human eye not having evolved for such dim-

lighted endeavors. The splashing, twig-breaking critter—in a plunk-plunk amble, erratic but steady in direction over the course of twenty minutes—moved on south, navigating the up-creek waters. It was the moose, surely the moose.

In its northward meander down the valley, the Bitterroot River can be depended upon only for its fitful instability— channels, over time, braiding and rebraiding. The west bank's eighteen feet holds our barn well above any present-day floodplain; rising waters are destined to spread east across a wide pan. The trickling creek just below us, fed now by irrigation ditches and springs seeping from the bank, flowed as a main arm of the river a hundred years ago. Nature's rearrangements have left it marshy and bordered with cattails and alders, ideal for red-winged blackbird nesting, and pocketed with lazy backwaters, homes for muskrat, beaver, and duck. The creek and adjacent bottomland—the latter a mix of meadow, towering ponderosa pine and old gray-trunked cottonwood, brushy alder and bright copses of young aspen—support a rich population: great blue heron, great horned owl, Canada goose, common nighthawk; stately sandhill crane and prehistorically profiled pileated woodpecker; red-tailed and rough-legged hawks; Wilson's snipe, red-shafted flicker, belted kingfisher, and black-billed magpie, along with the occasional bald eagle and osprey and a teeming variety of smaller birds. Coyote pups, under cover of dark, yip like a chorus of pubescent girls on a carnival ride. Freewheeling bats snag beetles and moths between slurps from the creek. Day-snoozing white-tailed deer crush meadow grasses into gentle bed hollows. Moving about, for the most part unseen, are porcupine, mink, otter, skunk, raccoon, weasel, meadow mouse, vole, and shrew.

Nightly, after we crawl into our outdoor bedding, an odd star, Delta's 11:35 into Missoula, turns into a drone overhead. Sometime past midnight the whine and gear grind of traffic on the getting-less-than-rural highway thins out but never completely dissipates. Industrial-age noise is an annoyance to the requiem of outdoor slumber, yet it is mostly the piercing and preternatural that rock our sleep on the deck: pips, cries, and hoots, shrieks and howls, whirrings and drummings and croakings, quacks, flaps, snorts, and snarls all leap at us out of the dark. Toward the end of summer, when the countryside begins to dry out, it is the wider-ranging individuals of the higher mountain species that come to browse and prowl and clomp the riparian plain. Braving their way into the rural fringe, they are the big trio: moose, black bear, and mountain lion.

A strange year was upon us, our eighth in the barn. The backcountry was overrun with mice. Mountain Mary, returning from three days camping at Big Creek Lake, reported on their night games of ripping up and down her sleeping bag, over her head and through her hair. She dearly wished her gear had included a swatch of mosquito netting, for barring them from her mouth while she slept. I was told about an outfitter farther up north, in the area of Nine Pipe, who witnessed oceans of mice moving in waves ahead of him as he traversed mountain meadows. Another friend said Steller's jays were on the valley floor for the first time in seventeen years. Patrick, on a birthday hike into the heart of the Bitterroot-Salmon-Selway Wilderness, found not a huckleberry in the grandest patches—nor, for that matter, a bear. Mountain lions had moved down into the populated areas, curled up on porches, begun stalking hikers.

Over the next week, our neighbors spotted two more grown bears strolling through the river corridor. Three miles downriver, Katya, breakfasting on her porch, thrilled at a bear's lumbering across her lawn. A bear roosted in someone's apple tree, a bear pawed through someone's garbage. I was longing to see *my* bear! More than a few times in my years outdoors I had been the sole member of a river-running or hiking group singled out for a bear encounter: the last seen bear in the Stanislaus Canyon, the season's first bear in a Kootenai Canyon huckleberry patch.

The whole valley was a-titter with bear talk. The local papers carried pictures of bears, cute shots, mostly of adults perched in trees—napping, harvesting apples, or taking refuge from scary human commotion. The *Bitterroot Star* ran a full-front-page photograph of a little black cub exploring the potted geraniums on the front porch of an antiques shop. By the time the game warden arrived, the cub had vanished.

The black bear, or *Ursus americanus*—not the mountain lion or the moose or the jay—was lodging itself firmly at center stage and, in the manner that theater and human encounters with bears will, began to serve up scenes of comedy and tragedy that would stretch, as it turned out, into a long-running drama. For six weeks, Montana's Department of Fish, Wildlife and Parks (FWP) had their hands and their traps on wheels full trying to relocate town-strolling bears. In the relocation business, the agency employs a loose three-strikes-and-you're-out philosophy—the looseness determined on an individual basis, having to do with such things as a bear's gender, a bear's degree of habituation to humans, and a bear's aggressiveness. Bears that have attacked humans and "caused injury or loss of life" are destroyed, meaning shot or put down. (Yet, often, people have *elicited* the injuries—by stumbling too close, by inviting bears into cars for pictures, by thrilling to hand-feeding them, by urging baby Joanie to pat one's nose, by leaving around enticing edibles. Every bear is different, and every day in a bear's life brings—just as for a human—changes in mood. Black bears acting on their own are known more for wreaking havoc with such things as vehicles containing food, camp coolers and food boxes, and the insides of cabins, than for purposefully going after people.) Bears that attack livestock are also destroyed. It is the "nuisance" or "problem" bears—those getting into human foods or just too close for comfort—that receive a dose of tranquilizer, an ear tag, and a ride out of town. Adult and subadult males racking up second-nuisance offenses are destroyed, while females of breeding age or females with cubs are allowed a second relocation. Agency guidelines specifically state: "No bears will be relocated a third time." Hoping to short-circuit some of the tagging and black marking with what was looking this year like a gang of hungry and potentially bothersome bears, the game wardens sent out warnings for valley residents to gather up their fallen apples, bring cat and dog food inside, rake up birdseed scattered beneath feeders, secure garbage indoors until collection day, clean barbecue grills.

A poor berry yield this year was to blame for the abnormally high influx of bears. The entire range of the mountain berries—including huckleberries, serviceberries, chokecherries—had seriously failed. Dr. Charles Jonkel, a wildlife biologist and bear specialist of forty years, in addition to being father of the International Wildlife Film Festival and president of the Great Bear Foundation, said such an all-encompassing berry failure in the northern Rockies might occur once in five hundred years.

Huckleberries are the Rocky Mountain version of blueberries. In thick, low-bush forest undergrowths they generally thrive in the mountains of western Montana. For some time, I'd thought "Made in Montana" huckleberry products were fine and fitting presents to take when visiting out-of-state friends. I was partial myself to the jams and syrups and chunky chocolate bars, but there were also teas, soaps, lotions, ice cream, pancake mix. And they offered added enticement for a person who believed in shopping close to home. Then one day I quit buying anything with huckleberries listed as an ingredient. In recent years, local huckleberry factories have burgeoned into a $1.5 million industry, with workers scouring the mountainsides for the most lush and concentrated patches. Rumor had it that some pickers were yanking up whole bushes, carrying them home, where the work could be completed in comfort. In contrast, a bear, with remarkable dexterity of forepaws and tongue, may gently cull the berries from the branch or perhaps rip off the tops, giving the bushes a healthy pruning. Ludicrous as it may seem, these large-bodied mammals depend on the tiny berries to see them through the winter. These fruits are the main fat-building items that remain hereabouts on the bears' menu. In the intermountain West, we lack the variety in eastern nut tree species; our whitebark pine, infested with the pine bark beetle, is dying out. And the seagoing fish with high oil content are, for the most part, gone.

I was coming around to thinking we had taken enough berries from the bears: killed their calorically lucrative salmon runs with multipurpose dams; backed them into ever-shrinking territory with urban sprawl, clear-cuts, and our increasingly invasive high-tech wilderness recreation. Over the years, I'd given effort to cooperatively fighting the dam building and urban sprawl, and then chucked commercial backcountry guiding. The act of boycotting huckleberry products was simple and single-handed. Besides being painless, it required no gut-wrenching campaigns, no vast hours devoted to organizing. Although the black bear is a fairly adaptable species, in our building of industries dependent on wild fruit (not to mention the growing number of day hikers gathering berries for pies), we were squeezing the last "yield" from the bear's diminishing home range.

. . .

It was a mild last winter that had brought on an unusually early spring. People everywhere were speculating on the causes of the present situation. Dr. Jonkel's thought, when I caught up with him one Saturday at the Missoula Farmers Market, was that the berry bushes had bloomed before the pollinators—bumblebees and such—were up and functioning. In some areas, it was heavy rain and hail that decimated the blossoms. Then on the fifth of July, the wet had ceased, abruptly, as though someone had capped a pipe. Soaring temperatures followed. Only our new neighbors, just arrived from Tulsa, contentedly flourished in the heat. The month of August, too, blew hot and dry. As summer strained on toward fall, in a landscape parched and devoid of food, a parade of critters had begun marching down the Bitterroot's drainages and fanning out into the populated valley.

One morning the phone rang. It was Judy Hoy. She and her husband, Bob, a game warden retired from the FWP, run the Bitterroot Wildlife Rehabilitation Center. Had I seen a rare yellow-billed magpie reported to be in my neighborhood? I hadn't, but I said I'd keep my eyes open. Before hanging up, she mentioned they had acquired seven orphaned bear cubs—the mothers having stepped somehow into lethally devastating trouble—and it would cost two hundred dollars per cub to keep them over the winter. She was thinking of starting an "Adopt a Bear" donation program. Did I know anyone who would take pictures that she could then send to the nice donors? Did I!

The next day I grabbed my camera and drove the four miles east to the Hoys' place. At the west end of their hundred acres, a tumbledown row of old calving sheds stands as a windbreak. The bear pens were tucked against them, adjacent to a paddock with an old horse and a herd of goats, the latter milked to fill the bottles for orphaned fawns. Nearby stood an immense cage made of snow fencing, with fish netting for a top, that was occupied by a bald eagle with a bad foot and a red-tailed hawk with a broken wing.

The noon feeding, the second meal in the cubs' current three-a-day schedule, Judy said, would offer the best photo opportunities. She and Bob, over the past twenty years, had provided winter quarters for more than fifty black bear cubs, but this was the most they had seen in a single year. Two had already been sent over to the state-run facility in Helena, Bob knew of three more not yet caught and blundering around, and over the phone he had told me he expected stragglers into January and February.

"February!" I cried, it only being September.

"Any cubs left out then will be weak," he explained, "and easy to catch. We've gotten year-old cubs that weighed only twelve pounds. It takes them about three days to start eating, and then they put on about a pound a day. You can almost see them growing."

Cubs come into this world hairless and blind and weighing less than a pound. The bear is an anomaly as a species, mating at the lowest ebb of its physical fitness and bearing its young in the season of most inclement weather. The she-bear comes into estrus for thirty days, peaking about the middle of June. She mates typically every other year, driving off amorous adult males in her young cubs' first summer. After the summertime breeding, she carries the free-floating fertilized ovum until November, at which time implantation in the uterine wall occurs only if she has packed on the fat for enough winter reserves to supply milk for cubs. Once the egg implants, fetal development screams along over the last two to three months of the pregnancy, or until January or early February, when the cubs are born "preemies" in the den.

The black bear's winter den is generally not the extensive

cavity a grizzly will dig. More often, it is a tree hollow, an old stump, a rock overhang, a thicket, a burrow lined with leaves and grasses, or nothing more than a shallow dish scraped in the ground with a jumble of branches pulled over as roof. It is not uncommon for black bears to sleep smack on the ground, leaving winter to do the work of forming a snow cave over them. By curling up, turning her thick hair to the weather, and poking her nose between her hind legs, the female can keep her tiny cubs warm and nursed against her thinly haired belly. Hers is a thick, viscous milk, high in fat and protein content—roughly three times richer than that of a cow. In April or May the cubs (typically one or two, more rarely three or four) emerge from the den weighing four to ten pounds. Barring disaster, the family will stick together for approximately eighteen months. For the youngsters, this is an intense time of education about the bounties and perils of their home terrain. From their mother, they learn the elaborate chores of locating seasonal foods and the techniques of browsing, rooting, digging. They soon know, with any sign of danger or at Mother's signal, to scramble high up a tree. The second winter, mother and cubs again den together, the juveniles helping to prepare the den. Then, at the beginning of the following summer, the mother becomes essentially a delinquent mom, more interested in the pursuit of passion than in mothering. In accepting suitors, she becomes less protective of her cubs.

At the Hoys' rehab center, the cubs were first year, seven to eight months old. They'd had only about five months of worldly experience—turning over logs, looking for the fattest grubs.

As I pulled up, Judy and Bob were busy with feeding and cleaning pens. They are sixtyish and energetic, dedicated, involved-in-the-world people. Bob is quiet-mannered and soft-spoken, not a chatty person unless you ask a question pertinent to his work, and then he will warmly hold forth from the wealth of knowledge gained through his years of dealing with wildlife and the backcountry. For all his calm, Judy is the counterpoint—a nonstop, upper-octave stream of commentary and lobbying on everything that is her passion, from the protection of wildlife to the banning of pesticides. An old cowboy hat has a permanent home atop her still-dark hair, which she keeps in long braids—a testament to her cherishing what she is fairly certain are Native American genes. Her genealogical research pointed at first to a dark, never-admitted liaison but later to a set of Chippewa great-grandparents who fled the Great Lakes area to avoid being sent to reservations in Oklahoma. They never spoke again of their Indian heritage, not even to their children.

The Hoys' morning had been taken up building pens and den boxes. A pen of minimum size requires six, six-foot by twelve-foot, chain-link fencing panels—four for the sides (one with a door) and two top panels. New, a pen cost about six hundred dollars. Fortunately, a neighbor had just delivered a ten-foot-tall pen, on loan. They were taking anything they could make secure. Each cub also needed a den box, a hidey-hole for withdrawing and sleeping. Out of plywood, Bob had been knocking together rectangular boxes, open at one end and roofed with tin. A thick flap of carpeting—slit up the middle—hung tacked over each opening. The pens were strewn with fresh hay for bedding, and numerous black rubber feed tubs, the type commonly used for ranch stock, lay scattered about.

The first pen held triplets. Found in August strolling through the playground of a grade school in Superior (a town seventy-five miles west of Missoula), they were presently bunking together in a St. Bernard–sized doghouse, incongruously painted pink. A tire swing hung in their "yard."

All were black-bodied and brown-nosed, the coloring most characteristic of their species. Black bears range, in what are called color phases, all through the browns—of chocolate, tan, and cinnamon—over to blue and a stunning white, but always the brown nose.

"That's Smokey Bear," Judy said, pointing to the triplet by the doghouse, "he's a he. The one back there is a female, I call her Blackie, and the one at the feed tub is Honey, another girl." Females, she told me, are apt to have thinner noses. Much to Bob's chagrin, it appeared, Judy gave all the bears names—not particularly to call them by name but as a way of distinguishing them in conversation and in the records.

The three cubs were chubby, like big-bottomed babies bundled into fancy fur coats. Their posture when they sat down brought to mind a friend's pudgy-legged daughter when she was eight months old and swathed in diapers; she would sit hunched forward, one leg stretched out, the other bent at the knee with foot flat against the opposite inside thigh. At my approach, they all scrambled for the doghouse. The square spacings in the pen's chain-linking were too small for my camera lens, which forced me to squat in the doorway, while Bob with a quiet celerity portioned out among the feed tubs servings of puppy food and apple slices. Immediately three noses bobbed in and out of the doghouse door. Honey, too curious to stay put, in slow, timorous steps ventured across the yard. Blackie, more wary of me, was seized by a dance of indecision, while the slightly sturdier-appearing male stayed planted in the dark cavern. Moving methodically on to other chores, Bob left me propped in the doorway waiting for my shot. But it was not until Judy squeezed past to sling three globs of frozen raspberries, a heaven-sent donation from some woman's freezer, into their tubs that the three bunched up: Honey, after an immediate trip to the raspberries, brought the taste back to her siblings at the dog-house. Smokey licked the residue from her mouth and nose, while Blackie standing behind and peering bright-eyed over the center, took in my every move.

The adjacent small pen held a shy, cocoa-colored female, perhaps twenty pounds heavier than Smokey. She was a black bear, like the rest, but Judy called her Grizz. With Judy's shifting a piece of plywood canted over the den box's entrance, I had a clear view of the cub's face. She had a long, narrow nose. Her dark eyes were soft, and wearing an expression that hit me as terror-stricken and beseeching.

Next down the line was Yogette, a reclusive little black cub, cranky and gruff. She would nose out of her box only a few feet to gnaw on a deer leg (a plump piece of road-kill) that Judy had tossed her, and not without a fierce, stiff-legged jump and huff in my direction. *Good girl! You will make it.*

The last to need portraits, Raspberry and Huckleberry, from different mothers, were down at the end. For lack of sufficient pens at the time of their arrival, they had been housed together. Though each had been provided a den box, they had promptly taken to rooming together. As I sidled up, the far box vibrated with a series of thumps and bumps. A small oak brown cub shot out from the slit in the carpeting and darted behind the box. Then he leaped on top and delivered to the tin roof, over his partner's head, a resounding couple of wallops. Suddenly registering my presence, with a yikes-who-are-you? look, he again dived behind the box. Though in a minute his head popped up. He was standing on his hind legs, staring at me over the top, as if to ask, Who'd you say you were again?

Standing upright on their hind legs is something bears will do from the time they are wee cubs. It is not a stance meant to be threatening; rather it affords them a better look around, a better sniff of danger, and often an easier reach for food. My credentials were being checked out. With their having already cleaned up their meals, Judy dumped more sliced apples into their tubs to lure them into another walk-about.

There is a wide range of difference in approaches to rehab-ing bears and, as yet, no established standard for care. I was told about a woman in Alaska who never spoke in the pres-ence of the cubs she raised. She took them for walks and by example taught them how to dig for grubs, pluck berries from bushes, and drink from a creek, always letting them taste what she had in her mouth. This latter is proper bear etiquette, their way of learning from Mom or siblings about foodstuffs. Then there are rehabists who take it the opposite way, trying to totally eliminate human contact by wearing gloves and staying hidden. The Hoys, with their easy mov-ing about the pens, seem to be in their own category. They feel confident the care they've given to their charges has helped the little ones on their way. It is an assessment, how-ever, more held in their hearts than based on scientific study. Many of the cubs they have kept over a winter were ear-tagged or tattooed, and Bob says, to his knowledge, none has ever turned up—as a nuisance bear or a hunter's kill. Which is not to say, positively, they are still alive or even reached breeding age. But Bob gives extra effort to releasing their cubs far from human settlement, back in the wilderness Tim-buktu.

A few days later I was back for the next arrival. Lolo, named for the drainage where she was found, was a petite and gor-geous cinnamon cub. She was sitting in front of a grass green doghouse inside the tall pen on loan. When Judy opened the door and approached the feed tub with lunch goodies, Lolo stamped the ground with a front paw and chomped her jaws, emitting a clacking sound—bear behavior for "I am frightened, please don't come any closer, maybe this will scare you off."

A week went by, and Judy called again. "We've got a new, tiny one." Elkie, found wandering up on Elk Ridge. Would I come take a picture? And Grizz had escaped. Judy had left the padlock off, thinking Bob was on his way down. Sometime during the night, Grizz had figured out how to lift the hinged, U-shaped latches, top and bottom. She was obviously clever, she had a bit of weight on her, it was probably her best move. We wished her well.

A long drawn out winter—in Montana they usually are—lay ahead, but not an especially cold one. Lots of snow piled up in the high country, but only a few inches, intermittent and fleeting, fell on the valley floor. I had stepped into a world of bears and it began, not unwelcomely, to engulf me. I curled up with a stack of library books, a reading list from Dr. Jonkel, whom I was by now calling Chuck. And occasionally I drove over and peeked at the cubs. A particular concern for them began to tug at me: worry about their human contact. Sponsors, potential sponsors, and classes of schoolchildren were stopping by. My visits, by rights, were no healthier; I decided to limit them. I sat in my truck, as a rule, down the way, and watched them through binoculars.

One school of thought holds to the belief that in the long run there is no good contact (for the bear) between bears and people. In reading Robert Franklin Leslie's book *The Bears and I,* an endearing early-twentieth-century account of his years spent thoughtfully rearing triplet black bear cubs in Canada's north woods, the dangers become apparent. As hard as he tried to teach them everything they would need to survive on their own, it was, in the end, a canoe that became their undoing. Having journeyed with him as infants far into the northern wilds by canoe and continuing to like riding in his canoe, the cubs as three-year-olds did not differentiate when hunters arrived by canoe.

I was beginning to grasp how little we comprehend about the rescue and salvation of the bears that ended up crossing paths with humans. There are no real data on the success rate of pen-kept, winter-fed cubs. It is difficult to track an individual bear's development. They roam over large territories and, for the most part, live as loners—the exceptions being females with cubs and the groups that form where food sources run plentiful, at garbage dumps and fish spawning grounds and expansive berry patches. Bears, amongst themselves, may have a broader sense of social relationship than we have previously assumed, including recognition of past partners and knowledge of one another's territories. But that doesn't tell us the story we're wanting to know: the precise fate of a released cub.

In addition to their habituation to humans and human foods, these young cubs were destined to have other big troubles. The mountains are full of hazards—wolves, mountain lions, big burly male bears covetous of their territories, well-armed hunters—and there was always the possibility of injuries and starvation.

By one estimate only 45 percent of bear cubs survive the first year, by another only half reach age three. At five years, they have an 80 percent likelihood of lasting another year. Bears, in the whole earthly scheme of things, with their low birthrates and precarious food supplies, are a species far more orchidy than weedy. Siblings in the wild, after Mom boots them out, will sometimes keep company for a couple of years. Releasing them in pairs, Jonkel told me, or, in the case of the triplets, in threes, would give them a better chance—an "I know you! If all hell breaks loose, we'll stand and fight together!" chance. They would become surrogate mothers to each other. In twos, they were better at picking up early signs of danger. They could forage cooperatively. Learn from each other, even comfort each other. "They get scared and rush into each other's arms," Jonkel said. "Same as we do."

I began to keep in touch with Beth Sorenson of Wildlife Return, another rehab center 130 miles north, in Kalispell. She was receiving cubs almost daily, the numbers pushing thirty, and her project coffers were sucking zero. The Department of Fish, Wildlife and Parks funded the state-run animal shelter in Helena, which kept no paid staff over the winter. They occasionally sprang loose small, and always appreciated, amounts to assist the home-based nonprofit enterprises like Sorenson's and the Hoys'—places that in years like this one carried the load in orphan care and rehabing. The flyers Judy had made up with the cubs' pictures and posted around the valley were sparking interest and donations. She and Bob had also received a small foundation grant. Beth was not faring as well. In years past, she'd always had her income to fling on rehabing. Recently divorced, she was having to live on the money she made at her day job, as a physician's assistant. Interviews that she gave to the local papers, along with calls to relatives, brought in donations of puppy food, calf formula, and a chunk of cash. Yet for the past month, as the cubs poured in, she'd been building pens with a fury, maxing out her credit card to the tune of five thousand dollars.

But there was also the good news. The high media profile of orphaned cubs was providing rehabists a needed exchange of information. Beth would purposely throw four cubs together in a good-sized pen to determine which ones liked each other. If they got to scrapping, she broke it up with the blast of a hose and then adjusted roommates. Judy and Bob were just finding out you could put two unrelated cubs together, but they dared not experiment further. Without the option of larger pens or plumbed water in the pen area (each day they hauled the cubs' drinking water from the house), they were concerned about the potential for serious injuries.

Shortly after New Year's, the Hoys received two more cubs. A small, glossy female Judy dubbed Black Velvet. She'd been caught at the buffet table of a rancher's grain bin. The other was a latte-colored two-year-old, emaciated, with a blue ear tag. He became Blueberry. The state-run shelter in Helena was at its limit with nineteen cubs, all in hibernation boxes, and caretaker Steve McMorran not technically working but routinely checking on them. The count at Sorenson's, with the latest—a seven-pound shell of a cub—had risen to thirty-four. And the evening news carried a story about Sally Maughn, a rehabist in Boise, Idaho, on the far other side of the Bitterroot-Salmon-Selway Wilderness, caring for nine. Then, a few days later, an eleven-pound cub ran through the door of a house in Kalispell and hid under a couch—Sorenson's thirty-fifth.

On a crisp January morning, riding before a cold front, Erik Wenum, the black bear conflict specialist for FWP's Region 1 out of Kalispell, started denning Sorenson's cubs. The first to go were the fattest, those eighty pounds or more. For some time they'd been gorging on a rich calf replacement formula Beth mixed with Mazola oil and sugar. Then a week ago she had withdrawn their food to nudge them toward denning-mode behavior and they had gone to sleep. Wenum took twenty-four cubs over the course of the next few weeks. He and his crew trucked them into the backcountry—to the ends of plowed roads—where the cubs were tranquilized and ear-tagged and then transferred in pairs to special winter denning boxes. With the boxes strapped on the backs of snowmobiles, the young bears were spirited away to spots of seclusion. There they were packed into snow banks that would supply good insulation against subzero temperatures. Wenum picked his spots with care: for good drainage, nearby water, and southeast-facing slopes offering early spring vegetation. To the plinking of snowmelt three months from now, two little cubs would wake up, nuzzle each other, sniff and stretch, then trundle out the opening Wenum had left them and paw through a banked pile of brush. A short saunter, following their noses, and they would tumble into a meal of Rocky Mountain wildflowers—glacier lilies and spring beauties.

The denning program, Wenum told me over the phone, had been seven years in operation. "It's been a learn-as-you-go process," he said. Yet he was getting a 100 percent success rate in den emergence, meaning the cubs were staying asleep when they should and climbing out in good shape. In the beginning years, there was worry about their being able to store enough energy in their fat. Rehabists can't perfectly mimic a bear's diet in the wild. "The fat that a human puts on is different," Wenum said. "It's strictly pure white fat, low in energy, high in water content." Deer and elk lay down adipose, or brown, fat—what is called true energy fat. The bulk a bear piles on is different yet: white fat that's fairly high in energy. Pen-kept cubs receive processed forms of sugars that cannot match the sugar of huckleberries. Pouring the weight on these cubs was a way of making up for lack of quality.

The winter denning program is seen as beneficial because it shortens the period of human involvement. Pen-kept bears, even if in a feed-them-by-remote-control arrangement, become food-conditioned. Time on the mountain, beneath the snow, provides denned cubs with a break—one hopes particularly in their minds—from human contact. (The Hoys' cubs were scheduled for spring releases because they were in FWP's Region 2, which for reasons of budgetary constraints has not instituted a denning program.)

Of the sixty-two cubs that Wenum had denned since the program's inception, he was familiar with the long-term stories of six. Rambo, one of Sorenson's denned as a yearling six years ago, had been encountered the previous year (due to incidental capture in a snare set for a female grizzly that was scheduled to be recollared) as a two-hundred-pounder: a grown bear leading a good bear life! Three others had been shot by hunters, two as three-year-olds, one a two-year-old. The fifth had been hit by a car on Highway 93 north of Whitefish. The sixth became a problem bear, was captured and rereleased with aversive conditioning (more about this later), and so far was staying wild.

In the wild, it is not winter weather alone, as is commonly thought, that triggers denning. When a bear has accumulated a righteous padding of fat, sometimes as thick as five inches, its stomach refuses further food. Anatomically this is because of the growth of fat deposits in the bear's abdominal cavity, which cause the stomach and intestines to constrict. The stomach deflates into a pancake or, some say, shrinks into a hard ball the size of a fist. A bear in this condition sidles off to a den site and slips into a state of inactivity, content not to eat, drink, urinate, or defecate for as long as six or seven months. During this time, the animal's sensitivity to danger drops to nearly zero.

Over the course of a bear's denning, it may lose 15 to 50 percent of its body weight, a nursing mother losing the most. Yet a healthy, well-fed-in-the-fall bear will emerge in spring in good condition with a splendid coat. Its first meals will be light vegetation consisting of grasses and forbs, flowers and leaves. Bears are the largest of the omnivores, or generalized eaters. They have teeth adapted for herbivorous chewing but retain the short digestive track of the meat eater. Black bears consume considerably less meat than grizzlies or polar bears (the last, of all the bear species, eats the most meat). A black bear's meat intake amounts to a small percentage of its diet, and much of the meat, at that, consists of insects, grubs, frogs, lizards, birds, and small mammals. This diet light in meat is due largely to the energy cost of "playing predator" to larger species. Even the young calves of elk and moose can entail an energetic chase. Bears, with their formidable stature, find it easier to plunder another animal's kill. But when fresh out of the den—just as after a fast one can't leap straight to gorging on red meat—they sometimes pass up winter-killed carrion directly in their path. For a few months, they tend toward a negative calorie intake, expending more energy than their foods supply them, and often dropping further poundage. It is a time rather for rebuilding muscles. By the close of spring, bears will be looking lean and their fur scruffy from shedding their winter coats. In the days when hunting went unregulated, it was during these first months of summer that bears were not prized. Then, as breeding season winds down, they start to put on weight again.

"After that it will be sugar they need," says Jonkel. "Pounds and pounds of berries, every day!"

On January 16, Patrick and I were eating breakfast, layering on our own fat—Patrick in his twenty-pound winter gorge that he loses again in summer, me in my slower and more permanent fashion—when he pushed the "Outdoors" section of the *Missoulian* toward me. The headline read: GUIDES OUTRAGED BY ONTARIO SPRING BEAR HUNT BAN.

Outfitters with bookings for the coming season were up in arms at the provincial government's ending of the traditional spring bear hunt. The official reasoning was stated as such: "It would no longer tolerate cubs being orphaned by hunters mistakenly shooting the mothers." Ontario has one of the largest populations of black bears in North America, an estimated 75,000 to 100,000. Though shooting females is illegal, approximately one-third of the 4,000 bears killed in the spring hunt are judged to be female, leaving in the neighborhood of 270 orphaned cubs. (It's difficult to determine the gender of a bear by casual sight in the wild. Even the obvious mother with cubs may have stationed her offspring up a tree a good distance away.) A second complaint voiced by the opposition to the spring hunt flowed from the less than challenging aspects of killing a bear at its den. Like anyone waking up warm from a nap, say on a couch with the sun beaming in, the big mammals are slow to get functioning. Because they are behaviorally laid-back and with digestive tracts that need to adjust gradually, they don't at first stir around much. A bear might sit at the edge of its den for a couple hours and then return to sleeping a few more days. He might repeat this routine two or three times. Not being a deep hibernator in the physiologically comatose sense of a bat or a ground squirrel, a bear can, it is true, within a few minutes of sensing danger, rally energies and bolt. But during the low-reactive, lounging-outside-the-den time, a hunter downwind has an easy kill. The *Missoulian* piece had come over the Associated Press from Toronto, the byline David Crary's, and it contained this statement: "The spring hunt was popular among affluent U.S. hunters, who sometimes received guarantees that they would return home with a trophy." And this, a quotation from Rob Sinclair of the International Fund for Animal Welfare: "The idea was to offer a guaranteed kill. If you don't get a bear, come back next time free."

A call to Toronto and a check of the Internet turned up a few more details. As compensation, the Ontario government planned to extend the fall hunt and provide monetary relief to outfitters with losses of revenue. But clearly the government was hearing only the initial outrage. Lost client fees for the coming spring would tip $10 million; lawsuits were in the making. Hunters, meanwhile, were being directed to other provinces. I found the following blurb promoting an outfitter in Saskatchewan: "In the spring bears are hunted from tree stands located near the edge of the lake or river, looking over baited sites, this has been a very successful method of hunting for many years." And this one from a New Brunswick lodge: "Untapped bear population. Careful site selection activated by tons of bait. This gives you a terrific success ratio." Beyond being an unconscionable, to my mind, tactic, baiting creates unnatural associations—with food deposited by people. It teaches the bears bad behavior. (Though some hunters use roadkill, many bears that visit bait sites walk off knowing the taste of human food.) Baiting also alters bears' habits and their relationships with other animals of the wild, in that a bear pursuing the smell of bait is detouring from the path it might have taken.

In Montana, bears begin rolling out of their dens sometime in April or May, the hungrier ones first, the nursing mothers last. Montana holds spring hunts of varying duration. Baiting and hunting with dogs is illegal. Shooting females with cubs is illegal. In the Sapphire and Bitterroot Mountains, just east and west of where I live, the season begins April 15 and runs for six weeks. Eight, ten miles back into the mountains to the west is the Idaho border—any bear wandering across is met by luring with bait and hunting with dogs ($7.50 for a hunting license, $7.50 for a bear tag, $1.50 for a bait permit). The season for Idaho's Units 12 and 17 in the Clearwater Region, the territory lying directly west of the Bitterroot Valley, was to begin this year on April 15 and end June 30 and June 15 respectively. That meant somewhere up in those mountains, hunters would be putting out their butcher scraps and grain just at the time the Hoys would be wanting to release their cubs.

True to Bob's predictions, he and Judy received their final cub early in February, found in the Lolo Creek drainage near Traveler's Rest. Judy named him Louie, after Meriwether Lewis, who had camped at the spot with the Corps of Discovery. She gave him the pen beyond Blueberry and Black Velvet. Later, around the time of the cubs' release, Louie was found to be a probable twin to Lolo, who herself was discovered high on the pen wall sporting a big-as-life penis. When put together they fell immediately to playful brotherly tumbling—"Where have *you* been?"—and were subsequently sent on their way as a team.

In tallying the final rehab counts, including three at Sorenson's from the Confederated Salish and Kootenai Tribes, I came up with seventy-seven orphans—their famished mothers shot for getting into someone's garbage, killed mistakenly in the fall hunt, body-bashed while crossing busy highways and train tracks, one accidentally relocated without her cubs. On one of his trips into the mountains, Erik Wenum witnessed a female grizzly trying to abandon her starving cub, who couldn't keep up; he theorized this was being done on a larger scale by mothers that in this time of famine considered their youngsters competitors for food. Mother bears we fairly worship for their attentive caring for and defending of their offspring. Many knowledgeable people believe a bear mom would never desert her little ones. What Wenum had seen indicated the most desperate of circumstances.

.   .   .

The following week I awoke one day before dawn to the beeping of Patrick's alarm clock. In his rolling over to hit the snooze button, a handful of snow dislodged itself from the flannel-covered comforter that is our top layer and splatted onto my cheek. In walking my fingers around the exposed top of my head, I came upon another such blob, this one frozen into my hair around my barrette. Only two inches of snow had fallen during the night, but it was sufficient to wrap the world in a profoundly peaceful stillness. Patrick, with an early appointment to shoe two arena-working horses—the grist of his winter farrier trade—soon leaped up. I hung on, watching a corner of the sky lighten.

The river bottom lay deep in shadow, the wild rosebushes, aspens, and cottonwoods swathed in new shawls of white. A royal golden glow spread out, ever so slowly, ahead of the sun. Before peeking its life-giving face over the Sapphires, the fireball caught in the west on the pointy tips of the Bitterroots. From where I lay, I counted eleven snow-clad peaks simultaneously turning a flaming pink. For the dozen times I've marveled at this sunrise-on-mountain-tip scene, the only feeble likening I am able to dredge up is that of a candlelit birthday cake. The spectacle is beyond metaphor. For a person who'd given up on organized religion in second grade (upon being dished out an F in Sunday school: I didn't do my homework assignment), the grandeur of a dawn like this is a religious experience, one that pumps faith into a flagging heart. After a time I rolled up onto my hands and knees and settled into a satisfying back stretch, still gazing out from the envelope opening of my red-plaid snow cave. Perhaps like a bear, I could just stay tucked in here through March and lose fifteen easy pounds!

Legends of people turning into bears twine through the myths and traditions of many native cultures and are traceable back through the circumpolar tribes of the Northern

Hemisphere, even to Paleolithic times. Northern indigenous cultures almost universally place strong spiritual significance on their relationship with the bear. Of all the animals, it is the one that humans most closely resemble—in body shape and movement, in eating habits, in phases of holing up and venturing forth. The bear is a swimmer of rivers, a climber of trees. The bear is a dweller of terrestrial terrains from salty seashore to rocky mountaintop, from inland swamp to rolling plain, from dry southern thicket to Arctic ice field. It was from observing the bear that the earliest peoples learned of the locations of seasonal berries and nuts and honey, the timing of salmon runs, even applications for medicinal herbs and the healing powers of mud. From the bear came the art of the hunt itself. Robert Franklin Leslie, in the account of his cub-raising, wrote: "The heaviest animal on his feet in the North American forest, the bear walks flatfooted on the entire soft, naked soles of his paws, and that is why he can sneak over an acre of dry twigs and leaves and sit down beside you without your knowing he is there."

Today we are still learning from bears. Especially hibernating bears: how their bodies process proteins and fats and manage a usually life-threatening buildup of urea when not passing urine. Through the study of bears, medical science is retrieving information helpful in understanding diabetes, kidney failure, thyroid functioning, muscle atrophy. After months of inactivity, a bear's musculature is still in good shape. Delving into why will potentially aid athletes, the elderly on bed rest, anyone with a broken bone immobilized in a cast, and astronauts, who with weightlessness experience muscle wasting.

Another aspect of bear medicine centers on the proven curative properties of bear bile. Synthesized bear bile (from cow bile) is prescribed by Western doctors as a treatment for various illnesses: hepatitis, cirrhosis of the liver, blood cholesterol, the dissolving of gallstones. The peoples of Chinese-influenced cultures not only value the gallbladder's bile salts but sup on bear paws for their presumed medicative benefits—and also as status symbols. Paws and gallbladders, of course, come from dead bears. With the development of readily available and inexpensive synthetic bile, it was hoped some of the illegal trade in bear parts would diminish, but there remains that irresistibility of a "real item," especially if it's priced out of this world. Asian prices for gallbladders, in the early 1990s, ranged from U.S. $1 to $210 per gram—at their high end on a par with China White heroin, according to Judy A. Mills, author of the chapter "Bears as Pets, Food, and Medicine" in the book *Bears: Majestic Creatures of the Wild*. She writes: "Black-market vendors in the open air markets of China peddle bear gallbladders by the kilo. Wholesalers of traditional medicines in South Korea travel to North America to buy their bear gallbladders fresh from bears killed before their eyes . . . leaving in their wake whole bears dead, with nothing but their gallbladders missing."

There is something eerily human about a skinned bear. I know avid big-game hunters who for this very reason will not hunt bear. Over the winter, I had observed the gray, coatless bodies of little Blackie and Honey; the girls had lost their hair, due to what, no one knew. Naked, they further resembled, save for their snips of tails, pudding-fat, huggable infants. My friend Katya is forever encountering dead or hairless animals, which causes her great upset. She once pulled her car off the highway in order to drag from the shoulder, and reverentially cover up, two dead intrauterine fawns ejected from the belly of a roadkilled white-tailed doe. At seeing what hunters (hunters of sorry sorts) had dumped on the highway opposite her driveway entrance, she came unstuck: a stiff, skinned bear corpse, missing head and paws.

The age-old veneration of the bear and the bear hunt, in-
stilled generously in indigenous cultures, is not something
slid easily over the counter with the random purchase of a
gun. Indian peoples hunted bears (though some tribes did
not), killed them as they emerged from their dens, even
scared them from their dens. Traditions surrounding a bear
slaying originated long before the advent of automatic weapons. A crude handheld knife and a club were likely the in-
struments of combat. Generally, the hunt, the kill, the
consuming of the bear were accompanied by elaborate rituals of preparation and procedure and, at the finish, sacred
burial. There were honorings, fastings and offerings, absti-
nences, prayers, dances, chants, special handlings of the
body and feastings on the meat, as well as rhythmic reenactments or pantomimes wearing the fresh bear skin. "Mimic
performance," Paul Shepard and Barry Sanders suggest in
their book *The Sacred Paw*, "may be as old as, or older than
speech itself, and the dance of the hunt may have served to
communicate about it before storytelling emerged." With
First Americans, a multilayered sustenance was taken from
the gift of the bear's body, and reverence given back.

Today many different Indian ceremonials venerate the
bear. Autumn's honoring dances are for putting the bear to
sleep in the den; spring rituals sanctify the bear's awakening.
For some tribes, it is spring's first clap of thunder that signals
the bear's emergence from the den, and around this weather
event sacred ceremonies are planned. The sacredness is often
guarded. When a good friend from out of state invited me to
a bear dance, she wanted little of its whereabouts or ritual revealed. It would be some months yet in Montana before
thunder rocked the heavens. If my going to a bear honoring
could somehow transfer benefit to these cubs, it was an invitation for me to accept.

.   .   .

Tossing a duffel bag in the bed, I climbed into the old truck—still running well, ten years after departing California, though its white paint was now measled with rust. With a plane to catch, I parked in the long-term lot at the Missoula International Airport. A few years back, the old Johnson-Bell Field had been renamed and enlarged from four gates to six. It is a brick edifice now, with timber-vaulted entry and plains of tile, offering displays of art and Montana-made crafts, a combination tourist boutique and newsstand, and, as the Treasure State's welcome and send-off representatives, two large stuffed bears. In the downstairs entry stands Bruiser Bruin, this name printed on a gold plaque above MONARCH OF THE GOLD CREEK DRAINAGE OF THE SWAN VALLEY. HARVESTED MAY 24TH, 1997. In smaller lettering there follows the location of the kill, the hunter's name, and the name of the taxidermist. Such use of the word *harvested* has always struck me as peculiar; it's a word I might apply to garden produce, orchard fruit, farm-raised livestock. Our Mr. Bruin is positioned in an upright stance atop a chunk of imitation granite in a six-sided glass enclosure. His coloring is Lipton tea brown. He has small, narrow-set glass eyes and on his chest sports the white V-patch characteristic of many members of the black bear species. In my freshman opinion, he came out a bit too flat-headed between the ears. That, coupled with his fixed expression, gives him a beady-eyed, sober stare. Arrayed at his feet today were three airport goers, each commandeering a four-seater bench and highly absorbed in novel-reading, anxious ticket-fingering, or cell phone deal-making.

Upstairs, in the central lobby leading to gates one through four, looming like a lone tree in a clearing, is an encased, erect grizzly. He is amazingly happy-faced, with an open-mouthed smile and a friendly glint in his eye. A plaque holds this inscription: WELCOME TO MISSOULA—HOME OF THE UNI-

VERSITY OF MONTANA 'GRIZZLIES.' The bear's coat is a milk chocolate color woven with soft yellows—the hue lighter on his snout, chest, underchin, and lower abdomen. Coming up the stairs, I noticed on the outside of the glass, at the two-feet-off-the-floor level, nine small handprints and a few nose smudges. As I stood for a moment gazing up into his great ursine face, a man trotted by and tossed out, "Ugly, huh?"

The next night found me in an isolated outdoor sanctuary; all around, the dark heads and shoulders of mountains poked into a star-strewn dome. The spirit that moves in circular ways between the earth, the heavens, and the underworld is the bear's. The bear is the symbol for rebirth and renewal, the steward of seasons, the driving force of night's pulling the sun up into day. Bear is the metaphor for death and decay, from which comes fresh new growth—in plantings and in passages from one stage of life to another. Bear is the trustee of fertility and a woman's menstrual moons. Upon invitation to enter the ceremonial circle of bear medicine, out of a respect for bears, for the orphaned cubs back home, and for tribal customs, I removed my boots and socks. Stepping in, my bare feet lit on cold, tamped earth and took me straight to places I had so long missed. Below hemline, my ankles caught the brush of chill night air. But the roundel of soil was warm near the fire at its center, and polished from the feet of those gone before. My freed toes, eager in their communion, sought out the small imperfections inherent in a hand-compacted dirt, felt as slight rises and hollows—pressed in first by bear wisdom that was to honor and to follow. Three tribal dancers, inhabiting the skins of bears—eyes lowered beneath jutting bear jaws, hands spiritually bonded at paws and claws—embodied the heart of the bear. Song. Dance. Kindling consanguinity. Twice, at the pop of fiery sprays, my thinly callused soles settled onto the sting of tiny, bright embers.

Most of all, the nightlong vigil provided me a slowing down that began to open me up, warm me up, lift my blunted instincts from all that goes with our cluttery modernity of virtual gadgetry and maniacal schedules dictated by two-income households. Above the clouds, in the plane flying home, ancient rhythms of the drum still reverberating in my core, I browsed back over the events of the past eight months. I had seen bears confined in cages, stuffed behind glass, offered as trophies over the Internet, held tightly in the hearts of friends, sketched and photographed for newspapers and calendars, pressed into lines of type on the pages of books, come to life in vision and story and song, wrapped in ritual and myth and sacred ceremony. An overpowering urge took hold: I promised myself to find a bear in the woods.

May. A glorious, sun-soaked, blue-sky mountain morning. More so, coming after weeks of spring's dull overcast and pathetic spits of rain. Any weather with a soul would have satisfied—a drenching downpour, an infamous Big Creek Canyon blow, or today's beaming sun. A lazy string of puffer-belly clouds dangled just above the Bitterroots. Snowy peaks gleamed as though satin, birds chirped, lilac buds swelled to bursting, and laughable clumps of dandelions studded the roadsides. I drove up to the Hoys' full of hope: This was a day *made* for the cubs to hike back into their forest. Five would be released—the triplets, Black Velvet, and the two-year-old, Blueberry.

Already having arrived from FWP were Warden Captain Jeff Darrah—"the new, young, big cheese of Region 2," I'd heard him called—and, also having come down from Missoula, Derek Schott, game warden. Each had driven a pickup that trailered a culvert trap, a two-wheeled contraption painted bright yellow, with the black-lettered warning DAN-GER STAY BACK. A few minutes later, Joe Jaquith, FWP's war-den sergeant from the Bitterroot, pulled in, and we all began strolling around looking at cubs. As soon as Judy and Bob ar-rived from the house, Joe, who is a tall, strapping man with an open, friendly face and confident manner, took charge of the morning. He had the most experience with darting. Four of the bears needed to be sedated and ear-tagged. Blueberry already carried a tag, the one that had inspired his name. Males were given blue tags, females red.

Though tagging is something more easily accomplished when cubs are smaller or if they are tranquilized at the time of their capture, the plan to tag all handled bears had gone lacking over the years, for want of a game warden's time and energy. Darrah saw today as a prime opportunity for tagging; he believed in its importance for documenting histories. As bears then turned up, their tag numbers would supply infor-mation to a central data bank. Short of the expense of radio collars, Darrah was determined to drag the countryside for answers to questions rolling around in his head: "Keeping these cubs over the winter, hand-feeding them—is it just a warm fuzzy feeling for us? Are we actually helping the bears? How can we help them the best?"

Tags, however, could not tell us everything. The cubs might end up being illegally poached or devoured by large predators. Once they were turned loose, we all frankly hoped never to see them again—that would mean they hadn't shown up as "nuisance" bears or been killed during a hunting season, yet it wouldn't necessarily mean that they were leading long, healthy lives in the mountains.

The tailgate of Darrah's pickup came down, and the three uniformed men—in blue jeans and tan FWP shirts—huddled around a compartmented fishing tackle box holding needles, vials, charges, and darts. A dart or "automatic flying syringe," containing the drug Telazol, would be fired with a .22 blank. Telazol was considered the newer, safer tranquilizer. It came without the worry of convulsions and the sometimes crazed behavior associated with its predecessor, Sernylan, which had the same composition as angel dust. Darrah had brought along a new gun that fired factory-sealed, nonreusable darts; they were a step up from the old system of hand-load, sterilize, reload.

Joe, wanting a record of the morning's events, asked me to shoot the roll of slide film in his Pentax. Then he prefaced the actual darting (surely for my benefit, as I was the only uninitiated person present) with the following statements: "It's a given that 'things happen' when handling bears. These cubs are wild animals. People and animals can get hurt. Animals can die. There is always the possibility for things to happen."

Judy is a fanatic crusader against pesticide and fungicide poisoning. I think of her as the Karen Silkwood of the Bitterroot. Most of us will believe her only when half of us are dead. She was certain Blackie and Honey, the two females of the triplets, had an unusually high chemical sensitivity, evidenced in part by their loss of hair over the winter, and she was afraid they would die if they were darted. The decision, however, was not hers; the cubs had only been farmed out to the Hoys for care. I knew, myself, that any time I had undergone surgery I'd been required to sign a cheerless little paper that said I was fully aware I could die on the operating table from the anesthetic. The rate of loss from tranquilizer for bears is placed at one in a hundred—termed in the records as "died from unknown causes."

The females of the triplets, utterly oblivious to us, were pacing one side of their pen in synchronized wheelings that reminded me of choreographed swimming. They'd worn a groove into the dirt in the past weeks: they were hyperactive with cage-craze. Joe poked the barrel of the new gun through the pen's chain linking and planted a dart in Blackie's haunch; her flinch was barely noticeable, perhaps it was my own. He fired one into Smokey, the little male, but the dart popped right out and Derek, from his vantage point, saw at least part of the load squirt onto the cub's coat. Joe tried for the third, but the cubs were riled and continuously revolving around one another and the doghouse. Not wanting to hit Honey in the face, he came up with two misses.

We backed off to the trucks and the gun was reloaded. The backing off after darting was an actual part of the procedure, to let an animal calmly go down. A churned-up animal produces adrenaline that fights with the drug, neutralizing its effect. Fifteen minutes passed, and Blackie was still fervently pacing, throwing her head with every pivot. We headed off to the pens at the far end to dart Black Velvet. Joe took careful aim. The dart needed to hit muscle. If the drug dispersed into fat, it wouldn't do its job. The gun fired, the dart hit her in the backside and bounced out almost as fast as it went in, uselessly spurting the drug again. Probably the friendliest of the cubs—liking to stand on top of her box and almost preen for visitors—Black Velvet reacted to the dart's sting as though personally betrayed. Shock in her eye, she dove for her box. It was a look to break a heart. I tried to console myself with: Better now than later in the woods.

The new gun was impressing no one. Gears shifted.

Joe and Darrah went off to hand-load darts for the old gun, while everyone else concentrated on moving out the already tagged Blueberry. Save for larger head and paws, the two-year-old was the same size as the yearling Velvet. Bob stepped through the door and gently tipped him out of his den box, then dragged it from the pen. Judy lugged in a carrying box, essentially the same type of plywood affair except for chicken-wire fencing at one end, a door at the other, and convenient carrying handles. Blueberry immediately darted into the carrying box, and Judy slid the door shut. It took three people to heft the box onto the trailer hitched to Judy's four-wheeler. With the turn of a key, she drove off and sidled up to one of the culvert traps. We checked Blackie in passing. The drug was having little observable effect, knocking not even the edge off her frenzy. The bright eyes I remembered from our first meeting, when she stared me full in the camera, couldn't hold still. Blueberry was transferred easily into the culvert trap, and an audible sigh of accomplishment arose at having one bear ready to roll.

Everyone met over the tackle box again, the conversation centering on darts and guns and doses. The darts for the new gun are equipped with a small wax barb designed to hold them in place until, in a short time, the wax melts, allowing the darts to fall out (an advantage on a bear that sprints for the woods). Everything working there. The charge in the gun is what sends the dart flying. Upon impact, a second charge, inside the dart, ejects the drug. Prepackaged charges for darts were known to lack consistency. These particular factory-sealed darts, it was being guessed, may have contained too much charge, which upon impact had the effect of firing the dart backward. Should an initial dart not solidly connect and deliver its entire load, the dose of tranquilizer for each sequential dart must be individually calculated, keyed to the animal's weight and how much was received from previous darts—a system, at best, of guesswork. Bob took a trip up to the house for his old-standby applicator, a homemade device he had used for years. He called it a jab pole—literally, a steel stick with a dart on the end, administered by hand. Jab poles are commonly used by rehabists for medicating animals they can't safely hold in their laps.

In the lull of activity, Derek related a story about having

to relocate a bear that had camped in a tree. When he darted it, the bear took off up the tree until he ran out of trunk or good branches and then fell to the ground, landing on his head. "You never know *what* will happen," he said. I asked if the bear had made it, and he said he couldn't believe it but the bear had lived. Bob, I was to learn later, had through similar circumstances lost two bears during his years as a game warden.

With his return, we focused our attention again on the triplets. Judy nailed plywood over the doghouse door, and with the thought to remove at least one cub from the chaos in the pen, coaxed Blackie into taking shelter in a carrying box. The box was then hoisted onto the tailgate of Joe's pickup. While Judy distracted the little cub at the chicken-wire end, Joe, with flashlight in one hand and the help of Bob working the door, darted her in the rear with the jab pole. They checked the load; it was still in the dart.

"How," Joe asked, "does the mechanism work?" He was fingering the mystery of the slim stick, this one not spring-loaded.

"You have to give it a darn good push," Bob said. The dart itself stops once it is in the bear; the pole keeps sliding along to plunge in the drug.

On the second try he was successful; they shut the door, draped someone's cotton shirt over the wire end, and, with the sun coming on hot now, Joe moved the truck into the shadow thrown by a tall cottonwood. Telazol causes the bears to breathe rapidly and has a dehydrating effect. Parking Blackie in the shade would help. Smokey, visably uneasy, was standing now—as though wanting to compute all the proceedings—on top of the doghouse. Using the new gun again, Derek successfully sank a dart, but in the cub's lower hind leg. The time was noted, and we would wait to see if it took.

Judy headed over to check on Blackie. She soon hollered, "You've got a dead bear!" her realized fears hardening into anger. The cub's lips and tongue were purple. Instantly, everyone was on the cub, checking her airway, looking for a pulse, applying artificial respiration. It was no use. Her shining eyes had gone dull. Her long tongue, to have aided her in reaching special tidbits in the wild, hung full-length out the side of her mouth. I backed away, not wanting a picture of this. It seemed somehow too private a moment. The feeling was similar to the one that seizes me when I'm in a line of drivers rubbernecking bodies strewn around a highway accident. Joe reached for the camera, took it from me, and clicked off a frame. "People need to know this kind of thing happens." His words were steady and firm.

For ten, fifteen minutes, we stayed hovering around the cub, in a brief mourning, asking the "why" questions, the "how" questions, each of us inwardly trying to plumb our part in the unknown causes. Our hands went to her body. In a need to touch her? In our disbelief? Out of remorse? In our wanting her forgiveness? At the horror we couldn't assimilate.

Her limp body was transferred to Darrah's truck; she would be taken to Missoula. Judy wanted her autopsied for the kidney and lung damage that she suspected from farm chemicals blowing in on storm fronts from agricultural areas in neighboring states upwind of us. With a time schedule imposed on our day, and other cubs to tend to, we were provided distraction. Joe easily planted an old-style dart in Black Velvet, then one in Honey. He radioed for another culvert trap. Bears coming out of Telazol can be fine or they can be nasty and hurt each other; he wanted no more than one bear in a trap.

Over the course of the next hour, I kept returning to the back of Darrah's pickup. Others did too. I met Bob there, and we conversed, clinically, about the weight of Blackie's paws, the feel of her fur, the configuration of her teeth, the length of her claws. All the while, I couldn't help running my hands over her still-warm body, massaging her ears, her forehead, her foreleg. The last was jointed for motion like my arm. After Bob walked off, I pressed my nose into her ruff. She gave off a sweet, animalish odor, that of my mate's scalp when his hair doesn't smell freshly of shampoo.

Black Velvet was soon conked out. With tagging pliers, or punch tool, in an operation similar to ear piercing, Derek gave her a red ear tag. She was placed in a carrying box and loaded into the bed of the pickup that trailered Blueberry. They were pals, to be released together.

Honey was down. She received her red tag, and with the second culvert trap positioned near the pen, she was carried out and tucked in. Joe's radio blared his call letters. The game wardens Doug Johnson and Ron Jendro were a few miles away with the third truck and culvert trap. The little male now sat down and presented Joe with a clear shot at a still ham. His third dart. The accumulation finally began to take some effect, but he fought it all the way. We stood back by the trucks and watched as he lifted one paw and plopped it back on the dirt in front of him, ten times. He swung his head from side to side with a dipping motion in the middle, as though trying to get wind of or shake off whatever it was that was taking hold of him.

Fifteen minutes passed. Johnson and Jendro arrived, and the trap was backed up to the pen. Smokey was not going to go down. He was woozy enough though that three men, suited up in leather gloves, picked him up as you might a sack of flour, by the corners, a fourth person supporting his head, and carried him to the open trap.

The whole operation had taken three and a half hours. Heading out, we made a quick stop at the first gas station.

Two of the FWP trucks needed gas. I hopped out to check on Honey. Her eyes were open, her head was up, her breathing was fine. A large-framed woman from another vehicle came sauntering toward to the traps. "Moving bears already this year." She said it as a statement. One of our party explained they were last year's orphaned cubs, to which she gruffly responded, "I hate seeing people feed bears!" She stalked off, leaving me to wonder if she understood the alternative in these cases: euthanizing upon capture. I had talked to one person recently who believed that was the only humane thing to do. I was of a different mind: How could we not help but give these little guys a crack at life with the best we could summon? I had the feeling that if this huffy woman were told about Blackie's death she would offer another judgment, something I had heard on more than one occasion: "That's what happens when we begin messing with Nature." The game wardens of FWP were not in charge of messing with Nature. That had already been done, by every one of us—from urban center to rural fringe—who lived under a roof, threw up a fence, drove a car, cultivated natural land, hiked in the woods, ate wild berry pie. Not even Ms. Huffy gets out of this one. The wardens were merely working at the tail end of the monster messing.

Tanks full now and bears checked, we steered a course for a far-off region Jeff Darrah had purposely chosen—where the spring bear hunt was finished.

Suddenly alone, uncoupled from the morning's turmoil, settled in my truck for the long ride, tailing the three pickups towing the strange traps, all of us caravaning along the highway's yawning bends, the sun's rays still glorious, fields now full of dandelions, I began turning over in my mind Joe's phrase "things happen." The next thing I knew, no one to hear, I was shrieking. "*Things happen* maybe for you! Things like this don't happen to me!" And I was driving through my tears. It was for the little girl cub that I cried. For her brother, and her sister. It was for the game wardens, especially Joe, who must have felt awful. It was for other bears, and other animals. For people, the ones who cared, and the ones who didn't know enough to care. A heavy sorrow tore holes in the insulation of my initial shock. I was crying then for myself, crying the pain of impotence in a fast-hurtling world.

Sometime in the afternoon, in a town I'd rather leave un-named for the sake of the cubs, we pulled into a U.S. Forest Service facility, and the parking lot was abuzz with ambling people, all sorts of vehicles, and dogs. Some of the dogs were wardens' dogs. Three were Karelian bear dogs. Four or five state and federal agencies, representatives from all over west-ern Montana, had gathered for an afternoon of introduction to bear dog techniques. The event was an outgrowth of the Wind River Bear Institute in Heber City, Utah, founded by Carrie Hunt, a career bear biologist and bear conflict spe-cialist. For years, in the western United States and Canada, Hunt had worked her bear dogs in research and conflict situations, helping to lower the incidence of occurrences that cause the most problems between bears and people: close encounters, bear habituation to people, and bear con-sumption of human-associated foods. She was presently busy lining up permanent funding for a program called Partners in Life, people and dogs working together to conserve bears. Karelian bear dogs, bred for centuries in Finland and western Russia, are said to have an instinct for safely working bears— herding, turning, tracking, warning to stay away, bringing to bay. They are small dogs for a large task, the size of Bor-der collies with the build of huskies, born with a distinctive coat of appealing black and white markings and a raccoon-like mask. Their job is to increase a bear's wariness of people, to modify a bear's behavior, to teach a bear to steer clear of people and people places.

But first we had a set of cubs to release. I quickly parked my truck and jumped in with Jeff Darrah, who was trailering Smokey. Doug Johnson followed with Honey. Leading the way was a local game warden, guiding us into the high country. On the drive, Darrah had time to share a bit of FWP's, and quite obviously his own, philosophies. The agency's bywords were "living with wildlife" (emphasis on the *with*), around which they had developed a multilayered educational outreach program. "We need to change people's thinking," Darrah said. "We're trying to help the suburban resident understand that wildlife is not 'invading' their backyard: they are living in the wildlife's front yard." He felt it was important to promote neighborhood awareness and to stress the need for "responsible action." For instance, the highest percentage of problem bears shot each year are those raiding beehives. Bees, by state law, are classified a livestock, and their owners have the right to shoot a predator. The department would prefer that beekeepers ward off bears with electric fences, and to that end they make an increasing number of the battery-operated chargers available each year. It is then the bee owner's responsibility to purchase the poles and wire and maintain the fence. Bears respond well to electric fencing, usually steering clear; game wardens can then apply their energies to something else; the beekeepers present no big predation bills; everyone, especially the bears, wins.

As we ground upward on the dirt switchbacks, Darrah recounted a story that is telling of his character. One day, while headed up to Lolo Pass, towing a culvert trap containing a bear for release, he was followed by a hunter. At the release site, the hunter, ready with his gun, stepped up to the trap and announced he was going to shoot the bear when

Darrah released it. It was the middle of hunting season and, though criminally unsporting, the action would technically have been legal. "I pointed to the Idaho border," Darrah said, "and I said, 'I'm going to drive down there and release this bear. If you shoot it without an Idaho permit, I'm going to arrest you.'" Darrah seems to know innately that the black bear, despite its strength and bulk, falls far short of being a weedy being.

Around a few more corners, our own release site showed itself. The traps were backed in at the level edge of a meadow, the sparkle of a creek trickling through it. When the doors clanked open, Honey tumbled out, only to land in a lump, unable to move her hindquarters. It had been explained to me that bears come out of Telazol front end first. She seemed alert and perturbed, peering around at us. With her front legs, she dragged herself a few feet, then gave up. Smokey loped out of his trap. Paying us no heed, he beelined for Honey, sniffed her all over. Then, with his hind end flopping sideways at every fifth or so step, he ambled off a little distance, turned to face us, and sat down. He began chewing on grasses. A jet black bear against shades of forest green, he was a hell of a handsome young cub; we all remarked on his roundness, his thick, shining coat. We took pictures. I said little prayers. Pushed my terror and longings for his safety into a box. There he was: all I'd been craving for my "bear in the woods."

Darrah volunteered to stay behind, watch over them until they shook the drug, keep them from becoming grizzly lunch. The rest of us headed back. I climbed in with Doug Johnson, both of us anxious to take in the Karelian instruction. A "hard release," or aversive conditioning, was planned as a demonstration, with Blueberry and Black Velvet. As we stepped into the conference room, Tim Manley, the grizzly bear conflict specialist for FWP, was explaining hard releases and sharing the success story of an adult black bear that was one of the first bears he had "worked" with the Karelian dogs. Manley is slight of build, a sandy-haired man in a baseball cap, who gives the first impression of someone with the adventure threshold of a Little League coach. It rapidly becomes apparent, however, that in his chest beats the heart of a Viking: he is out there with his dog Tess working grizzlies in the middle of the night. The previous year, with the help of Carrie Hunt, he had worked twenty-nine grizzlies and thirty-nine black bears, mostly in and around Glacier National Park, teaching them to keep their distance from humans.

A hard release starts with the bear dogs being held on six-foot leashes while they bark at the bear in the trap. When the trap's door is raised, the bear in most cases immediately runs. I noticed a large can of pepper spray handily strapped on Manley's belt—but he said a bear had "never come over the top of the dogs." While still in close range, the bear is fired on with beanbag loads, the same devices used to quell prison riots: these, one-and-a-half-inch squares of a heavy muslin stuffed with bird shot. At midrange, a volley of rubber bullets connects with the bear's behind, and then cracker shells, items one might covet for the Fourth of July, are shot off. All the while, the release team chants, *"Get out of here, bear!"* Sometimes, for a finale, the dogs are set loose.

The particular black bear Manley spoke of had ventured into a campground, banqueted on horse feed, and broken into an unoccupied camper shell. "We captured him," Manley said, "put a radio collar on him, and hard-released him right there." Two years had since passed, with the bear's not reentering the campground, though he ranged all around it, even chose his winter denning spot a mile and a half off.

A report from Erik Wenum contained more good news about hard releases *at the site of capture.* He was experiencing a near-perfect success rate with black bears, meaning they were not getting themselves into bad situations again. Relocated bears, historically, have not fared as well. They have tended to repeat their behavior and ended up being destroyed. With an at-the-site-of-capture hard release, the bear—a mammal said to be smarter than the dog—receives the most direct and immediate message of "No!"

Piling into vehicles again, we were soon hauling up another mountainside. This time I hopped in with the game warden Bill Koppen, tall, red-haired, and from the Seeley Lake area, a small mountain community nestled between the Swan Range and the Mission Range. His career, he said, had spanned the "Department of Parks, the Forest Service, and Fish and Game." In Seeley Lake, he fields 250 to 300 calls a year on black bear annoyances; sometimes they're about the same bear. "People say thanks for taking care of their problem. What they don't understand," he said, "is they are the problem. It's their garbage, bird feeders, and dog food that attract the bears. A bear will return to a food site [after it's been cleaned up] ten different times."

As a game warden busy with bears and wolves and mountain lions, Koppen doesn't go out unless he thinks people actually have a problem: a bear strolling through a backyard is not, in itself, a problem. His biggest lament concerns the people who move to Montana seeking a communion with wildness. "After a year or so and something has taken after their dog or cat or kid, then they want to change things and make it not so wild. If you come to this country," he said, with a weariness, "wildlife is an assumed risk. You got to be able to take it."

Hearing about Bill Koppen's exhaustive strivings to protect wildlife put me in mind of a situation in Snowmass Village, Colorado. I had recently talked to Laurie Smith, the animal and traffic control officer with the local police department. In 1994, community residents had adopted a town wildlife protection ordinance, the first in the state addressing the human factors in bear problems. Then recently, with the whole community heartsick at the euthanizing of a mother and three cubs right in town—the mother, a problem bear, had taught all her cubs to feed on garbage—the towns-people revisited the ordinance and fashioned some teeth in it. The ordinance now reads: "No person shall knowingly leave or store any refuse, food product, pet food, grain or salt in a manner which would constitute a lure, attractant or en-ticement of wildlife." From mid-April to mid-November, all bird feeders must be suspended from a cable mounted in such a way as to be inaccessible to bears, and the fallen seed debris kept cleaned up. (There is further suggestion that feeders and suet be brought in at night.) Strict rules were also instituted for prompt removal of garbage from local con-struction sites and heavily attended community events; the rules included outdoor garbage holders being those explic-itly approved as latchable, wildlife-resistant metal contain-ers. Residential garbage cans had to be secured—indoors, except for certain hours on the day of curbside pickup. Now for the teeth: violators were subject to penalty assessments (fines), the third offense requiring a court date.

Officer Smith—who previously, in her pains to keep town-visiting bears from becoming tagged (receiving their first black mark), kept finding herself in races to stay one jump ahead of the interlopers, soliciting people to tighten up on attractants—had high praise for the new ordinance. "I'm get-ting compliance right off the bat!" she said. In addition, a new Bear Awareness Task Force, focusing on public educa-tion, was to begin meeting once a month. And just down the road, Aspen's city council was adopting a similar ordinance.

.   .   .

The forest suddenly opened out, and sun poured into an old clear-cut. Everyone pulled over and parked. The pickup carrying Black Velvet and trailering the trap containing Blueberry was backed off the dirt road. There were fifteen people, video cameras, guns, high anticipation masked by placid professional expressions, and three leashed bear dogs barking at Blueberry's trap, opposite end from the door. The rubber bullets for the midrange, Tim Manley explained, would not be used on these little cubs. His assistant this year was Tonya Chilton, a statuesque and poised young woman in jeans and khaki fisherman vest, her smartly styled black hair under a billed hat. I couldn't help thinking that if this job had existed twenty-five years ago, I too would have jumped on it. She was being contracted out through Carrie Hunt: FWP and various foundation grants were funding her work with Manley. Today the dogs were his reliable Tess, a four-year-old male named Oso (the Spanish and Italian word for *bear*) that Carrie Hunt had sent along for further training, and Blush, a six-month-old pup out getting a taste of bear work.

The trap's big door clanging open set everything on fast forward—Blueberry galloping up a rough incline and into the pines, beanbag shots, cracker shells, the dogs turned loose, and all of us on their heels. At the terrifyingly mad barking of the dogs, my heart sped to Blueberry. He'd been confined in a small cage all winter, *My God, would he remember how to climb a tree?* Black bears, Manley had said, will tree in thirty seconds. I needn't have worried. With the still-barking dogs circling the trunk as I raced up, Blueberry was sixty-five feet up a seventy-five-foot tree.

Then it was Black Velvet's turn. Her carrying box was lifted out of the truck and positioned on the ground. I was suddenly wishing the young students at Lone Rock School, who had sponsored her keep for the winter—even had T-shirts printed with her picture—were here with us. The crowd's standing back gave Velvet a clear path to the same knoll up which Blueberry had scrambled. We were wanting to drive them in the same direction, not separate them. The excitement was high now, professional covers be damned, everyone animated, as if we were all injected with rodeo fever. Chilton stood braced, in a solid one-hip-forward stance, holding back the two leashed-again adult dogs, their noses just off the chicken-wire end of Velvet's box. "Bark at the bear," she said, every time they let up. "Good dogs! Bark at the bear." And bark they did, for the longest time, while Manley prowled the bushes for Blush, who in the commotion with Blueberry had taken a side hike.

Finally, everyone stood ready, and Derek Schott flung open the door. Without a backward glance, her eyes trained solely on the trees above, her little legs digging for purchase in a run for her life, up that broken slope she charged. Bang! A beanbag nailed her in the butt. Boom! Boom! Cracker shells filled the forest with flashes. *"Get out of here, bear!"* we yelled. Camera in hand, I followed. Fifteen feet this time from the top of a seventy-foot tree, with all of Karelia barking up at her, Black Velvet had wrapped herself safely around a branch, upside-down against the trunk, and was staring earthward, anxiously monitoring us.

We all stood around for a half hour, chitchatting about the successful send-off. Then we drove off—leaving in the big forest two little frightened cubs to climb down and find each other.

A horrible sinking feeling about Smokey and Honey stuck with me all the way home. Would they smell a grizzly in time? Would they intuit the presence of a mountain lion soon enough? When they came fully to their senses, would they remember the sting of the dart, know humans were to be avoided? The all too placid scene in the meadow where we left them kept coming back to me. I imagined their sweet little souls setting up a beach umbrella over a lemonade stand at the side of the dirt road. Imagined them walking up to the first hunter asking, "Got any dog food?" I ached to go back to them with Tess and Oso, the beanbags, the cracker shells—but it had been only a day of demonstration, a posing of possibility. The bear dogs were a pilot program for Region 1. Just as Jeff Darrah's Region 2 didn't have funds for a winter denning program, it didn't have access yet to bear dogs.

The next morning, sitting at my desk with the long view of the forested mountains, I was moved to phone Gordon Belcourt, a member of the Blackfeet Nation and a man familiar with broad cultural country, even the world community. Gordon, Dr. Jonkel had told me, was someone to whom I could freely pose questions, questions that just in their naive asking might be offensive to tribal custom. The Blackfeet have a sacred relationship with many animals, the beaver and bear among them, all of which they consider as brother and sister and do not use as sources of food. The tribe's meat once centered on the buffalo, supplemented with elk and deer. Though their hunting culture has long been shattered, tribal elders still carry deep traditional beliefs—and also concerns about human "management" of bears. I needed to hear them.

"The Blackfeet have never hunted bear," Belcourt started out. "You just don't go eating your relatives and allies."

Bears are valued for their spiritual guidance, he added; the Blackfeet had mimicked and adopted the bears' lifestyle as their own. To Belcourt's mind, the bears' current situation is analogous to what happened to the Blackfeet themselves, with their land's being subjected to separating demarcations.

The drawing of the U.S.-Canadian border first cut their territory in half. What remained after reservation confinement in this country lies nowadays in two counties, Pondera and Glacier. Competing federal, state, and county jurisdictions create a further shredding effect on daily lives. Any present-day bear management plan "can't help but be a convolution similar to what we as Indian peoples and the bears have had historically.

"Tribal elders," he went on, "would say to leave the bear alone, to do what bears do." Relocating bears to unfamiliar territory would be thought of as invasive, though killing a bear might be considered appropriate in situations of self-defense. With any other instances of killing, there would be a desire for the act to be holy and performed by those sacredly sanctioned. When using bears for medical research, there would be concern about what is taken from them—blood, fluids, muscle tissue, hair—and its being returned in a respectful manner. This stems from a belief that the bear needs all of its parts to make the transition into the next world.

Convoluted and tricky it all is, yes. But what better place to start than spiritual guidance from a bear. We closed our conversation with Belcourt's sharing his idea for helping bears that end up as problems, those on the to-be-culled list. Acting as a bridge between tribal traditions and science, and working with the reality of nuisance bears, he was proposing a sanctuary where the adult bears could live out their lives. He had in mind not a moneymaking attraction for tourists but a holy sanctuary.

It was the following evening before I realized what I'd really wanted to do with Blackie was to crawl up in the truck bed, draw her limp body into my arms, and rock her to sleep. The childless woman-who-wears-the-bear-coat drawn to cradling the motherless cub.

That night, clouds drifted in, covering over Ursus Major and the hunters and dogs that follow her across the sky. I'd been studying the heavens' Great Bear recently and learned the middle star in the Big Dipper's handle was actually two stars, easily discernible when looking through binoculars. *How many things in the course of my life would I look straight at and never fathom the whole of?* Rain splashed on the deck. For a while, I counted the heavy drops bathing my cheek. Later the first lightning storm of the year sailed out of the Bitterroots, and along with it the first clap of thunder. The sky lit up, a million cracker shells at a pop. Piano-rolling crashes bashed us about the head. I jumped, squeezed Patrick at the sizzle of a strike close in the paddock. Its horrendous crack fractured the welkin. I waited for half the heavy sky to flatten us. It was instead an odd, quiet darkness that settled.

Into the Big Hole with Covered Wagon
and Inflatable Raft

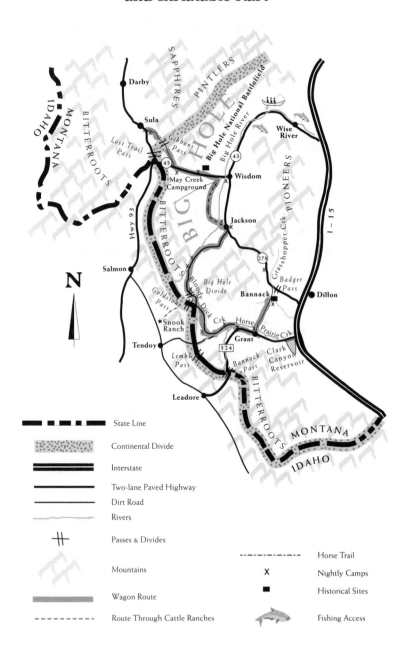

6

Ancient Currents to Egg-Sucking Woolly Buggers

Matters of Spirit and Sport

I'm not a fisherwoman, small chance that I ever could be. That said, I worked a summer, some twenty years ago, as a fly-fishing guide for a white-water rafting company in British Columbia. I didn't know a caddis fly from a nymph, a rod from a pole. My saving grace? I rowed a mean boat for the white-water end of the excursions. Our clients fished Dolly Varden, while the Fraser River headwaters hosted the largest run of sockeye salmon in twenty-five years. On the shallow, gravelly bends of the Horse Fly River, every dip of an oar sent a dozen bloodred streaks shooting away like a bursting Dixie cannon on the Fourth of July, huge spawning hump-backs breaking water all the way.

One afternoon downstream from the outpost of Likely, I was crouched on a canyon wall, scanning the more formidable waters of the river called the Quesnel. We'd pulled over our two boats to scout Quesnel's Pickle, as my companions had christened the course through the canyon. This was to be a fun run, not one we would likely take clients through. It was, by all accounts, one humdinger of a rapid. The fast-breaking, blind entry around a tight bend with a tree protruding horizontally from the bank left positioning guesswork for the slick-water tongue—a liquid conveyor belt delivering us into a jumble of standing waves, boulders, sous holes. All around, the sheer granite canyon choked down, giving water noplace to go. Either side of the central current it boiled upward—round-topped and glassy—out of a menacing black abyss. Midway through we planned to ricochet off a pillow of water forming against the left wall, as the setup for an oar-tucking plunge through a narrow chute: a momentary ride atop the entire force of the river. Directly after the plunge, a three-foot eddy fence, a wall of water thrown up by opposing flows, stood to flip a boat just where the banks fell back, forming a broad course blasted into water craters. This last—zigzagging around barge-eating reversals—required a lightly loaded craft for deft maneuvering. With these being the days before self-bailing boats, crews could count on bucketing with a fury-driven madness.

To fight the river's force would be useless, foolish, disastrous. The idea was to weave a path through this killer mess, plying the flow. I was to be at the oars of the second boat. It was not lost on me that salmon swimming for spawning grounds on the Horse Fly were laddering straight up the current through churning and thundering drops as though the task were nothing. From my perch on the bank, I studied their dark, sleek forms slipping through green towers of water. In writhing aerial displays, they flung themselves upward against pour-overs and through raining curtains of spray, each body a svelte, glistening muscle activated by slight flicks of the tail. With unfailing instinct they knew where they were headed. I needed to feel my path as precisely—down to the marrow in my bones, through the squint of my eyes, in the sinew of my thighs and shoulders. All parts of me had to synchronize with the river, move in perfection with its roiling currents. The assurance that I could do this came from somewhere unknown to me. I did not question it. I sat and picked my route down to the smallest side curlers and back cushions, memorizing it by en-visioning how it would look from midriver. With the adrena-line surging through me on the walk back to the boats, the smallest of apprehensions was quelled by an odd whimsy: *If I dump, I'll just wiggle my tail and track those salmon back to the top!*

Thus it was my wild—and, not to leave anyone hanging, upright—ride through the Pickle that gave rise to a kinship with fish. Ephemeral as that bonding was, it is the closest I have come to a relationship of the sort an angler develops. Water was the connecting element. In early Greek science, the River Ocean was thought to flow clockwise around a cir-cular, flat earth; it begat all rivers and oceans, and therefore all flows and floods, trickles and lappings. Thomas Farber re-minds us in his book *On Water,* "The water created 3 billion years ago is still in existence." From liquid to gas to solid, and back again; from the clouds above to the groundwater below; from ice fields to ice cubes and great salt seas to alpine drizzle; from the water I drink to the sweat I pour, the many-directioned, multilayered, continuous cycle moves. For one afternoon the salmon of Quesnel's Pickle and I took our lifeblood from the same ancient watery currents, those 3-billion-year-old droplets that flowed for the moment as a Canadian river.

When I hooked up with my itinerant horseman, the focus of my life changed—all but the writing—to draft horses, wag-ons, and *relationship.* Not a strange progression when you think of Neptune's having created the horse. My boating life subsequently dwindled to a once-a-year float down the lazy Bitterroot—with its growing state-fair feel: canoe parties; marshmallowy family rafts full of kids, dogs, picnics, coolers of beer, a spreading beach umbrella (I swear it!); strings of guided fly-fishing boats; Jet Skiers when they could sneak on; flotillas of rubber duckies and inner tubes.

Then one spring before the dandelions bloomed, a man

came visiting us. (Patrick says I should feel free here to call him Mr. Poopy Pants—disaffections such as ours sometimes do happen—but I'll settle for the name Cecil and, at the man's request, disguise him.) Working as a freelance scriptwriter for television and theater, Cecil lived in one of our nation's larger metropolises. He was seeking a full-blown Montana experience. Jim, a longtime friend of Patrick's, an ex–English literature teacher and avid fly fisherman recently moved to the Bitterroot from Michigan, offered to take Cecil fishing. "I can get him going in a day" is actually what Jim said. As for me, I didn't waste a minute in offering to row two literary gents down a nearby blue-ribbon trout stream.

On the appointed day, Patrick was up before dawn and mixing pancakes from scratch. He had a full day of horseshoeing lined out but wanted to contribute to our trip. Jim arrived early, peremptorily knocking as he stepped through the barn door, excited to be spending a day at his most cherished pastime. We were soon gathered around the table with Patrick delivering us cakes, two and three at a time, which we slathered with plain yogurt and rich B-grade maple syrup. Jim and I dug right in, forking up mouthfuls, but Cecil sat immobile, staring into his plate. He was not accustomed to this much food this early in the day.

"Take 'em with you," Patrick said. "You can have a Big Two-Hearted fishing trip, pretend you're Nick Adams stashing pancakes in your creel."

"A creel's just an encumbrance when you're backpack-fishing," Jim corrected. In addition to being a fisherman, he was a Hemingway aficionado. "Nick stored the pancakes in his *pockets*."

Cecil—also no stranger to the legendary author but with his own manhood cut from newer patterns—thought of Hemingway's short stories as posturing, his novels overblown, and said so.

Clearing his throat, Jim rose to the challenge. "The Nick Adams stories are some of the finest writing in American literature," he said, and with resolute squaring of shoulders, "I'll keelhaul you if you bad-mouth Ernie while we're fishing!"

I had loaded my pickup the previous night, tossing in my old Avon Pro, ten-foot ash oars, steel rowing frame, a bag of tie-down lines, gathered items of rain apparel, and, in a dry bag, sweaters, mittens, extra pairs of socks and shoes. Just handling the equipment had my juices moving. Then I was up at four, something unheard of anymore. By five I'd finished loading the truck, adding a foot pump, three life jackets, and the 180-quart Igloo cooler that served as my rowing seat in addition to carrying lunch—and, today, leftover pancakes. We stood in the glow of the barnyard light surveying everyone's gear. At Jim's offer to throw in an extra rod for me, I declined so clearly I startled myself, only a small taunt issuing from the back of my mind. *You may regret this if you're dying to fish by afternoon.*

We were aiming for the Continental Divide and the next valley over, the Big Hole, with its river of the same name. As we caravanned up the Bitterroot, the sun broke over the Sapphires. I was thrilled to be heading to territory more isolated. The precious "outer rural fringe."

The Big Hole Valley is an apostrophe lying down on land—a big bowl with a long, narrowing and curving tail that pinches down to barely enough width to let the river escape. It is the highest of Montana's large western valleys, six thousand feet at its floor. Snubbed against the spine of the continent, it is ringed by mountains—the southern Bitterroots, the Anaconda-Pintlers, the Pioneers. *Bison latifrons* and *Bison antiquus,* the larger, bigger-horned ancestors of the modern-day buffalo (*Bison bison*), are thought to have roamed here.

The ancestors of the Salish came seasonally to hunt elk, deer, antelope, and buffalo, and to gather bitterroots and camas bulbs. The valley is yet a base for hunters and fishermen. The towns are small—Jackson, pop. 50; Wisdom, pop. 101; Wise River, pop. 50; Dewey, pop. 40; Divide, pop. 25. They give off a steady feel for what life was, not too long ago. The floor of the valley is famous for its grassland, which has ever been the draw for grazing animals. Nowadays, it is the domestic species cattle. Maybe somewhat for keeping of traditions but certainly for ease in traversing snowy fields, the winter feeding of herds is often still accomplished with bobsleds and draft horses. Summer's haying season employs beaverslides, three-story wooden contraptions, the design of which originated in the Big Hole. By means of shivs and cables and skids, powered nowadays by tractors, piles of cut hay are winched skyward and then flung, in the building of barn-sized stacks. Thus springs the name Valley of Ten Thousand Haystacks. The Big Hole's ranches remain for the most part in large holdings, which, with summers short and winters severe, all saves the valley from radical change. Land of Big Snows is its other moniker. On a forty-below January night, the silent, hollow desolation emanating from the few widely scattered barnyard lights—lone circles of yellow thrown onto hard white expanse—comes stinging the traveler-through. More than once I've been that traveler, steering the eighty-odd miles from Dillon through the Big Hole in my old truck.

In the one-block town of Wisdom, we stopped at Fetty's Café to fill a thermos with black coffee. Just outside of town, Patrick and I had once camped with Pancho and Lefty, along with the families from eleven other covered wagons. The townsfolk had turned out with a welcoming barbecue and country band, and we'd all danced in the street. Back today a

fishing party, we trailed on downriver until the valley narrowed and the river swelled and the clouds sank in. The
hours ahead were to bring an alternating series of sprinkles,
showers, and hail, mitigated only by fleeting moments of
dryness. To a Montanan the weather was mild, but cold
enough that there would be no insects hatching, few fish
feeding.

The previous afternoon I'd called Frank Stanchfield at
Troutfitters, directly on the river, trying to get an idea of
which stretch to run and if anything were hatching. Born
and raised on the river, Frank had been catering to fishermen
most of his life; he had established his own guiding service in
1983. He reported the water as high and murky, only eight
inches of clarity. But it didn't matter. Floating a muddy, ram-
paging river was a story Cecil could take home. Jim took the
conditions as a challenge to his skills. He said we could
bottom-fish, troll, or use maggots.

"A fly fisherman would do that?" I asked, incredulous.

I had thought to a one, they were, die-hard purists. I'd
seen fly fishermen give bait fishermen the squint-eyed looks
cattlemen have for sheepmen. And the underlying feelings
ran back a long way—in the Bitterroot alone to at least 1910,
as evidenced in Percy M. Cushing's account, "The Cutthroat
of the Bitter Root," published in that year's November issue
of *Outing Magazine*. Cushing had worked his way up the valley to Stevensville and was on a mission to find a guide,
someone local who knew the river, when he ran into a young
lad who told him that the barber, Gene Cottrill, could " 'pour
out a stream of water from a bucket an' ketch fish in it—he
shore can.' " So Cushing kicked around the barbershop,
waiting, until Cottrill finished shaving a customer, at which
point the Stevensville man expounded on some of his fishing
philosophy. Referring to trout: " 'I caught a few yesterday—
just twelve. That's two meals for my family—two meals

even, I never catch any more than that—it's wasteful. There's plenty'll catch all they can—catch 'em on hoppers, angle worms, and beefsteak, and say they use flies. They did, too, because they put the bait on the fly hook. But they ain't exactly respected around here.' " Cushing stayed the night in the town. When he met Cottrill at five the next morning, the barber asked to see his box. " 'Got any bait hooks in it?' " Cushing writes: "I assured him I hadn't. I had taken them out before starting. . . . remembering . . . People who use bait weren't 'exactly respected around here.' "

But our trip was shaping up to be more about *catching* a fish than about fly-fishing. With a hint of the masterful and the mysterious, and I sensed on occasion chicanery, Jim said, "When you're not a snob, there are any number of ways to catch fish."

My own first encounter with a hook and line had come at age seven on a lake in the Adirondacks where my parents together with another family had rented a summer cabin for a week. Two things from that vacation still hang in my mind: that boys can pee through a window screen, while girls must hike the requisite path through high weeds to the spider-ridden outhouse; and the vision of me, scrawny-legged in a pair of overly baggy plaid shorts, falling off the dock and into the lake out of sheer excitement at catching my only fish—a little yellowish sunfish of some sort—which I promptly lost.

Later in life, I had a boyfriend who was a bait fisherman. Summers we fled to Mount Lassen in Northern California to fish, camp, hike, and romance—and, now that I think of it, in that very order. I dangled my carefully collected hellgrammites and store-bought worms and salmon eggs into pristine lake waters and lazy mountain streams and never once in three years caught a fish. No matter—I raked in points as a female not squeamish of skewering worms and as the best fish gutter in western states. More to my liking were the hours spent building rafts of downed timber and reading and dreaming, languishing on sunny banks, my hook dangling peacefully—and quite baitless.

One year, as a raw and wholly superfluous crew member, I flew into King Salmon, Alaska, for what can only be described as a herring fishing holiday aboard a thirty-two-foot gillnetter captained by my friend Walt, whom I'd known since kindergarten. It was another ill-fated encounter with fish: I was there, the herring were late. We whiled away the hours with an excursion into the Eskimo village of Togiak and a stop at Round Island, home to walruses reclining in heaps. We visited a tender and a processor, the larger boats that collect the fish from the gillnetters and house the crews who separate the fish bodies from the fish eggs. We gazed up at the aerial trials of spotter planes over Bristol Bay, listened to the banter of shortwave updates, circled the hulking Japanese tankers that would haul home the roe. Nine days passed. We took up hunting ducks. We bird-watched and whale-watched. Finally, the Alaska Department of Fish and Game called for a test to see if the herring were starting to run, and Walt volunteered to set nets. In two hours, we caught six fish. I saw how the operation worked. The next morning, just minutes before the season opened, I climbed into a Cessna 206 on the beach, clutching a nonrefundable ticket for the flight home from Anchorage.

In my forty-five years since losing the sunfish, there had been one other day of fishing, for salmon somewhere off the Golden Gate. I recall only the green waves of nausea that rode upward inside me as the boat rose on great glossy swells and then heaved into the troughs—and I as well.

I was thinking today would be a last test to see if I received the throbbing call to fish. It seemed a serene activity that I ought perhaps to get serious about taking up for my declining years. If I planned for it to feed me in any way beyond occupying idle spiritual hours, I would have to become a little more proficient. I didn't seem able to get a fish to the pan.

Upriver from the town of Wise River, the East Bank fishing access offered an easy put-in. We unloaded and ran the shuttle to park my truck eleven miles downriver. Then topped off, rigged, and everything tied down, we were floating free, batting off a few voracious mosquitoes tagging us aboard. The well-worn wood of the oars in my grasp, pressing against my palms, took me straightaway home. My spirits soared! The power of the river mounted the blades and road to my armpits; it seeped in under my rib cage and I breathed it. The boat went where I sent it, and I whirled us in dizzying circles until at last settling back to soak in the contours of shoreline and ridge line, and then the water itself. We were riding atop something akin to simmering chocolate pudding in a burnt-bottomed pot.

"Rather like used motor oil," said Jim. "I'd say clarity is more like two inches."

"It's a black-and-tan," Cecil tossed out, meaning a Guinness stout and Harp lager.

The river fairly barreled along, threatening to spill out of its banks. Runoff from spring snowmelt was yet on the rise in what was being called by ranchers dependent on summer irrigation a big water year.

Jim began rigging rods in anticipation of the first casts—a fly rod for himself, an ultralight spinning rod for Cecil. It was a ten-minute float to the Dickey Bridge, downriver from which the season was open for catch and release. I'd broken this news to Cecil the night before, expecting protests, but he had been too excited to complain. A man of ardent passions and adamant beliefs, Cecil didn't cotton to the practice

of catch and release. It was nothing more than medieval tor-
ture. "Bullpucky!" he called it. He was wanting to eat his
catch.

I was rather in agreement. As new aspects of almost everything are continually showing up, so, too, is it with fish. Traditionally, fish have been regarded as a class of cold-blooded
vertebrates too far down the phylogenetic ladder to experience a conscious awareness of pain and suffering. Lately we
were beginning to learn differently. A study conducted in
the Netherlands on thirty hooked carp concluded that fish
experience fear and pain—and to a degree comparable with
similar reactions in humans.* Another study, this one from
the United Kingdom, showed that endorphins, associated
with the perception of pain and the production of analgesia
in humans, were recorded at equal levels in fish.[†] What all
this will mean is probably still anyone's guess, yet it doesn't
bode well for our present human-fish relationship.

But as the nonfisher on the trip, this was not a subject for
me to leap into. And Jim, I knew, could get exceedingly testy
if you intimated that anything to do with his sport might be
a little slippery. Yet within the fishing community itself some
careful consideration seemed to be taking place, as evidenced by a fellowship of anglers going by the name Beyond
Barbless. They delight not in the fight or the landing but in
the sheer trickery of drawing the strike.

We shot beneath the silver-bottomed Dickey Bridge and
Jim sent his first fly sailing. Large and garish-looking, the lure

*Verheijen, F.J., and Buwalda, R.J.A., 1988. *Do Pain and Fear Make a
Hooked Carp in Play Suffer?* A publication of the University of Utrecht. En-
glish summary obtainable from Dutch SPCA, P.O. Box 85980, 2508 CR,
The Hague, The Netherlands.

[†]Royal Society for the Prevention of Cruelty to Animals, 1980. Report
of the panel of enquiry into shooting and angling. RSPCA, Horsham,
U.K.

sported a fluffy tail of purple marabou (the dyed downy underfeathers of ostrich, turkey, or pheasant) festooned with green, gold, and silver threads of flashabou. A sexy black chenille yarn wrapped the body, and a bright salmon-colored fuzzball stood in for a head. I would have pronounced it, without hesitation, a Glorious Flaming Drag Queen, but to an angler it was an Egg-Sucking Woolly Bugger. Cecil worked a plain Woolly Bugger—nappy brown with black marabou that, once wet, dangled leechlike from the end of his line.

Today we were fishing for Salmonids, or species of the trout family—rainbows, browns, Yellowstone cutthroat hybrids, arctic graylings, west slope cutthroats. The arctic graylings are glacial relics, or the small southern end of a population left after the last ice age. They have since recolonized waters in Canada and Alaska, but the Big Hole hosts the only remaining fishery in the contiguous forty-eight. Along with the arctic graylings, it is the west slope cutthroats (don't ask, yes, Big Hole waters drain down the east slope of the Continental Divide) that are this river's natives, while the rainbows, browns, and Yellowstone cutthroats are sorts of claim jumpers. Around the end of the nineteenth century—close on the heels of the first Anglo-American settlement in the West—fishing enthusiasts from the East, thinking to brighten prospects for exhilarating fishing, introduced exotic species to western rivers. Rainbows came originally from the West Coast, browns from Europe, and Yellowstone cutthroats from farther east in Montana (they are native only to the Yellowstone River system). In the Bitterroot River, the bull trout (another name for Dolly Varden) and west slope cutthroats are the indigenous; the rainbows, browns, eastern book trout, and Yellowstone cutthroats are the introduced.

For a long time, fish were trucked all around with the

good intentions to improve matters. Introducing foreign fish was demanded by anglers and encouraged by Montana's (then) Department of Fish and Game, as well as aided and abetted by the old federal fisheries commission. Bruce Farling, executive director of Montana Trout Unlimited—a man who likes to talk fish almost as much as he likes to go fishing—imparted a bit of icthyological history from behind the desk in his Missoula office. "It was a 'we can do better than nature' outlook then," he said. People were trained to raise fish; there were big hatchery bureaucracies to maintain. "The rivers of the Northern Rockies, before human intervention, had but a handful of Salmonids and a handful of dinky little non-Salmonids." Montana's rivers were looked upon as considerably lacking in diversity—as compared with streams of similar size in, say, Arkansas that boasted hundreds of native species. Thus Montana was in line to receive its fair share of fashionably lively fish.

Rainbow trout, in particular, showed themselves to be highly coveted as sporting fish. "The hard-core angler, who's in it for the sport and not necessarily the harvest," Farling said, "really digs rainbow trout because they jump and leap. Cutthroats rarely do that. Bull trout are a pretty muscular fish, and a big one will bite a little, but they don't dive down to the bottom, they don't jump up, they're not acrobatic. Browns people really like because they're very tough to catch, they're challenging. Especially the large ones. They're smart. And they get really big."

All this introducing, as we might have an inkling today, did not go without its consequences. Three things occurred in the relationships between species to upset the once prevailing balance: hybridization; competition; predation. As for the first, in the words of a layperson now: The new fish on the block and the original inhabitants, when put together and left to do what fish do, apparently develop wandering gonads. West slope cutthroats like to cuddle up with rainbows and produce "cutbows." West slopers also find it fun to cross species with Yellowstone cutthroats, while bull trout and eastern brook trout fall into each other's arms. The upshot of all this outside-of-species hanky-panky is diminished populations of the pure native strains. A bull trout female, for instance, lays her eggs, and, if it's an eastern brook trout that swoops in to lay his milt on them, she has just lost a season in bolstering the population of her own species. Then this further spinning of wheels: Bull trout hybrids are often sterile, making them, so to speak, dead in the water in terms of contributing to any enlargement in fish population.

Native fish, not so surprisingly, are genetically well-adapted to their habitats: the local water chemistry, water temperatures, high-water seasons, predator communities. "They have this tremendous knowledge," Farling says, "they *know* things." With hybridization, their genetic heritage and behavioral traits begin to disappear. Bull trout of the Bitterroot, for example, may have lost their genetic disposition to migrate; that is our guess, anyway, from finding that other fisheries of bull trout travel a hundred miles in refreshing their gene pools. Basic conservation biology tells us—and this is Farling's biggest worry—that fish are being created which are less fit to deal with local conditions.

Competition and predation, when added to hybridization, bump up the complexities. In fish societies, just as in human societies, those with aggressive temperaments tend to shoulder others out. The brook trout are the bullies, commandeering the best feeding spots; food comes floating by and there they are, body-blocking to grab it. In terms of predation, any of these fish will eat the young of other fish. Yet the bull trout take it one step further; they are piscivorous, meaning they eat *mainly* little fish—however, their range in the Bitterroot has gradually come to be confined to the tributary creeks, which leaves the many wee fish swimming in the main river as snacks for the brooks and browns and rainbows. Meanwhile, the strong-arming brook trout are busy breeding at two years of age, whereas bull trout do not mature to spawning until ages five to seven. This kind of Cuisinart action of competition and predation decidedly alters population sizes, with some species being shoved toward extinction.

In addition to the fish-relating-to-fish upsets, there are the stresses to riparian and aquatic habitats—the whole gamut that comes with humans inhabiting the landscape. From such things as the presence of livestock, septic systems, paving, building, logging—and I suspect to some small degree just our recreational activities, of camping and hiking and horseback riding—we tend to increase water pollutants and nutrients, or add to siltation from bank erosion. To get from one side of a river to the other, we build bridges, usually too short, and they promote the buildup of gravel deposits upstream and fast, deep water downstream; the hurrying current subsequently hooks hard for a bank, carrying away a few acres of land, at which someone then screams and starts riprapping. Over time, the river's banks become more and more stabilized, increased water velocities carve deeper channels, and the wandering river is lost. For fish, this means their favorite hangouts—shady pools and feeding eddies—disappear. (Throughout greater Los Angeles, as well as in other places that I haven't so personally witnessed, they skip all this slow agonizing over the erosion of riverine characteristics and just go ahead and encase the river in concrete.)

But that is not all. In the agricultural West, including the Big Hole and Bitterroot Valleys, fish populations must also contend with what is called dewatering, pulling water out of the river and tributaries to irrigate crops. In drier years, the low, slow, end-of-summer flows give rise to a number of problems: water too warm (bull trout tolerate only the colder temperatures); drops in fish food production (many bugs spend part of their life cycle underwater, clinging to river cobbles, and it is the cold, moving water that carries down the teensy particles they eat); lowered levels of dissolved oxygen (fish are equipped with gills—underwater respiratory organs that remove needed oxygen from water taken in through their mouths); and increased concentrations of pollutants (something affecting all the planet's species). These hot-weather, low-water stresses on fish can eventually translate into aggravation for human fishers, who may be asked to fish limited hours, or sometimes not at all.

To cap it all off, the networks of ditches and dams and headgates that often are part of irrigation systems pose serious challenges for fish. At best, the mazes cause fragmentation of habitat; fish swim up the ditches and can't get back down. At worst, the water is shut off, leaving them high and dry. (In the Bitterroot, there is a fish rescue day, an annual volunteer effort headed up by a member of Trout Unlimited.)

Small wonder the bull trout has landed on the federal Endangered Species List, with a threatened species designation. The west slope cutthroats and Yellowstone cutthroats currently are candidates for listing.

We were drifting now in the rain. The swollen current carried us like a bobbing toy from one river bend to the next, while I maneuvered from bank to bank, catching as best I could any semblance of an eddy. In our coming abreast a low-lying island of clump willow, my gaze suddenly met with a pair of alert brown eyes and a big flabby nose: the face of a moose, hanging between two bushes and stock-still as any wall-mounted head.

"Look left," I whispered. No response, the river was loud and the literati busy—Jim rhythmically casting off the stern, Cecil silently absorbed, hunkered into a carbuncle of hooded green parka on the front thwart, smoking and trolling.

"There's a moose on your left." I tried again.

"Oh, yeah" came Jim's croon.

"No shit!" yelled Cecil.

The moose spun with surprising speed for such a coconuts-and-boxes profile and, with the crack of fracturing branches, plunged into thicker brush—but not before Jim took note of the beginnings of antlers and declared him a bull. I was more entranced with the stark whiteness to the backs of his legs. The remainder of his body was mahogany and ebony, the latter perhaps hide wet from the rain or swimming the river. A moose can swim at eight miles per hour. My Peterson's *Field Guide to the Mammals* says a moose can swim as fast as two men paddling a canoe. (There is, strangely, no mention of the paddling speeds of women.)

The sun appeared for a few moments, glittering the water, brightening the not-leafed-out-yet twigs of bankside bushes. I took stock of the turgid water—not much in the way of waves but a definite speed course—and picked out several more split channels and, far down the river, a large black animal lumbering along a beach.

"It's a bear!" we chimed. Then it turned broadside.

"Nah, it's a cow."

With only two bites, Jim was going to something heavier, a spoon to get to the bottom: a Little Cleo with the letters WIGL inscribed below the outline of a hula girl. He rigged Cecil with a spinner, a Mepp's Black Fury—treble hook fitted with a black teardrop dotted with bright orange. An earring, I thought, with a case of fluorescent measles.

No luck.

We pulled into Troutfitters, scudding into a half circle chomped from the bank. Just then the sky split open and fired frozen pellets at us. We scurried for the cover of Frank's small fishing shop; inside it was cozy, with a fire burning in the woodstove but no one around. Frank sold a little of everything for the fly fisherman. The walls were hung with trappings of the art: hats, vests, neoprene booties, nets, hemostats, sinkers, snipers, and all manner of fly-tying paraphernalia. My favorite was a sealant good on rafts, waders, tents, boots, trailers, you name it—you probably could fix a flat tire with it. In Montana, the sport of fishing is an industry.

Indeed, most fly fishermen fish primarily for the sport of it, according to Chris Clancy, a fisheries biologist in the Bitterroot with the Department of Fish, Wildlife and Parks. Clancy himself, who can't warm up to the taste of trout, says he would sooner be fishing catch-and-release than catch-and-eat even were the seasons all thrown open. In chatting with him, I came to understand that, except in cases of precariously endangered species, the catch-and-release seasons are imposed not so much to protect fisheries or regenerate populations, as I'd been inclined to think, as to satisfy the sport—in essence, to keep the larger, feistier fish in the river and available for catching. Because of the increasing pressures on fish, including the pressure of fishing itself (as this book goes to press, the Bitterroot River is registering 100,000 angler-days per year, or double the count of eight years ago), seasons of catch and release are here to stay. Nonetheless, in the present design of fishing policy, some stretches of river will always remain open: for those archetypal fishers still after a dinner, for the bait fishers, who can have a hard time with catch and release because the worm and hook have ended up in the fish's stomach, and for the starting-out fishers—especially the younger set—who thrill to the classic snapshot of themselves holding up "the big fish."

Capturing my attention next were Frank's dozens of plastic cubicles displaying a seemingly endless selection of weird fake bugs with wondrous names: Ugly Rudamus, Grizzley Wulff, Blond Humpy, Madam X, Flashback, Renegade, and Bead Head Hair Ears. The San Juan Worm was tiny, yet unmistakable—a less-than-two-inch snip of Day-Glo orange yarn skewered with a petite gold hook. A highbrow fly fisher, who would never stoop to fishing with a live worm, would, in an instant, secure one of these look-and-wiggle-alikes to the end of a line. "What a concept!"—I could almost hear Patrick saying—"a fly miming a worm."

For Cecil's and my edification, Jim rattled off a succinct tutorial. *Fly-fishing*, by definition, means fishing with artificial means. Flies come in two general types, imitators and attractors, and three categories: dry, wet, and nymph. A dry fly floats on top of the water, a wet one sinks just under the surface, and a nymph, weighted with lead (nowadays lead substitute), fishes the bottom.

I picked up a Bitch Bugger, one of the wet flies, and saw in it a caricature of a cantankerous cleaning woman, all bobbling mops and brooms and flapping dustcloths. The Yuk Bug had hackle, what looked like the hair of a delicate paintbrush once a child twirls it hard on paper. Both Yuk Bug and Cantankerous Cleaning Woman possessed jiggly white legs and antennae, patterns stemming from the 1970s Girdle Bug, which made use of rubber cording stripped from outdated women's girdles.

While Cecil browsed for a billed hat and souvenir fly, Jim expounded further, almost in response to what I was thinking—that a fisherman, to cover all the occasions, would need two or three each of these elaborate bug impostors. "I always thought matching the hatch is more for the vanity of the fisherman than the fish. And they aren't that smart."

Of course, he meant the fish.

Just then Frank stepped in, and immediately he and Jim fell to conversing in an alien language. "I like to crossbreed flies," Jim was saying. "I've had good luck with a Royal Bitch, combination Royal Coachman and Bitch Creek, but I also like a Goofy Bugger, that's a Goofus Bug and a Woolly Bugger." My wandering eye suddenly caught on something familiar: the Mustad company name printed on a box of fishhooks! Mustad makes horseshoe nails. Perhaps at this very moment Patrick was nailing a shoe on a hoof with a handful.

My fishermen companions at last invested in Yuk Bugs, and Cecil walked out sporting a hat befitting any respectable naturalist—woodsman brown with a bill of charcoal gray. Well-supplied, we again donned life jackets. Annoyed by the bunglesome character of my old Mae Wests, and coupled, I could only think, with an insufficient familiarity with the random powers of nature, Cecil dubbed his a "life inhibitor."

The next bends of the river yielded a kingfisher stationed on a branch over an eddy, several eared grebes bottoms-up diving for lunch, and on the bank a pair of Canada geese herding along a gaggle of miniatures swaddled in chartreuse fluff. At either end of my boat, devoutness to fly fussing ensued. The bow held Cecil, the quintessential novitiate, proudly attaching his new Yuk Bug. Weighing down the stern was the wise old sage, looking the part in his military surplus wool trousers and a dark rag-wool sweater under a many-pocketed fisherman's vest. Jim was eerily the picture of an early forties Hemingway—the heavy, dark beard tinged with white, the rounded face and broad torso, the thinning frontal hair, even an Ernest-profile nose.

Just as my riders were focused on flies and knots and casts,

I was drawn inexorably to currents. On this Big Hole, I was rapidly reconnecting with the lure of the river. In my earlier years, I had sought solely hydraulics, chasing the classic pool-and-drop rivers, tolerating the pools to get to the next Widow Maker, Sockdolager, Hell's Kitchen. After years of navigating big stuff, the desire for challenge had fallen away and I had grown to relish the calmer stretches for what they offered in rhythm and serenity and scenery.

The running of a river is different—at the core of its sport—from the fishing of one. Current is not a thing to be conquered. In the final round, the river is bound to win. Large chunks of humility are required for running rivers. In pushing the limits of body and gear, one finds skill and luck and providence unfailingly intertwined. A successful big run should be celebrated, celebrated for what it was. Project it into the future, use it to pad your self-esteem, lace it with anything arrogant, and next time through the river will eat you. Today, with the oars in the water, it was all coming back. It was that melding with the spirit of the river and my role as spotter of wildlife that truly sang to me.

Tucked up against an island, a small, circling backwater offered us a lunch stop, and miraculously the rain eased to a stop. The fishermen piled out to try their luck from shore, and I opened the cooler to layer bagels with cream cheese, thin slices of sweet red onion and tomato, and lox of an otherworldly shade of pink. We were going to have fish today, if it had to come from Norway.

As I worked, I watched Cecil. Two days in the country of wide skies and he was beginning to look the outdoorsman. His chestnut mustache and beard had grown past their usual snappy look, and his face appeared crinkled and ruddy—if only from straining to hold a cigarette in his mouth while both hands worked the rod. He stood in the dried grasses at water's edge and contentedly fished.

With our pushing back onto the river, Jim pointed to a

large eddy coming up at the end of an island. "Right there, right there!"

Cecil cast. His pretty fly took off with the winged flight of a sparrow and landed in the top of an alder tree. The current swept us downriver; Cecil wildly jerked and tugged. Suddenly the line snapped—souvenir Yuk Bug, good-bye!—and Cecil committed Fisherman Sin Number Two, leaving forty feet of line behind in a tree, a lethal entanglement for birds. When he reeled in the other forty feet, straightaway it took a loop around my left oar, then the oar clip. Once it started going places, there was no stopping it. It locked a half hitch on my torso and then knitted a stitch to the frame. In complete exasperation—and just in time, I might add, to save me from becoming a monofilament mummy—he tossed the rod to Jim with a trenchant "Here!"

It was, admittedly, a lousy day for fishing unless one's skills were highly advanced. Water conditions were not conducive to teaching, and my lack of a drift anchor, essential equipment for a professional guide, only added to the possibilities of leaving line all over the river and banks.

Despite my empathy for the sportsmen in my boat and their not having a day more accommodating for their pursuit, there was something else absent—something on a larger scale. What this angling pastime needed, to my way of thinking, was a little more balance on the sporting end. With a hellbender rapid there was always the possibility of its thrashing you. All a fish could do was hide or, once caught, get away. Now, if the fish and the angler were more evenly matched, namely, if the fish were to develop some added characteristics—say, the temperament of a Spielberg velociraptor, the aerobatics of a circus performer, and the beak of a snapping turtle—the fisherman's focus would forcibly shift. Much as for the fish, to stay alive would be the point.

As it was, we kept drifting and trolling. The rush of the

water rose to our ears in unbroken accompaniment, menacing in its power yet soothing, like a stiff wind running through trees. A pair of high-stepping sandhill cranes with biscuit-colored bodies and red foreheads picked their way like anorexic ballerinas across a bankside meadow. Sandpipers bobbed in the ripples at water's edge. That we hadn't seen another boat all day said the weather and river conditions were purely for idiots. This is about what it takes anymore to capture solitude. An idiot then, I'll jump to be—this was my kind of day! Like the Salish of old, I came gathering my sustenance—though it be not buffalo—from the Big Hole. Yet the river's hold on wildness, extended well beyond a day of bad weather and high water. Its riparian corridor had a tenantless appeal. No big, new houses butting their decks into your time with nature, no riprap, no yards landscaped to river's edge, no keep-out, security-system signs. "Look!" I said it to everything—to the massive sandstone-looking rock standing in a sweeping curve of the left bank. Centuries and harsh elements had rounded its great shape and peppered its surface with pocks and divots. Mesmerized by this foreign configuration—Big Rock it was called—seemingly plunked into the middle of a soft-shouldered valley, we missed the Wise River confluence just opposite, the one spot where clearer water might have produced a fish.

A steady drizzle returned, further flattening spirits—though other species of fishers, unvexed, went about their day. I noticed the top branch of a towering cottonwood arching over the river, supporting a huge nest. As though on cue, we were treated to the seamless flight of this year's resident: a great blue heron that went all gangly upon landing and then incredibly folded in its unwieldy extremities as neatly as a piece of origami.

Every trickle and tributary broadened the body of river now. In an enduring determination to rearrange itself, it would eat whole trees, swallow acre-chunks of its lining. I was laughing at its apparent glee to be a big, muddy torrent somersaulting to New Orleans, when out of the muck there emerged the distinct lines of a long, strong opposing flow— circling its invitation—in the lee of a stately row of old cottonwoods. I caught the tail, and we floated midway up, tying off to a gnarl of undercut roots. Cecil, eager, teetered along a tube and in one leap landed ashore. The bank was strewn with cow fops that were oddly stacked like construction abutments or some bizarre form of clay sculpture. Mindful of our landings, Jim and I followed.

The fishermen headed for the top of the eddy, just short of where it spilled back into the turbulent mainstream. For a moment I watched Jim, the master, easily looping long S-curves in the tight space between trees. Cecil was casting a bright yellow jig—Yellow Parrot in a Bathrobe I called it, with its black eye set in a yellow parrot's head and its body wrapped in yellow chenille.

Back from the bank two grassy benches rose in stair steps to a broad pasture. I wandered over the top and came face-to-face with the forgers of the gargantuan cow pies: six Red Angus bulls! My stroll cut short, I turned just in time to see Cecil's rod bend. Jim jumped in behind, yelling, "You've got one!"

The sun broke through, the water's raw sienna color glistened. The long line shimmered. I could hear Jim saying, "Turn him into the eddy. Keep him out of the main current. Don't let him fight too long." A thoroughly spent fish is good only for the grill; it can't survive catch and release. Even from where I stood, I caught the excitement of its dazzling jump and the little Chubby Checker twist it danced on its tail—a beautiful big trout, in its prime.

Cecil stood braced, lifting the rod over his head. Jim waded in to grab the fish. Then, abruptly, Cecil flung down the rod and sprinted for the boat—to get the net, I'm absently thinking. No, it's the camera. "It's a fourteen-inch brownie," he yelled as he passed. "We gotta let it go."

Jim worked at removing the hook, gently easing it out. Cecil skipped back through the bull pies, stripping off gloves and life inhibitor as he flew. With camera tucked into a pocket, quickly he dipped his hands in the water, lest he commit Fisherman Sin Number One—disturbing a fish's protective mucous coating by handling it with dry hands. They exchanged fish for camera, and, with a deft jerk of his head, Cecil jettisoned his new hat into the grass, assumed a victor's toothy grin, and presented the fish in front of his chest. Jim, framing with one knee bent forward, swiftly repositioned closer, then crouched—to make the fish look bigger, he later told me.

Posterity records completed, Cecil marched his Mephisto, Italian leather tennis shoes into the water and bent to support the fish until, drawing oxygen from large gulps of water, it powered up. So anxious in their hovering, the fishermen seemed the ones barely breathing. After a long moment, the trout swam away.

The sportsmen shook hands. They clapped each other in a bear hug and laughed. Cecil danced a little jig, then leaned backward, a great arch to his back. "Weeee got one!" He yelled it to the treetops. "I change my mind," he shouted as I approached. "I can do catch and release! That fish was so pretty. So pretty and strong, one giant muscle in my hands. I *had* to let it go!"

"It was gorgeous!" I said. "The tail and fins were an incredible yellow."

Jim came strolling up the bank, buoyant, quoting from his friend John Voelker (known to most by the pen name Robert Traver): "I fish . . . not because I regard fishing as being so terribly important, but because I suspect that so many of the other concerns of men are equally unimportant and not nearly so much fun."

A final navigation of the amazing construction abutments put us back in the boat. I broke into the cooler, folded pancakes like tortillas, stuffed them with cream cheese and blueberry jam. We polished off the lukewarm dregs of coffee, passing the cup, each taking a swig.

They were conscientious, these fishermen, Jim and Cecil— Jim's knocking the barb to a nubbin before giving Cecil the hook, their not completely exhausting the fish and helping it to revive, their protecting it from deadly fungus by handling it properly. They were playing by the best of the rules. It was just that the rules were part of a doctrine first set in place by the early fishing enthusiasts from the East and their turning loose exotics. From there, it had grown by similar twist and turn, across almost a century, to become a system whereby survival of fish as a whole—the acquisition and preservation and reclamation of habitat, the salaries of fisheries biologists—had become dependent on the moneys derived from fishing licenses. Fish now *needed* fishers.

We shoved off, Jim hauling aboard a jumble of stern line to coil. The boat drifted up the eddy, until my sticking an oar into the main current kicked us on our way. My mind ran on, and the fishermen sank into their talk. I could hear Jim's throaty Hemingway-esque: "It was a big fish. It ran strong and hard into the deep current."

"Maybe I'll pick up *The Nick Adams Stories*," Cecil said.

Whoa! In So Many Ways

View from the Wagon Seat

Dawn broke, raw and blustery, the dimmest of light seeping through dusty canvas. Slowly, my little womb-against-the-weather emerged to vision: six steam-bent oak bows carrying cloth high in a churchlike arch—to me, more claustrophobic than ethereal. *What unused space!* came a first groggy thought (how well-trained my mind). My body parts, steeped yet in sleep's dormancy, were nonetheless braced for their surroundings; neither this hundred-year-old covered wagon nor I was outfitted for a plunge to 0°F.

It was my first day alone in two weeks of traveling, and I felt marooned rather than sprung free. I lay encased in my Carhartt coveralls inside my sleeping bag as though in pupa phase. A lethargy of dehydration, exaggerated by the cold, had boulders sitting on me. With monumental effort, I wriggled an index finger up to where I could snug down the blue fleece hat I wore. Oddly, I had slept well, out of sheer exhaustion and the wagon bed's easy swaying on its springs to the buffeting wind.

The glow of morning, coming on like a low-watt lightbulb through a soiled lampshade, heightened my feeling caged. But there was cheer in the gloom, floating to my ears. A soft, rhythmic munching. Pancho and Lefty, more comforting than any ministerial rite. Perhaps because they were big blacks with blazes (broad white facial strokes), someone had originally seen fit to name them Amos and Andy. After we'd bought them, seven years ago, they had readily taken to re-baptism, as though as much desirous of the change as were we. Ten feet away now, they worked on the hay I had strung the night before through a cow corral—a pen with a loading chute for gathering and shipping range cattle.

Yesterday, at the end of long hours of chill rain, wet, shivering, and hungry, we had unhitched on this spot, a pre-arranged camp atop a bare bench not twelve miles from a crossroads town I by now knew well. Wisdom, not infrequently, registers the coldest temperature in the contiguous forty-eight. After chores I had climbed into the wagon on a mission to find dry clothes and instead ended up shoving together two 180-quart coolers and a fifty-pound bag of COB, fashioning a pallet. I had blown out the candle and gone to bed in my clothes, without dinner, without reading, without flossing.

It was the third week of September—the last idyllic days of summer in many parts of the world—and at this measly 0°F any Arctic goer would have pronounced me sniveling. I thought about Patrick and our friends Rikki and Jon. Once they had departed last evening, all to return to their work, I had mused malevolently on how they were going to feel small and heartsick upon learning that, after a night of shuddering hypothermia, I had come up frozen as a fish snared in pond ice. But the sun's emergence told me I was not going to die. I was merely in for a spell of character-developing misery, self-inflicted, and with no one even satisfyingly to blame. "Go home and get warm, I'll stay here tonight," Patrick had offered. "You can come back in the morning."

Just how would it be for a woman on a quest to cave in at the hard part and leave it to her man?

"I'll be all right," I'd lied, thinking of how susceptible I was to frostbite, how the first winter I'd lived in the barn large patches of my skin had turned red, then black. But I stood firm, nonetheless, jaw clamped viselike on better judgment. I also was not to be comforted. Rikki, who by then had been riding with me for a week, reached in over the tailgate and gave my hand a lingering squeeze coupled with a look of sisterly earnestness and said—a little too breezily, I thought—"Make yourself a cozy little nest, make it real cozy." The sole thing to have sufficed would have been for all three to have dragged me kicking and clawing home to a snuggery of genuine bed and woodstove. But no one was reading my mind. I was being accorded a most proper respect for my capabilities and decisions. With Jon at the wheel of their pickup—he'd been fortunate enough on this lonely road to catch a timely ride to retrieve it from our previous night's camp—off they had driven into the coming night.

Now I had survived the storm, fortunately slept through it. The horses needed water, their buckets surely empty or frozen. I, too, needed water. For some twelve hours I had lain stiff, virtually motionless over the warm spot beneath me—yet it was, to my mind, too cold to get up. I'd brought one heavy shirt; it was red, the material some forerunner of Polarfleece. I had carelessly allowed it to get wet to the elbows while driving the team through yesterday's rain, and it now hung from a hastily strung clothesline above me. Reaching up to examine one cuff, with the fleeting hope that overnight the high-tech material might have dried, my fingers closed on something I imagined to be fibrous raspberry ice cream—unmalleable as a Popsicle. I would have preferred to greet the morning from beneath the wagon, where I commonly slept, from where it was easier to pop out for a morning pee, and from where with my first eye open I could survey the world—the mountains, the weather, the horses, what kind of day lay ahead. I would have preferred even more this morning to drop back into a dreamless coma. For the moment, though, I seemed able only to lie still, awash in self-pity, dwelling hard on how a cockamamie plan of this sort—to drive a covered wagon through the high country, fall coming on—had got started.

Some 150 years ago, with the European settlement of the West, it had been almost universally the men who determined to strike out across the country. For the most part, the women on wagon trains, though not always lacking in enthusiasm, had been joiners—of fathers, brothers, and husbands in their pursuits of gold and adventure and what the Homestead Act of 1862 had designated land free for the filing. For fifty-odd years the wagons had rolled, a few on into the 1900s. People hoped to reach Utah, Oregon, California, Montana—alive. There were those who arrived without belongings, and having lost children and spouse. The hazards were many: smallpox, cholera, snowstorms, rivers in flood, stampeding buffalo, Indian attacks, childbirth on the trail, little injuries of mishap that could kill. Much of the stock died along the trail. A combination of sparse feed, irregular waterings, and hard pulls decimated horses. Now, in vastly different times and at an age well past the average prairie woman's life expectancy, I had set out by team and wagon from the once territorial capital of Montana—Bannack (these days a state park and picturesque ghost town)—to wend my way up Horse Prairie into the narrowing canyon of the Bloody Dick, over the Big Hole Divide lying in the shadow of Mount Selway, down across the Big Hole's wide sweep of cattle ranches, up again into timber over the Continental Divide by way of old Gibbons Pass Road, then once more down, along the steep switchbacks leading to the Bitterroot Valley. I planned to reach home with my scalp only dirty, with my wagon intact, and with my horses in top condition.

Horse-and-wagon touring I knew intimately after Patrick's and my having covered parts of Montana, Wyoming, and Colorado. When not traveling with officially organized centennial trains, we had rolled by twist and by fancy, moderately smug about rebuilding a one-hundred-year-old wagon and watching countryside unfold from over the haunches of our earth-friendly horsepower. Mantied up* and buried in the wagon, we carried one bale of hay for emergencies but never had occasion to unpack it. As evenings came on, we would stop at a ranch and inquire about camping and buying hay. Had we stepped out of a pickup, no doubt we would have been told to move on, but there is something magical about traveling in a wagon pulled by horses. Homes and hearts flew open: frequently, we were *given* hay, offered dinner and showers, even beds. Friendships were instant and unguarded, perhaps because of their impermanence but certainly because of the romance of witnessing a bygone mode of travel. People had heartily invested in our endeavors, invested from that place of their own unfulfilled dreams of a slower, off-the-mean existence.

The idea for this year's journey had hatched deep in the cold of the previous winter. Jim Rieffenberger, a farrier, teamster, and friend, was employed feeding cows on a ranch out of Salmon, Idaho, about 120 miles to the south. On a swing up to Missoula, he'd stopped and over a cup of tea got to

---

Manty is a western word, not in my dictionaries but employed probably for a hundred years as noun, *manty*; as verb, to *manty, mantied, mantying*; and as adjective, *mantied*, meaning a sheet of canvas used to wrap up gear, usually for a pack animal's load, but also the load itself, or the action of the packaging, and taken from the Spanish word *manta*, or horse blanket.

lamenting the woes of ranching winters. "Gets blame tiring these below-zero mornings keeping the truck running through the start-and-stop of kicking off bales," he said. "There's a lot to be said for old-fashioned horsepower." Patrick and I didn't hesitate in offering him Pancho and Lefty. Having traveled on wagon trains with Jim, we knew him to be good with a team. Our horses needed something to do. They were a feed team before we owned them, they could feed cows in their sleep.

The following week, when Jim came with a horse trailer, I went along for the orientation. The ranch was an old one. A collection of barns, sheds, sagging corrals, ramshackle rows of calf pens snugged against lazy bends at the confluence of Sandy Creek and Lemhi River, where water and willows carved large fields into a maze of smaller ones, all of it bordering national forest that backed smack up to Goldstone Pass, over the Bitterroot Mountains' southern reach. "You know," Jim said, as we were making our first sled run through the snowy fields, "in spring, we could just pop over one of these passes and drive around in the Big Hole."

"Hell," I said, knowing the team would be toughened up by then, "we could drive them all the way home!"

The fire had us. Our minds were already traversing unfettered country, palms curled to the draw of long leather lines, changes in the weather felt instantly upon cheeks, spoked wheels laying down their twirling shadows on the land, skies skittering in a kaleidoscope of patterns. There would be the daylong fillings of lungs on sweet open air, the nights of crystalline stars canopied over bedrolls—this was the real world, we knew it—the rest we would leave in suffocating buildings far behind, our only earthly concerns the keeping of a wooden wagon rolling and the care of two good horses.

For three months the phone calls flew back and forth. While a neighbor commuted two hundred miles every day to work, and the Montana Department of Transportation pressed their agenda to lay five lanes of pavement through our mountain valley, I was devising a plan to roll across a piece of western Montana at an insanely pleasant three miles an hour—a pace at which I could again count petals on wildflowers. The idea was at once romantic and ecological: traveling at an old-world pace, requiring no petroleum. We could schedule the trip for *after* the last snow and *before* the onset of tick season, I was thinking—when the phone rang on the first of April. It was Jim. Cattle prices had been up slightly. The cows had all been sold. He was out of a job and loading our team to haul them home. Plan A dissolved. By June, when the heavy snowpack melted and backcountry passes opened, our outlaws were soft, fat, and running around unshod. Patrick had been plagued for two months with a vile flu, and home horses came last on the list in his harried schedule. I began rescheming; Plan B was for taking off in late summer. This time *after* the last of the infamous Big Hole mosquitoes and *before* the first snow. Planning in Montana is, of course, a joke: It can snow any day of the year. As the sayings go: "Only fools and newcomers predict the weather." "Don't like the weather? Wait ten minutes!"

It was about this time that I began to have the barest of inklings of what this trip would entail: first, that September would still be high season for Patrick's shoeing business; second, that Jim likewise would be occupied with ranch chores too toilsome to allow him time for bringing his saddle horse and outriding; third, that Pancho and Lefty would have to be worked daily for six to eight weeks if they were to be in shape for such an arduous trip; and last, if I had a prayer of pulling this off, it was I, and I alone—the so-called footloose writer in the crowd—who would have to do it, starting with harnessing and driving horses. Rain or shine.

There are some things in life that a person just automatically and blindly rises to, and this was one of them for me. When you live with a man who stands six feet six and beats steel on an anvil for a living, a man who wears a size sixteen shoe, is limber and lean and runs the Mountain Goat Marathon (a local, twenty-five-mile, cross-country event, up and down mountain peaks), I'm talking a man who unconsciously cinches down jar lids as though fillings such as peanut butter and mayonnaise require protection from imminent nuclear attack, then to keep your inner balance, you must—every little once in a while—plan something empowering. This trip had the stink of it, and I relished it. You think I can't do this by myself? (Not that anyone, except me, was thinking that.) Watch me! Those two little words became my challenge.

First was to shoe the ponies. Pancho and Lefty wear what are called clipped, fullered plates, forged from steel bar stock (a straight bar, ½ inch by 1¼ inches). Plates are fairly simple flat shoes, though in size, for these horses, impressive. Pancho, with the larger feet, carries on each front a shoe measuring eight inches in diameter and weighing three pounds. The fuller—or crease—is a groove into which the nail holes are punched, the clip a thin triangular tab of steel angling up along the hoof wall. Clips are drawn, or hammered, out of the steel when pulled pink-hot from the forge. Beginning with a length of bar stock appropriate to the size of the horse's foot, Patrick, by means of forge and anvil, turns a shoe. For a draft horse, he draws one clip, at the toe. Then, before completely cooling the shoe and nailing it on, at the time it is hot-seated, he also burns the clip into the front hoof wall. Burning a shoe onto a horse's foot is a painless procedure, when done properly, amounting to a person's pressing a hot match head to the end of a long fingernail. It creates the perfect fit while sealing the horn tubules from the damaging passage of moisture. And one clip, Patrick always says, is as good as two more nails for keeping a shoe attached to a foot.

While my favorite farrier-man shoed the horses, I took a three-day spin south to scout Idaho-Montana passes, acquire Forest Service maps, check backcountry horse regulations, hunt history in Salmon's museum and library, and talk to the magistrate for Lemhi County, Judge Snook. Freddie Snook to his friends was a hobby historian as well as owner of the ranch where Jim Rieffenberger had been employed—it was Freddie's cows that Pancho and Lefty hauled feed to. Everyone in Salmon said I should talk to Freddie. Though I never did meet him in the flesh, we chewed up the phone lines, and, as it turned out, he was well connected to the Big Hole ranchers, whose properties I was hoping to traverse once into Montana.

The Goldstone Pass, which led conveniently out of Freddie's, turned out to be impassable to wagons. The next one south, Lemhi Pass, was a backcountry route used by not much more than ranchers, the occasional tourist out exploring, and hunters. Its western ascent culminated in three miles of one-lane, dirt switchbacks that had given horses trouble as far back as 1866, when it was the main stage line from Red Rock, Montana, to Salmon, Idaho. Not infrequently Concord coaches had overturned and sent wagons, horses, and passengers spilling off the abrupt edge. Nowadays, during a west-side climb, there was every chance of meeting a descending pickup truck with horse trailer—and only a few spots where one of us could pull over. Any rig coming down on me would have the right-of-way, and, with my not being at all enamored of backing a loaded wagon down hairpin turns, the situation called for a support team with walkie-talkies for traffic control.

Bannock Pass, therefore, became my choice—over the

advice of locals, who warned that Bannock had heavier through traffic. They were right, of course: on the day I scouted, I encountered two cars on Lemhi and four on Bannock! It was the approach I liked—the long, steady grade of the wide gravel road and its open, sweeping curves, where drivers zipping along would not blindly run up on our slow-paced outfit. I planned two camps on the Idaho side: the first a staging ground where we would rig and load the wagon near the town of Leadore; the second beside a creek two miles from the summit. The following morning, Pancho and Lefty would pull the last of the grade to the Continental Divide and drop us into Montana.

Full of plans, laden with long lists of things to do, find, fix, buy, I blocked out my mornings to work with the horses. Creatures of routine and handling, horses tend to go feral when left alone. The first few mornings I needed a pail with a little grain to entice them into halters. With Pancho, I could set the grain outside the gate, walk in, slip his nose through the loop of red nylon, and buckle it around his neck. Lefty was never so easy. Both horses had been sorely mistreated somewhere along the line. When we acquired them, we couldn't at first raise a hand near their heads—to scratch an ear, to brush a neck—without them whipping away as though they would be beaten. We spent the first month leaning on them, walking around and around. In time, Pancho softened and began to trust, eventually tagging us about like a puppy. Lefty had remained the cat, aloof, the world on his terms whenever he could manage it. I attributed this to his past abuse having been more severe, but perhaps it stemmed in part from his breeding. Patrick purports, except for the rarest of teams, there is always a worker and a thinker. Pancho offers up his undivided heart in honest work; Lefty is the crafty boy, ever the shirker, the dallier, the teenage runaway.

It was not unusual to find him staring at a gate, kneading its workings through his mind. Yet, whenever the going got tough, in the real pinches, he unerringly came through, putting his head down, pulling like a son-of-a-bitch, right with Pancho, step for step.

Their conditioning period would extend over more than twice the length of the trip itself. I started them eight weeks in advance to allow for my scheduling additional reconnoitering trips and meetings with ranchers to seek permission to camp on and cross private land. Afternoons were for making phone calls, gathering up scattered camping gear, laying in supplies; evenings I drew up lists, made repairs, read history and regulations.

Yes, regulations.

The U.S. Forest Service, for the area I was heading into, had an enforceable closure order, permitting (on national forest lands) only weed-seed-free hay, certified by the standards of the Montana Department of Agriculture. This meant for all the high country of my trip. The weed in widest contention was spotted knapweed, or *Centaurea maculosa*. First reported in Montana in 1927, it arrived as a contaminate of alfalfa seed coming from Eastern Europe or Western Asia. In the summertime now, the fields of pinkish purple flowers draw delighted comment from tourists unaware of the darker side—that native grasses and wildflowers disappear as knapweed takes over. Of the long list of human-introduced species, knapweed is one of the more invasive, with 4 million acres of Montana rangeland succumbed to it. On our little five acres, we fight it continually. Summer evenings, for a couple hours, I will hand-dig the toughly rooted and sticky-leafed shanks as a kind of therapy. With resolute attention, I've been able to eliminate it only in the small yards directly adjacent to the barn.

.   .   .

The man possessing an intimate knowledge of spotted knap-weed is Research Professor of Entomology Jim Story. A few years after my wagon trip, I would make arrangements to meet him where he works at the Western Agriculture Re-search Center, a part of Montana State University residing in the Bitterroot Valley. The buildings that house the center were constructed in 1906, as Montana's Horticulture Re-search Center for Pomology, the science and study of fruit growing. In the early 1900s, when the Bitterroot apple boom was still in full swing, workers in these buildings were im-mersed in studying orchard cultural practices and cover crops. In the old horticultural barn Jim keeps a small office; the walls are hung with mountain, meadow, and river scapes—all pleasingly overpowered by a large picture win-dow onto the Bitterroots, snowcapped the day I am there. A tall, lanky man, bespectacled, and graying around the edges of a trim haircut, Jim is attired in jeans, a rugged style of ten-nis shoes, and a plaid shirt. He sinks only lightly into his chair, but with a core of calmness and patience that bespeaks a viewing of things in their longer-term runs. For twenty-five years, his entire professional focus has been the biological control—by deliberate use of natural enemies—of spotted knapweed.

Several other genera of knapweed plague various parts of the country, but Montana, Jim says, "has the lock on *spotted* in the United States." The Bitterroot Valley is the center of its invasive universe. Ranchers began seeing aggressive infesta-tions in the 1960s. It was spread, and still is, primarily by means of vehicles moving along roadways and railroad beds. In the roadless high country, it gets its start from feed that is packed in by (and for) horse, mule, goat, and llama; hence, the certified weed-seed-free hay dictate from the Forest Ser-vice.

Spotted knapweed propagates only by seed, but one plant

can produce anywhere from 25 to 18,000 seeds annually, in correlation to the number of flower heads it develops, which is in turn dependent on soil, nutrient, and water conditions. Knapweed seeds are extremely persistent, remaining viable—able to sprout—for ten years or more. The roots and leaves have their own randy nature. By exuding a chemical into the soil (with the leaves, it's when they decompose), they create an allelopathic effect, or a retardation of growth in surrounding vegetation. This aspect of knapweed is not fully understood: Studies have shown the plant can have an allelopathic effect on itself. A further characteristic that gives the species a competitive edge—in helping newly established plants grow toward monoculture pink blankets—is a deep, stout taproot. In our yard, when the ground is still moist in late spring, I've pulled up plants with two- and three-foot-long taproots. With this built-in straw, knapweed can drink down the water table, making survival increasingly hard for adjacent, more shallowly rooted species.

Knapweed is the robber baron of water, yes, but it actually does not like boggy spots and cannot gain good purchase in flood-irrigated hayfields. Our barn acreage came with no water rights, all of them having been sold off before our arrival, attached to larger pieces of hay ground. With ours being the last plat on the ditch before the creek that joins the river, we did receive "wastewater" for several years— until new neighbors began sending it all south. From our south paddock the knapweed has vanished, the horses having stomped it out in their turning the whole plot to dirt. Some good grass remains in the north field, which I try to nurse along, not allowing it to become overgrazed. Still and all, without irrigation water, knapweed files across it in a bigger way each year.

For Bitterroot property owners, the future is likely to hold only fiercer county weed regulations; so far, just the roadsides are monitored. One friend of mine, on an extremely limited budget, was recently outraged at having to purchase the new, metal, fifteen-dollar NO SPRAY sign, to (somewhat) prevent herbicide from reaching her chemically sensitive daughter. In the past, a homemade cardboard sign was acceptable. The shiny new one comes with a shiny new contractual agreement—a promise on the part of the landowner—to keep roadside stretches free of knapweed. Or what? The sprayer police will soon be tooling along in their toxic tank truck squirting out a fine suffocating mist. (More than once while driving down the highway, I've suddenly come upon it and tried frantically to get my windows and vents shut.) But hand-pulling knapweed, when it comes to people with long frontages, requires nothing short of a chain gang. Patrick and I have managed to dig it out along our five hundred feet for two consecutive years, yet inside the fence line the rangy plants know no bounds. Anyone willing to spray has an easier time of it. Ours is a position of predicament: Weeds or poisons? If a sea of knapweed did not lie off two of our borders, I might feel a higher level of guilt. As it is, I cling to the hope that biological control will eventually benefit us.

"It already is," Jim says.

Twelve species of insects, he tells me, have been released since 1974. When spotted knapweed first hitched a ride to Montana, it arrived in a place unpossessed of its natural enemies. With help from the U.S. Department of Agriculture, Jim works with insects—moths, weevils, tiny flies—collected from knapweed's homeland. Before being let loose on American soil, the introduced species are comprehensively studied to ensure they are host specific. Meaning "they won't feed on wheat, barley, or bananas," Jim says.

"Bananas?" I look up from my scribbling.

"A joke!" he says.

Out of the twelve insects, eight attack the flower head and four the root. Jim's job is to follow their progress—their capability of establishing themselves in the Bitterroot's ecosystem and climate—and to build up populations that one day might be available for someone like me to take home in little boxes. Out of the twelve, a few are doing better than others. One has proved highly adaptable, establishing itself across the entire state; it is the knapweed gallfly, *Urophora affinis*, looking like a tiny ant with wings. Its larva stage develops inside the knapweed's seed heads and, feeding on tissue from which seeds would normally form, causes the growth of a gall. The larvae of another species, *Agapeta zoegana*, a half-inch-long, yellow-winged moth, chew on the knapweed's roots. But there's a snag. *A. zoegana* has a slow rate of reproduction—one generation per year, with each female laying, at the outside, one hundred eggs.

I inquire about the overall picture.

"I'm just beginning to see an effect," Jim says, explaining the goal will be not to eliminate knapweed but to "manage it" at a tolerable level. There presently aren't any insects available for purchase. That could take another ten years.

We step outside, and Jim points to a freshly turned tract in which he will be—of all things—planting knapweed. Everything else is dried up and dormant. The established fly study areas are crowned with plastic pipe frames that in summer will carry netting. Bands of metal flashing encircle the weevil plots, to keep the tiny, long-nosed critters from crawling out. Back again in Jim's office, while he is out copying a pamphlet for me, I take note of the small bird feeder attached to the window and the double CD on his desk, *The Best of Mozart*. Tossed on the middle shelf of a floor-to-ceiling bookcase, crammed with bug tomes and little vials of flies and larvae, is a tape of Irish dance music. Is this a man just doing his job, or is there a sense of hope here?

I head home for a walk in our pasture, to break open seed heads and inspect for gallfly larvae.

So regulations it was! I was wholly accepting of doing what I could, even with what little I knew at the time about the tenacity of knapweed. Who wanted knapweed in the high country?

Then, a call to the first rancher regarding camping and my whole trip changed. "Not on my ranch you won't camp! I don't want any of *you Bitterrooters* on *my* property. Don't even pull off the road." Being still new to the Bitterroot, and more than a little curious, I gently pressed him to discover the source of his emotion. Fear of knapweed. I assured him I would be feeding certified weed-seed-free hay. He said I'd have seeds in my undercarriage, in the horses' feet, in their manure; he said the Idaho side of the pass was rife with it. I was stunned by the sourness in his vehemence, but his assessment was accurate. To have been even relatively certain, I would have had to mow and rake and vacuum the two Idaho campsites, power-wash the wagon, steam-clean the horses!

Yet by this time I was under commitment—to myself—to proceed: I switched my launchpad to Bannack, and I dropped the word *Bitterroot* from my vocabulary of introductions. Where did I live? In Victor. Furthermore, I determined to start feeding the certified weed-seed-free hay—as the Forest Service was recommending—ninety-six hours before our leaving home. This would stand in as a colonic, clearing seeds from the horses' digestive tracks.

In terms of the trip itself, the knapweed knot meant more elaborate planning. Instead of buying hay along the way or accepting offers, I needed to choose exact camps and make arrangements for hauling and stashing bales in advance. Things were beginning to take on a far different look than any of Patrick's and my previous touring.

. . .

With the horses in training, my mornings settled into a routine of tying the boys in the shade, mixing vitamins into their grain, and holding the pails for them to eat so as to conveniently rub them about the ears and face, getting them accustomed again to hands all over. I am a cooer, to Patrick's dismay, forever conversing with horses as though they understand my sentences. "Hi, Ponchi-Ponch! Hey, Left, how you be this morning? A gorgeous day for us, eh? Whaddaya think?" Then, with brush and currycomb in hand, tail comb in my back pocket, I would set to grooming. This was not show grooming, but it was thorough. Caked dirt, bits of hay, or foxtails under collars and harness can work up sores faster than anything. A daily close inspection also gave me a chance to doctor breast, belly, and sheath spots, where flies had gnawed, to watch for swollen joints, the beginnings of blisters, ticks when in season, and, in some country, cactus spines the horses picked up in rolling. Their feet came next. One by one, I held them up, braced on my knee, and, with a hoof-pick, pried loose the mud and manure, stones and corruption, packed into the bottoms. I checked the shoes for secureness—that a front hadn't pulled loose from stepping on the back of it, or a hind from hooking it on the fence. With grooming taking place just after the morning feeding, newly digested hay persisted in pushing out fertilizer, causing me to pause periodically to scoop up aromatic piles. Eventually it became time for a break—to wash my hands, to swallow my vitamins and a second cup of coffee, to grab my water bottle, straw hat, driving gloves, and carry them out to the wagon.

The very first day, I was fully recaptivated by these horses: the feel and shine of their warm bodies, their big, soft lips and pink-tongued mouths, the kindness in their eyes behind long lashes, their willingness. I settled the large leather collars around their necks; they take them over the head, like pulling on a sweater. I went next for the harness, thirty-five pounds of it. Sliding the breeching, hip drop, and back pad onto my right shoulder, I grabbed the steel hames just down from their top brass balls, one in each hand, and brought the entire harness off its hanger as a unit. Walking to Lefty's near side, I hefted the hames until the one in my right hand flopped to his off side and the short strap joining them settled into the depression in the top of the collar. Then I shoved the rest—what to the untrained eye seems an utter jumble of leather—one section at a time, onto his back. Again at the hames, I tucked them evenly into the grooves down the sides of the collar and snugged the bottom strap through its buckle. To accomplish the latter, to achieve the right leverage, I needed to lean my right shoulder directly into the knobby steel draft holder riveted to one of the heavy leather tugs (or traces, the other ends of which hook to the wagon). This daily task kept my shoulder black and blue as though bludgeoned. Next I buckled the belly band loosely and lined out the harness until the ring of the hip drop sat on top of Lefty's haunches and the breeching dropped around his buttocks. Then I lifted out his tail and began again with Pancho.

Hitching had its own routine. The decrepit old rubber-tired, flatbed wagon I used for conditioning the team has a low-slung tongue* with a hinge that allows its end to drop to the ground. You can ground-drive a team into place; one horse steps over the tongue. But our covered wagon, converted from a Selle, fifth-wheel-geared freight wagon, has a hip-high stiff tongue, so I stuck to the routine I would be using on the road. Patrick and I led the horses into position on

*The tongue—just as with a little red wagon—is the steering mechanism.

either side of the tongue. That Lefty works on the right is due solely to an Irishman's sense of humor. We guided on their headstalls, buckled the lines into the bits, clipped the jockey yokes into the harness, and slid the large center ring of the four-foot neck yoke over the end of the tongue. Then, following our rigid procedures for safety, which had evolved from Patrick's many years of working with horse-drawn vehicles and the public, he stood in front of the team while I hooked the tugs to the wagon, picked up the lines, and climbed aboard. It was our rule: one of us stood in front of the team until the other was at the lines. In unduly hairy situations, for instance, with fireworks shooting off—or when people were in the precarious position of clambering on and off the wagon—we would take up both positions. The routine of it helped the horses to feel secure. And a person who knew how could calm them, turn their attention from buggery things. Altogether, it was added insurance against having horses jump or bolt. "You got 'em?" Lines adjusted, my foot on the brake, I returned, "I got 'em." Lastly, attending to our final bit of precaution, Patrick removed from the rear wheel two five-pound wooden chocks. "Chocks out!" he yelled, and walked up and slid them under the seat, behind my feet.

Upon our return, the wheels were blocked again, the horses unhitched and walked to the shed. They were tied for an hour of cooling off, during which time I unharnessed and brushed the sweat from their bodies and mixed up a solution of Epsom salts for bathing their necks (an old-timers' technique for toughening skin against blisters). I washed the sweat from the collars with saddle soap, cleaned the breechings of manure. Finishing up, I walked the big guys to their paddock and then—for the first two weeks of this—I collapsed. Who was in training?

.   .   .

It was the dirt roads running west to the mountains that I sought for conditioning routes, and this meant crossing Highway 93. Though merely a two-lane, it had inspired the bumper sticker PRAY FOR ME, I DRIVE 93. Recent years had seen it grow busy with impatient, speeding motorists; long-bed loads of lumber and hay; cement mixers; delivery vans; still some logging trucks; pickups towing all manner of utility and horse trailer; oversized loads of new mobile homes, enveloped in flapping plastic; gargantuan weird things strapped on semitrailers; and all interspersed with tourons (Patrick's word) ensconced in their climate-controlled motor homes bedecked with lawn chairs, bicycles, canoes, motorcycles, and towing everything from power boats to Jeeps, even other motor homes.

In addition to the above road race, a young man brimming with testosterone was lately at the wheel of a bright red tractor-trailer hauling garage-sized boulders—repeated trips from a local quarry. This *gentleman* we'll call him here, as I was wont to call him many things at seven in the morning when he flipped on his Jake Brake in taking the first of his hourly turns at our corner.* Various city and residential sections of the country have adopted ordinances prohibiting any "engine-braking" that results in excessive or explosive noise,

---

*The Jake Brake Engine Brake is a compression-release braking system on diesel motors, designed to supplement wheel braking when stopping heavy loads, particularly on long downgrades. The term, seen posted along highways as NO JAKE BRAKES, stems etymologically from the Jacobs Vehicle Systems' Engine Brake. All of the company's braking systems, including their nearly silent exhaust brakes and driveline brakes, are called Jake Brakes. For the record: The Jacobs company feels it is unfair and inaccurate, possibly illegal, to use their trademarked name generically in "brand-specific" signs and references; they attribute the braking racket emanating from big rigs to poorly muffled, poorly maintained, unmuffled, or illegally modified brakes, as well as to other brands of brakes and truckers who simply take pleasure in sounding off. I suspected we had a case of the last.

and the laws are backed up with stiff fines and jail time—but nothing of the sort exists for our corner. If there were engine brake contests, say for shattering windows, then the driver of the red rig surely held the record. With a full load he was slamming out a quarter mile of what sounded like a Paul Bunyan jackhammer working on my cereal bowl. On his return trip, empty and plainly cruising uphill to the stop sign, he would squeeze out four more staccato rips. My worst nightmare was for the engine brake to sound off behind me while I stood poised with the horses to cross the highway. Some animals dig in and defend their ground against disturbance or threat, but horses are not among them. In the old fight or flight, at the onset of fright, they choose the second. At an unearthly loud blast from the rear, there was every possibility Pancho and Lefty would bolt, and we would become marmalade beneath a second eighteen-wheeler.

For my first two practice runs, Patrick squeezed a break into his schedule to accompany me. Walking in front of the team the first morning, he led the way down our back driveway and past the farmhouse. When the coast was clear, he waved me onto the side road. In similar manner, we journeyed to the blinking red light at the highway intersection, where I hugged the center yellow line: this allowed anyone turning right to slip around us and forced those planning otherwise to wait. My strategy was to prevent impatient drivers from peeling past us on both sides while we waited for a good opening. (Over the weeks, the drivers behind me were wholeheartedly patient. As I think about it now, they were probably holding their breaths.) We clattered across the pavement, and I stopped to let Patrick leap on.

Seemingly anxious to see the world again, Pancho and Lefty settled into a brisk walk on the packed dirt. These July days were righteously bright, blistering by afternoon. By going mornings, we were avoiding the worst of the biting deerflies and the truly menacing horseflies that are deserving, I always think, of a place next to backhoes in the excavation business. I had mapped out three-mile jaunts on fairly level ground for the first week, with plans to add miles and grades as we progressed.

Patrick, with his long history of horsemanship, has taught me to condition my horses to the tasks I will ask of them. And plan not to ask for more than they have. Teamstering had started early for him, on the family forty-acre subsistence farm. At the age of three he was holding the lines, at six he was driving his father's big mares, Minnie and Blanche. With a powerful stubbornness his father resisted progress, refusing to "have a tractor on the place." Patrick's uncle Raymond drowned when his first tractor rolled over an embankment and pinned him in the Munoscong River. No surprise then that my sweet buckaroo failed to develop the national pervasive fondness for gasoline-powered machinery and managed instead in this speed-racked culture of ours to spend almost as many of his days behind the bums of big horses as might an Amish farmer.

By comparison, mine was but a brief and fanciful career with horses—fairly well-broke and decently dispositioned horses at that. At the time of this trip, I'd been at it about twelve years, all starting when the Italian dairyman, Silvio Piccinotti—nearing eighty and with one shoulder gone to a bursitis that precluded any more slinging of harness—was game to take me on. I was an equine greenhorn in the city-est sense of the word. Except for riding stable for-hire horses when younger, the closest I'd come to western horsemanship was to know how to stuff the pant legs of my Lees into a pair of Tony Lamas and dance the tush push.

Seven draft horses roamed Silvio's Northern California pastures: four Belgians, two shires, and a Clydesdale. In his scattered barns reposed a unique and priceless assortment of old horse-drawn conveyances, the bulk of them in advancing stages of ruin. Over several years, I came to drive each of his horses (one to four at a time) on various antique vehicles—a high-seated covered wagon; a small red spring wagon; a goosenecked orchard wagon; a dusty, paintless stagecoach once held up by Black Bart; a velvet-upholstered vis-à-vis for weddings; and four brightly painted and pin-striped high-wheeled carts. For the work I put in readying his horses and outfits for parades and fairs, I logged hours of instructional driving. Then I bought a doctor's buggy and a Clydesdale mare.*

Pancho and Lefty, even this first day out, would have been perfectly behaved in a field full of cows. From their feed team days, they had a terrific *stop* on them—just say "whoa," hang up the lines, and head to the rear of the sled to bust open bales. Now, with a couple years of not being out in public, they were no longer road-wise. I regularly walked these western roads for exercise because they are not paved and are peaceful with traffic and offer spectacular views. This morning, I was a bit concerned that for horse training they might be too dull, not enough exposure to weird goings-on.

In answer to my thoughts, we had gone no more than a mile when an empty stacker—a tall, wide contraption of mostly framework and strapping used to collect hay bales from fields—came clanging and flapping toward us, determined to hog the road. Slowly we squeezed past each other, the stacker missing Pancho by about two feet. The horses remained calm. I had acted "as if"—as if nothing were scary. On down the road there were four people working fence out

---

*The mare has since died of old age, but we have her bay filly, grown into a beautiful horse.

of a pickup, two young boys pitching old fence posts into the truckbed, one man in the field loosening wire, and another winding it onto a big wooden spool he was rolling down the middle of the road. *This ought to be good!* The biggest of my concerns, the rolling spool, had, by the time we arrived, been shoved into the weeds on the right side of the road; we marched by the whole operation with some curiosity but not a wrong step. It was on our return trip, with the spool still resting in the ditch but now on Pancho's side, that more than a horse showed up rusty. The spool screamed at Pancho's small horse brain, "Dracula! Son of Sam! I eat you!" As we drew nearer, he began to step sideways, crowding Lefty and taking the wagon toward a roadside irrigation ditch. My working of the lines to ease him back left, coupled with a plaintive cheerleader's "Come on, Pancho!" did nothing to save us. He merely torqued his body into a C-curve, allowing his head to follow my pull while his midsection continued pushing Lefty right. Patrick grabbed the lines (something he is always reluctant to do) and, with a swift snap of one to Pancho's butt, to get his attention, accompanied by a commanding, deep-voiced, *"Pancho!* Step around there!" the horse reconnected to us and shook off his goblins.

The third day, Patrick waved me across the highway and I was on my own: I practiced my baritone deliveries and acted "as if" the whole way. At one turn, a flashy paint horse came barreling down a hillside of brush—a black-white-green, black-white-green freight train. Pancho threw his hinds into a triple-time stomp, but I gathered him in so quickly I didn't have time to think we were headed for the border. "Easy, Ponch, it's one of your kind." With Lefty, it was the llamas that were lions. Or the thirty little calves chasing us along the fence line, just out of view, behind his blinder. When we had completed the loop back to the highway, the elderly neighbor ranch hand scheduled to help me across was nowhere to be found—and here came the monster red tandem full of boulders. Gulp. I stopped a good twenty feet back from the intersection. *At least he's not behind me.* The driver, for once, was asleep at the switch (and it is a switch), or else he had the eyes of a hawk and had spotted me. As he turned the corner quietly, I gave him the benefit of the doubt, elevating out of the dirt my original appraisal of his Samaritanism. The boys stood quite placidly while we waited for a totally clear road. I trotted them across. Once in the barnyard, I faced them into the front wall of Patrick's shoeing shed, climbed down, and, lines in hand, unhooked. When I had them in their halters and tied, I paid homage to the neighbor man: He had inadvertently delivered me into my confidence.

From then on Pancho and Lefty and I were a *team.* It was their job to trust me. It was my job to trust me. And it was my job to be broadly vigilant: to anticipate and talk them through anything frightening, "It's okay, big fellows, it's only a silly (rolling) garbage can"; to work the lines maintaining an easy but I'm-right-here tension on their bits; to see that they pulled evenly, sharing the load; to haul them in when they jumped to run—"Here, here. Waaalk, just walk"; to let them stand and blow on the hour or after a long pull; to monitor the fit of the harness for adjustment as they hardened up and changed shape; to keep an eye cocked for leg-breaking potholes and an ear trained for overtaking traffic; and finally to wield the long buggy whip, mercifully flicking off flies they could not reach with the swipe of a leg or brush of a tail. Day by day, we put on the miles, building a mutual steadiness, an interlocking dependence. Three weeks along I was not fazed when Lefty, chasing an itch, caught his headstall on the end of the jockey yoke. He came to an easy stop to my easy "Whooaa." I climbed off, holding the lines, and untangled him.

On our longer jaunts in the August heat, I was comfortable pausing now to water my good workers from two pails that swung, sloshing a bit, from hooks beneath the wagon bed. Otherwise, we joggled and bumped along to a music of our own cut: the jingle of tug chains like a cantata of small bells, against the *whomp-whomp* percussion supplied by the dry-rotted wagon bed's bouncing on its rear bolster as we hit chatter bumps, and all accented by an imperious booming of tuba, Lefty's resonant farting. I sang. Loudly and not particularly on key, tossing out into the countryside nonsensical lyrics on melodies of the moment—from sprightly marches to operatic croons.

My soul was wholly at peace.

Afternoons I returned to the inglorious ground-level tasks, things that were becoming the real challenges. The most up-to-date list I could find for growers of certified weed-seed-free hay was two years old. I called all across the state and found that many ranchers had already promised their entire supplies to hunters using it for packing into base camps. Others were not bothering to grow it this year. Weed-seed-free hay can bring a higher price, but to earn certified status, it must be inspected within seven days of its being cut—at a charge of a dollar fifty an acre, plus the inspector's mileage. Just another something for a rancher in this climate to juggle: We are sometimes lucky, between ravaging thunderstorms, to get a four-day window—to cut hay, dry it to the optimum moisture level, bale it, and get it under cover. Crews sometimes work all night.

Finally, by word of mouth, I stumbled upon a nearby certified field that had just been baled. It was partially alfalfa, which I didn't want; we prefer feeding working draft horses straight grass hay, supplemented with three-way (COB) and vitamins. To collect the ton I needed would require two trips in my old six-cylinder, half-ton pickup. I backed up to a sky-high stack, and the rancher began tossing down bales. Each bore a small red plastic tag with a serial number: the certified mark. The bales felt damp, a little warm, and there emanated from them a disturbing smell of chemicals. Most certified hayfields, I had been told, were not sprayed. It was economically unfeasible. Either you had weeds or you didn't. Our county's chief of roadside weed spraying might boast drinking herbicide for nightcaps, but I was not pleased at the prospect of serving it up to my horses. Then it came to me— this was perhaps proprionic acid (a fatty acid, sometimes mixed with acetic acid), functioning as a mold retardant; it's sprayed on hay too wet to bale. When I questioned the likelihood of the bales going to mold, reiterating my need for good horse hay, not cattle feed (cattle, with their series of stomachs, can better process imperfect hay), the man was insulted. This was *prime* horse hay, hunters would be glad for it! Terse in his tone, he said it was merely "going through the sweat." Did I want it or not? I'd seen a lot of people over the years unconcerned about feeding their horses rotten hay. I was not wanting my hay shed to spontaneously combust; I was not wanting to revisit my greenhorn days and come up a dumb, duped girlie. More than a little skeptical, but with no other known alternative, I chose to put on my blinders and believe him; he was, after all, the husband of a friend.

I left the second load in the truck and in the morning took off for the Big Hole, for a day of wrestling these heavier-than-I-was-used-to bales into secure, dry places—sheds, barns, old schoolhouses—my prearranged camps. The bales left at home would be delivered by friends directly to my high country camps; to leave hay, even mantied hay, sitting around in the woods for a few weeks is to invite elk, deer, cattle, even mice to dinner.

Not only would I require hay shuttled into four camps, something that was becoming a many-pieced board game, but I needed someone traveling with me at least during the days, as the West was built for bovines. Every mile or two in this country, on almost every back road, there is a cattle guard, a sunken grate over which vehicles can pass but cows and horses will not wander. By regulation (exactly whose I never figured out), installers of cattle guards must provide a detour for the moving of stock and for trail riders. The detours are gates, of every imaginable form, installed in the fencing somewhere off to the side of the road. On my research and hay runs, I was also scouting these detours. The predominate problem was in my getting to the gates. Many seemed years unattended, with obstacles such as high, hardened berms left by consecutive passes of a road grader. I would have to dig them out. Some merely posed challenges to my driving skills: gauntlets of rock and sagebrush, narrow squeaks through the gates themselves, tippy plunges in getting to them. A couple were built only wide enough for a horse. With others, stout starts of pine trees grew all over the cutoffs and even right up through the gates. I found one passage completely inaccessible down a sharp embankment into a borrow pit that had recently become an irrigation channel. We couldn't come *this* way. And I made a note to carry in the wagon a shovel and a saw.

As it would be imprudent to leave the team standing on the roadside while I sallied off to open gates and all that that might entail, I began signing up "companions in adventure." People who could open gates or stand in front of the team. Fortunately, there was no shortage of friends wanting to come along. My expedition lists were expanding, to riders-along, camp locations, addresses and phone numbers, bedding, clothes, personal toiletries, horse tack, kitchen gear, menus, groceries, first-aid and repair items, things yet to do.

Then one morning, it all started going awry. I hooked the team and asked them to back up, and the wagon did not budge. When they threw their hindquarters—sat their joint 3,400 pounds—down into the breeching, the wagon tongue rose, pointing its tip skyward, and nearly broke out of the old hounds before I could get them stopped. When you are driving a car, your senses send a signal to your brain, which tells, say, your foot to step on the brake, and the brake engages. When driving horses, there are additional steps to the process. This time my senses radioed my brain and instructed my voice box to holler "whoa"; the horses' ears swiveled on the word before delivering the message to their brains, where it was then relayed to hips, hocks, and feet. With such a long linkage, a teamster must always be thinking well ahead. On this occasion, it had taken my brain—second in the chain—a monstrously long time to come to consciousness, to understand we were anchored. It was our right front tire, hiding in the grass. Flat! There was only one nearby gas station with the equipment to change a wooden-hubbed rubber tire, and the crew there was backed up until afternoon. The day was shot.

The next morning Pancho came up lame. An elderly woman friend of mine, an astrology nut, would say of this kind of luck: "Honey, the planets are square." I called our veterinarian, and he scheduled an appointment for the following morning. By then Pancho was hopping on his left front, carrying his right. A stone bruise, the vet told me, had created an abscess inside the hoof wall; the abscess would either reabsorb or eventually blow out the top. I took the two bottles of penicillin and handful of needles he offered and was grateful he administered the first shot before leaving.

In the morning, Pancho had a gouge in his flank the size of two lima beans. Big Boss Lefty had bitten him; Pancho couldn't dance out of his way. I retrieved his halter and led him gingerly, one step at a time, over to our other field, where he could recuperate with our mare. She was at the bottom of the pecking order, and it would take her a few days to figure out he was presently incapable of being her lord. Patrick helped me with the morning shot, and I slathered salve on the flesh wound.

Come evening, Pancho was wise to the folks with the huge needles and getting hard to catch. I didn't have time for this or for patiently waiting for the abscess to pick its path. A call was in order to the hotshot horse vet, Doc Richardson, with whom Patrick worked on occasion. He came from Missoula the next morning, arriving when Patrick was off at a shoeing appointment, and had to pry off Pancho's big shoe himself. Then he laid the curved blade of a hoof knife against the tough sole and, following a dark line inward, dug away until he hit the abscess and a stinking gray fluid oozed out. He packed the bottom of the foot with old-fashioned ichthammol, a black drawing ointment, which his grandmother when he was little, he said, had plastered on him for everything—cuts, abrasions, splinters. Next was to wrap the salve as a poultice with four layers: a plastic bag, tan elastic wrap, bright blue leg wrap to the top of the hoof, and adhesive tape from quarter to quarter, round and round. All this he accomplished with the help of an assistant in twenty-five minutes. To my amazement, the poultice remained intact for the requisite four days. And Pancho walked less tentatively each day. The new antibiotics, intended to reach the foot with greater impact, were, at first glance, absolute horse pills, but I was instructed to crush them, twenty at a time, and lace them with molasses. For surefire appeal, I added a shot of Patrick's pure maple syrup. Twice a day I stirred this gummy glob into a little grain, and Pancho fairly skipped into his halter to get at it. On the final day, we removed the poultice, soaked his foot in a pail of warm water, and nailed his shoe back on over a leather pad sealed at the heel with oakum. Because the abscess had left a nickel-sized hole in the front hoof wall, I stretched several layers of duct tape across it to keep dirt and manure from entering at that point. Pancho walked out of the shop, silver-toed and sound. We hitched him and drove him four miles.

I had lost nine days' training.

When we came up on four days to leaving—or the ninety-six-hour Forest Service directive—as planned, I broke open a bale of the certified weed-seed-free hay. It wasn't particularly a shocker that I had to pry apart flakes glommed together with black-and-white mold, a big *poof* of choking spores engulfing my face. The real surprise came an hour later, when the phone rang: a rancher getting back to me from my inquiries of weeks ago. He had grass hay, just baled, no mold, and no herbicide—for the last two years he and his wife had pulled their few weeds by hand. Could he deliver? You betcha. Now? This afternoon. "Bring *two* ton!" I said, thinking I might recoup some of the money I had made up my mind to lose on the moldy ton—dilemma of a friend's husband—by peddling to last-minute hunters what I knew to be a rare commodity this year. When it arrived, it was by far the loveliest hay I had ever seen. I felt a new surge of something more than energy. The planets seemed to have lined out. The boys would have first-rate, almost organic feed. All would go right with this trip.

On the seventh of September, we were a parade heading for Bannack. Jim Rieffenberger had come to haul the horses for me, and he led out. Behind him my neighbor Joe, with his little girl riding along, fell in towing a flatbed carrying the covered wagon. I was at the wheel of my pickup with all the gear, and in the passenger seat sat my first companion, Audrey Sutherland. Audrey had flown in from Hawai'i (as she's careful to spell it), from a more watery sort of life. She is a small, fit woman with a blazing smile, and the author of two paddling books, *Paddling Hawai'i* and an account of her solo adventure, *Paddling My Canoe.* I had met her the previous year at a kayak symposium where we were both speaking. Because she was my senior by some years—just how many she never reveals—and because I stood in awe of her fearless quests for adventure, I considered her a shining mentor. When she was first exploring Hawai'i's wild coasts, on a severely limited budget, to reach coves inaccessible by hiking, she'd jumped solo into the ocean and begun swimming, dragging behind her a bag of minimal food and clothes. Concerned friends soon told her she would appear less like shark bait were she in a boat. She has been kayaking ever since. She came now to join me, curious to learn the ropes of horse travel.

We pulled into the campground at Bannack, just outside the ghost town proper, which allows only foot traffic. Across the creek stood a relic from gold rush days, an old stamp mill for crushing rock. I turned the team into a rustic round corral, and then we didn't look up again for an hour, unloading. Afterward Joe headed home with a sick daughter, and Jim, who'd planned on delivering my next five nights' hay, took off straightaway for an unexpected job interview in Idaho, dropping only the first night's two bales en route. Jim's departure was an unexpected blow. But wrenches to my schedule were a given, and agonizing over them only robbed me of energy. I turned to feeding the horses and setting them up with salt and water.

Leaving Audrey staking out her tent, I took off on a drive I would later dub the knapweed-driven hay run from hell, in that it ended up taking a mammoth bite out of my one planned good night's rest. I'm one of those people who needs eight hours' sleep to function well. From here on out, six was the most I could expect to snatch, and I sensed I was going to need a high, driving energy for the three weeks ahead, in spite of having scheduled only eight- to twelve-mile days with several layovers, a pace far easier than Patrick and I together would have set. Once we were on the road, there would be plenty more to add to my daily horse chores: cooking and dishwashing off the tailgate; dragging around hay bales and hauling water, in some cases, fair distances; evenings, unpacking the wagon and setting up the hot-wire fence; mornings, breaking down the fence and repacking the wagon; and, every fifty or so miles, the Jiffy Lube!—never seen in Western movies—of jacking up the axles, removing each wheel, greasing the hubs and spindles.

Eleven miles down the road, I came to the Cross Ranch and saw the bales Jim had left mantied by the roadside. The field we'd been given permission to camp in was chock-full of milling cattle. This was not your average KOA campground standing ready at the welcome; there had obviously been a change in plans with the cattle. I tossed the bales in the truck and drove on. This next stretch, to what would be our second night's camp, followed along the route Lewis and Clark had traveled with Sacagawea, struggling, of course, with many adversities—but at least not the rippling ramifications of knapweed, I thought. Winding on up Horse Prairie, I pulled into the old Stocker Ranch, belonging to Steve and Kim Hirschy. Here, Kim put me in touch with the Cross Ranch manager, and Steve took the rest of my hay with a generous offer to deliver it for the three nights following our stay at their place. About this time I realized I had enough gas to return to Bannack, but not enough to get out of there again, and so with directions I set off to the nearest service station, over on Clark Canyon Reservoir. It was dark when I hit the marina, and I missed it and had to circle up to Dillon. By the time I took dinner in a truck stop, climbed over Badger Pass, and parked again beside the wagon, it was going on two in the morning. Audrey, gone to bed, had left dinner on the tailgate.

Morning broke full of sunshine. After breakfast—the boys' and ours—I ran the last of the hay bales down to our new, idyllic creekside camp at Cross Ranch. At last, we began to organize gear and rig the wagon. First was the bolting on of bows, bought tall enough for Patrick to stand upright in the bed. It was a stretch for me to work the one-piece bundle—225 square feet of canvas—up and over the bows, one by one. Audrey fed me armfuls while I pressed them overhead, my face buried in the folds. The fumes from a fresh coating of Thompson's Water Seal ran up my nose with the zinging power of Chinese mustard. Like an ancient form of shelter, skins upon ribs, the covered wagon profile began to take shape. A little breeze billowing its sides, I fussed with adjusting the dozen-plus tie-downs. And smiled at the image of myself.

As a child I had been a vessel of jumbled longings, a cultural product, telling of just how pervasive were American frontier myths.

My hair was styled for me in pigtails beginning at age four; early snapshots show a cherubic smile flanked by thick, stumpy braids. That the plaits grew on down to my waist, that I wore them unfashionably into the eighth grade— other girls sported ponytails tied up in bright scarves—was due in large measure to my father's commandment for my hair to appear *neat*, a term in those days meaning "tidy." This entailed my sitting upon a small rush-seated stool every morning, while my mother—for some reason exceptionally unhandy with a brush and comb—yanked and tore through knots until often tears ran down my cheeks before the freshly woven braids stretched down my back. One day in a final fit of rage, defiance, and adolescent independence (shortly after my twelfth birthday), I walked myself into a barbershop, climbed into one of the leather-padded swivel chairs, propped my feet on the ornate, nickel-plated foot-rest, and to the smocked man said, "Cut these!" Two swift snips at the nape of my neck gave me a whole new other-side-of-the-world look. That of a Dutch boy. My father's not recognizing me in this bowl-over-the-head 'do proved a lasting thrill. And there would be no more mornings on the stool. Yet the braids themselves I sorely missed: I was an Indian wanna-be, without knowing the term. Coupled with my high cheekbones, my braids were the stuff of a young girl's voluble fantasies—fantasies wrapped around the appeal of pretty feathers and beaded clothing, not to mention an unparalleled appreciation for bold noses and an early-in-life rooting I had somehow acquired for the world's *hunted*. In addition, there was an imagined freedom: of fleet running, barefoot, through beckoning woodlands. I craved discovering a clandestine liaison (like Judy Hoy's) in the trunk of my family tree.

But that was only the Indian facet. There were also cowboy and prairie girl daydreams first spun in the era of Hopalong Cassidy (my mother, to coax me to bed at night, yodeled "Hopalong Kathidy"). My head-yarns grew throughout the years of Ward Bond in *Wagon Train* and the ranching *Bonanza* men, then ripened into a preoccupied crush on—who else?—*Rawhide's* Rowdy. For much of my life, I thought I had been born into the wrong century. I serially invented myself into all roles of a Manifest Destiny soap opera, plus I was surprisingly not rigid about the sex I assumed. When my great-aunt (the one with the pastel Easter bunnies) brought me a "Hoppy" costume for Halloween, I wriggled instantly into the gun belt with matching six-shooters, the spurs and cowboy hat and bolo tie—perhaps an early yearning for personal power? a precursor of my breaking with expectations? or a sensing that the better adventures in life for me would lie outside a traditional woman's role? What it said about my great-aunt, years dead now, is a longer guess. More to the point: What today are disdainfully branded Western myths—those unrealistic or romanticized versions of cowboys, gunslingers, God-fearing sodbusters, heathen Indians or glorified noble savages—I had as a child internalized as *life.* My savages all heroes. My sagas all tweaked to happy endings.

As I moved into adulthood, my longings took a stride toward the pragmatic, to coupling up with the right man and heading to the north woods for a life of homesteading. I outgrew this one without its materializing. The prospect then of traveling by team and wagon with Patrick would seem to have held out the perfect actualization of my earlier dreams. Instead, riding the high white prairie sail, posed acute internal conflicts. Having grown beyond childhood fantasies and learned some history—of displacement, degradation, expungement, extermination; having moved into the West and formed friendships with Indian people—Cherokee, Apache, Chippewa, Ojibwa, Blackfeet; here I was big-as-life traveling in a conveyance quintessentially symbolic of the cutting asunder of whole cultures; not to mention consummately symbolic of western settlement, gone now over the top to a grievous sprawl that daily, before my eyes, was wiping out lands and species essential to the lifted human spirit, essential to the planet's—vaguely as we know it—continuing.

I had some years back left any wanna-being behind. And though the makeup of my personal religion springs from perhaps congeneric earth beats—long tapestries of undisturbed landscape unfolding, wind whips, thuds and scuffles in the forest, bird peeps, naked soles upon the ground—I am now somewhat uncomfortable participating in Native Peoples' ceremonies, to do so feeling almost the final robbery.

.   .   .

By the time we hitched and set out, it was mid-afternoon and
with the weather threatening a change. An obliging park
ranger laid sheets of plywood over the first cattle guard, one
we could not scoot around. The boys clattered right over
(we had practiced at home). Waving the man our thanks,
and also good-byes to the folks Audrey had met in the campground, we sat atop our perch on the wagon seat and thrilled
to the working haunches of Pancho and Lefty, their jaunty
walk and pricked ears, as they carried us over Grasshopper
Creek. Ever enthralled by the flow of water, I peered upstream and down. A gem of a little watercourse, it had clear-
running bends shot with tropical aquamarine. "All was
a-shake and a-shiver—glints and gleams and sparkles, rustle
and swirl, chatter and bubble": I was feeling as jolly and be-
witched as Kenneth Grahame's Mole just come up out of his
hole and onto a river in spring. At long last, we were going
a-journey!

With ease we pulled the grade out of the creek, and Audrey opened her first gate, one that would have sneaked up
on us like an obscured freeway off-ramp, had I not in recent
weeks, five times, passed by it. The sky turned a solid slate.
To stave off a bitter breeze blowing a light rain in our faces,
we broke out winter hats and gloves and a two-layered lap
robe: wool army blanket and tarpaulin. Cheerily, we settled
in—save for Audrey's gate tending—for seven miles of winding through gently ascending rangeland, a mottled canvas of
yellow-blooming rabbitbrush and silvery sage, the latter's
pungency released by the rain.

The sky cleared toward evening as we topped out to a
panoramic view of Horse Prairie—a vista that would mean
almost nothing in a car, so fast would it come and go. With
our knowing every nuance of hill and curve in getting there,
we took in the long view with relish; it would be ours to
examine—fields dotted with rotund, blond hay bales and

dark cattle, a snake of willowy river bottom, the mountain-
scape on beyond—for the whole next hour. Audrey said we
had three miles to go, she could tell by the look of distant
trees. Our now ruler of a road ran through the middle of
the Cross Ranch complex: houses, barns, trailers, corrals, a
kitchen building for feeding large crews. At the roadside was
a now familiar sign: FIFTEEN MILES PER HOUR. As I came upon
it this time in the wagon, it drew a chuckle from me. Should
I be whipping the team to a gallop?

A mile or so farther and we pulled onto a side road, then
down into the corner of a hayfield beside a willow-lined
creek. Parking near our two certified weed-seed-free bales,
lying there like a couple of wrapped Christmas packages just
waiting for us, we threw in the chocks, unhitched, unharnessed, and began to unpack. I tossed out the bedrolls and
Audrey's tent, handed down the cooler, the propane bottle, a
five-gallon jug of people water, the fencing. Next was to adjust the tailgate to level; slide out the stove and the kitchen
box with its cups, dishes, utensils, and spices; hook up the
gas and set a pot of water to boiling for pasta.

Leaving the boys tied to either side of the wagon,
we walked out into the field—in twilight, the mountains
going to silhouettes—to set up fence. Carrying a short-
handled sledgehammer, I pounded in a waist-high steel rod,
paced off twelve feet, pounded in another. Audrey came
along behind with the bag of yellow plastic insulators, attaching one to each post. The electric wire—an orange plastic mesh tape, woven with silvery conductor threads—was
wound onto a spool the size of a lunch box. Shoving a two-
foot piece of bar stock through the spool and holding the
ends, Audrey walked along unwinding, while I fastened the
tape, nice and taut, to each insulator. The size of our corral
would vary with available field conditions and as time per-
mitted. I liked to give the horses as much room as possible to

work out the kinks from their hard labor. We always had more wire than we needed, and extra stakes. When we'd completed what tonight was a forty-foot-square corral, I pounded the piece of bar stock into the soil for an electrical ground and hooked up the small battery-run fence charger. In the dark, Audrey stumbled back to the wagon to work on dinner, while I kept the flashlight for stringing around hay and dipping pails of water from the creek.

Before we loaded up our plates with pine-nut-and-pesto sauce over spinach-and-cheese ravioli, we had one more chore: to show the boys to their bedroom. I led them in by their halter ropes, this time with Audrey out in front, shining the flashlight on the fence posts and wire as we walked the entire perimeter. In daylight, the horses could easily figure out their boundaries. Throwing them into a new setup after dark, without walking the line, was asking for a breakout. This was a tissue fence in reality, one they could run right through, snapping the tape if badly spooked, or in connecting with an electric jolt and jumping the wrong way. The fence's zap, were I accidentally to hit it with my hand, was enough to run up my arm, explode in my head, make me gnash my teeth together. When horses are first being broken to an electric fence, they will investigate it with their noses. I can't even imagine.

After we cleaned up the dinner dishes, Audrey retired to her tent and I threw down my bag, flannel comforter, and pillow beneath the wagon. Crawling in, I took along the gas lantern. I pried off my boots and propped them by the front wheel, then wriggled out of my jeans and rolled and stuffed them into the bottom of the bag for keeping warm. In lying back, I beheld the bottom of the wagon bed, its yellow wood aglow in the soft light. Almost over my head was the front cross-spring. I had once painted it, along with all the other hardware, an old-fashioned Brewster green. Farther forward, in the fifth wheel, a gear that sits horizontally, I could see the two small pieces of varnished wood that were the only two we'd salvaged from the original wagon. My gaze traveled along the bed's stout ash stringers, specially ordered from a mill in Salt Lake City, down to the tailgate, which I'd designed. At either side of my knees hung big oak blocks lined on one side with tire tread, the brakes, adjusted to a half inch of the rear wheels—and then the rest of the brake assembly, with its sturdy steel rod running back up to the driver's foot lever. The harness and collars, dangling from their wagon-side hangers, just grazed the ground. With all the gear I had slid under the front and back for the night, it was—axle to axle—a cozy little cave in here. I wondered how many pioneer women had tucked themselves under wagons. Those whose diaries I had read had slept inside, on actual beds or mattresses that often turned soggy when it rained and their canvas toppers leaked. Had those journeying women donned long flannel nightgowns, or had they retired in their lacy undergarments? I was pondering this while my fingers punched the numbers to reach Patrick on a cell phone. It was the first I had ever used—free from Cellular One for my checking the range from Dillon. Three snatched minutes of catch-up and libidinous babble were ours—across what might have been more than a century—before the connection cut out.

A medley of weather moved in the next day: fog, sunshine, buttermilk skies, and, by evening, drizzle. We motored along to the crunch of our steel wheels shattering pebbles to powder. Again I was tracing the steps of Lewis and Clark, who, themselves, had trod paths laid down over aeons by the seasonal migrations of indigenous peoples, the latter having followed the trails of the "animal peoples." By my best guess after poring over journals and maps, right in here somewhere, give or take a mile, Lewis had met his first Shoshone—his hope for horses—while the young Shoshone boy made his first acquaintance with white skin. It was a telling meeting, one that stands as a foreshadow of the entire future course of the American West. From my reading of Lewis's notes, he rolled up a sleeve "to give him an opportunity of seeing the colour of my skin" and held up "some b[e]ads a looking glas and a few trinkets." At a distance of a hundred paces, with another member of the corps pressing in, the boy "suddonly turned his hose about, gave him the whip leaped the creek and disapeared in the willow brush." The following day, the other side of Lemhi Pass, Lewis came upon a large Northern Shoshone camp, where fortuitously for the expedition he was supplied the horses that carried them into the Bitterroot. (Patrick has read nine of the fourteen volumes of the published journals of the Lewis and Clark Expedition. Most are heavy, big books. On an evening when he was wading through volume 5, he suddenly blurted out, "There's three different spellings here for the same word in one sentence! This is all before standardized spelling. When I'm through with our boys Lewis and Clark, I won't be able to spell *anything!*")

Audrey and I were to keep mostly to a dirt track ourselves today, some of it surely once early Indian road. I felt a little shiver of thrill in glancing about, wondering *who* might have been doing *what* here half a dozen million years ago.

When Patrick and I had traveled in Great Britain and been shown places dating back to the Normans, the Romans, to Hadrian's Wall, built in A.D. 120, we had mildly boasted we lived in the oldest "settlement" in the Pacific Northwest. (One side of our property is considered part of that very town: Stevensville.) This only prompted people's asking: "And when would that have been?" "Oh, 1841," we had said, at which utterance we were generally bestowed looks rife with pity. Poor things we were, we had no appreciable history!

Yet, in driving through Horse Prairie, open country still sparsely settled, no sound of a car or engine reaching our ears, and with Audrey and me on the seat of a covered wagon—setting us already a good deal back in time—it wasn't hard to stretch my mind further, down any one of many narrow dirt paths to the first presence of humans. Light footfalls trailing off around a stand of sagebrush.

I had found scant reading material on Horse Prairie's human inhabitants prior to the coming of Lewis and Clark, but the area exudes what surely is a whole rich culture of spoken, native nomadic history, predating the written—if misspelled!—Anglo, settled history. I am personally privy to little of it, though its existence I do not doubt. We commonly use the word *prehistoric* for events predating written history, my *Webster's New International Dictionary*, second edition, defines *history*, apart from being "a systematic written account of events," as a narrative of events, a story, a tale. In turn, *narrative* is defined as a recital, and *recite* as repeating from recollection, or something committed to memory. The legitimacy of oral history is contained within the life of the voices.

I remained preoccupied with my primordial flitting-amongst-the-sagebrush apparitions until we hit a stretch of thoroughly modern macadam on secondary Highway 324. We stopped at its edge, and Audrey climbed down to switch on our road-construction-type blinking light. Originally rigged up for Patrick's and my highway touring, it was wired to a twelve-volt car battery on the back of the wagon. The bulb is the sort that can be seen in daylight for a mile; I credit it with many days of preserving my life.

Sometime later in the afternoon, when we had pulled off onto the shoulder and Audrey was clutching a pail of water against her belly, offering the horses a drink, a car cruised in and parked alongside. Out popped a young couple handing us a loaf of freshly baked bread. In the brief visit that ensued, they expressed knowledgeable admiration of the horses' shoes—Patrick's beautifully fitted handmades—and sympathy for the rigors of our travel, having recently themselves, in moving to Horse Prairie, come all the way "honeymooning on horseback" from Colorado.

Well before dark we were back on dirt, crossing a wooden planked bridge over Horse Prairie Creek, skirting the broad base of a crumbling mound called Red Rock (different from the old stage stop), and pulling into the Hirschys' pasture.

Since my canoodling by cell phone with Patrick, it had been twenty-four hours of a whipsawing back-and-forth across centuries and millenniums.

By the Hirschy family we were warmly welcomed as western friends, offered showers, the use of a bathroom, shown to the corrals and water. The following night we were scheduled to stay at Steve and Kim's cow camp, the old Robinson Cabin. In the 1800s, it was the settlers and the First Americans—and throw in the U.S. government—who had fought the consuming, pitched battles that centered on land, territory, resources, and wildlife. Today, with the topics virtually the same and the issues not wholly different, the opposing players are people like the Hirschys and me—then add to the wrangling again government and First Americans, and now sportsmen. The Hirschys are the cattle ranchers, a family-sized business running a few hundred head, with pasture leased out to a few hundred more. I am a person agonizing over such things as stream degradation, the crumbling banks and fecal pollution, the siltation and cloudy flows with lowered oxygen levels, and the diminished riparian populations of songbirds. Here in the West, our communities stand fractured over these and similar issues of resources—sides torturously duking it out. Occasionally the skirmishes are fought skillfully, even amusingly, and publicly in back-and-forth letters to the editor; other times they are clandestine and humorless, a telephone's ringing with a middle-of-the-night death threat. Because the polarized factions rarely think to pull up chairs in kitchens, talk across the flowered print in the oilcloth, take in the chips in the coffee mugs, the scuffed paths in the flooring, it makes it all too easy for one side to stonewall, while the other seeks to banish a way of life: "What your family has been doing for five generations is no good anymore." In conversing with Steve and Kim, it was plain to see how they might feel not just the pinch of constricting federal regulations but the environmentalists' empathy-empty crush—however more pointedly leveled at larger, corporate, and international beef industries—threatening to bury their homelife.

Some years after my trip, I would sit at Kim's kitchen table, hearing about dropping cattle prices and her litany of money troubles, and sensing that any kind of fencing of stream banks would finish them off. As a ranch mother and seasoned Horse Prairie inhabitant, Kim is lovingly wedded to the isolation in her way of life, no close neighbors, forty-two miles to town. Before I left, she said something that, although I live with only *one* person, rang true to my core. "There's too many people here some days—I have my mom, my dad [recently moved in with them], Gene [a longtime ranch hand], my kids, and Steve." It was something we both knew (and seemingly a starting place for deeper understanding): Alone time is crucial.

The rain had quit sometime during the night. The weather gods seemed particularly considerate of our open-air touring, often delivering up just the needed break to set up or strike camp. We didn't have the fencing chores this morning; the horses had been lolling in the Hirschys' huge cattle corral. We promptly ate up the saved time, however, in a lengthy grooming away of the fresh cow fops the boys had lounged on overnight. Under our brushes and currycombs, the globby embedded patches, which had dried by the time we'd finished with breakfast and packing, produced clouds of particulate matter so dense I thought our inhaling alone would give us giardiasis.

Audrey was having a surge of morning energy, so I taught her to pick the horses' feet and check for looseness of shoes. "Heavier than I expected," she said, leaning into Lefty and hoisting the front foot he presented her with a bent knee. The shoe was barely visible beneath a thick, compressed, rank-smelling pancake of manure. "And messy!" I handed her the hoof-pick with its right-angled head, and she pushed it in like a spading fork in a garden and levered out chunks until unveiling the bottom of his foot. The shoe was tight. In this department, I hoped never to find anything amiss, as if I did the whole trip would stop dead while I sent for Patrick. We weren't carrying spare horseshoe nails or a driving hammer; I didn't feel competent to use them. I was trusting implicitly to my dear one's clips and nails. Beyond that, it was one of those things I threw to the gods in general. These gods of mine are not the types to come punishing wrongdoing; they're more a force, way out past the positive posturing of *"believe* all will go well, and it will." They are something not at all cognitive. A jet stream, perhaps: Ride it high and don't look down!

The day had begun on a gucky note, and it was to continue that way. We waved our thanks and good-byes, and a half mile down the road, a wayward hailstorm nailed us head-on. I could barely swing the team around fast enough to let them take it in the rump, white pellets zinging off their black hide as though a barrage fired from within. Audrey and I huddled in the lee of the wagon, the taut canvas creating a drumhead over us. The pummeling stopped as suddenly as it had started, and shifted to rain as we set off again. Another half mile and the road surface turned into a semigumbo that began to cake up on the wheels, more seriously, to close the gaps to the brake blocks. The horses could not drag the wagon. Audrey climbed down and, walking along the grassy shoulder, periodically waded in and took a scraping stick to the brake blocks. We cleared the first small rise, but I knew there was a longer, steeper hill not too far ahead, and the muck was gaining on us. At the first flat spot in the road, there being no place to pull off, I stopped. Audrey threw the chocks in and then planted herself in front of the team while I unhooked the tugs. I had to adjust the brakes, get them as far away from the wheels as possible. Doing this required my dropping the lines: I needed to dig tools out of the back of the wagon, crawl under the bed, pull two cotter pins, and ratchet the adjustment out several turns. The road was one of little traffic, but in the curves we could see only a short distance in either direction. For the moment, the horses were fine and Audrey was fine. Audrey, I knew, had lots of grit— but she was not a six-foot-six Patrick, and not a horsewoman. If we were going to have company, I wanted to grab the lines. I kept my ears cocked and worked as fast as I could.

I finished so quickly I impressed myself. We were hooked up and rounding the next bend when we met a stout pickup with a stock rack on back. The driver eased gently past, bringing his load—a saddle horse, I couldn't say now even what color—abreast of Pancho. A sudden registering of what an oddity we were hit this horse, and it blew up. The racket sounded like a tap-dancing class working out in a steel culvert. And the spasm was catching. The boys collided sideways, as though each hoped the other was its savior, and jitterbugged ten steps down the road before I had them. When we were at a walk again, my heart momentarily seized—at what might have been, had the spastic horse met us ten minutes earlier.

Rolling along more easily now, we pulled the longer grade, moved out of gumbo territory, and turned up the Bloody Dick—canyon, creek, and road—which over the next days we would trail to the Big Hole Divide. When I first learned of the Bloody Dick, I thought, *Now there's a story that'll sell a book.* Didn't folks blush just reading the road sign! Visions of Lorena Bobbitt. Or at the very least, an ax murder—Dick, the perpetrator or the victim—hacked body parts staining crystalline creek water red. Research, however, revealed something less gruesome: The creek was named after, yes, a man named Richard, an Englishman known to rail about the state of things—"bloody this" and "bloody that."

Before the Hirschys' cow camp appeared around a bend, we endured one final incident of the day. Audrey had gone ahead on foot, wearing an orange vest and carrying a road crew's slow-and-stop sign, this our program when coming upon blind curves and hills. From the top of another long grade, she gave me the coast-is-clear signal to come ahead. I was wanting to drive the team dead up the middle of the narrow road, where the dirt was packed, as the sides were a soft, deep sand. Halfway up, I saw Audrey wildly waving her sign. An old green pickup came flying past her, careening down the middle of the road—the driver rude, blind, or drunk. I wheeled for the shoulder, and a second later Pancho and Lefty were earning their feed, digging in, bellies down, struggling to haul us back out.

You could get killed on a backcountry dirt road driving horses three miles per hour. I was protective of my gee-gees (a loving term for horses adopted from our gypsying theater friends), knowing they would absorb any pedal-to-the-floor impact ahead of me.

During our most extreme rants about the advance of so-called progress, Patrick and I find ourselves *wishing* Highway 93 back to dirt—hungering to slow things down, localize living, build community over commuting. We sometimes muse on taking a sledgehammer into the night, organizing pothole gangs. Nothing would delight us more than a return to horse-drawn travel. There would be no more careening green pickups, no more motor home extravaganzas, no more engine brakes—not to mention the added benefit of a small reprieve for the troposphere. Correspondingly, there would be no more sushi-and-theater nights out in Missoula, not all in one evening anyway. For that matter, no more sushi for inland Montana. Even in the abstract, at the prospect of relinquishing these favorites of indulgences, I can see us flinching (me more so than Patrick, who generally prides himself on the ability to slip into austerity mode without a sign of martyrdom). Seduction by the exotic! We are, in the bald truth of things, like the aboriginal family with their first television, not wanting to give it back. Worse perhaps, we are like the dreaded multi-national corporation, positioning greed to feed hedonism ahead of sensitivity, sustainability, saneness. Most certainly, we are—just by birth, and as anyone else— sorry specimens of a self-centered and for the most part gallivanting species. There is always the hope that rising gasoline prices will force a national refocusing: public transportation, carpooling, solar-powered engines. But eyes, recent history has shown, would likely turn first toward how to buttress petroleum resources, the madness that gets us into wars, that drives us toward drilling in wildlife preserves.

I'd joined, even led, campaigns over the years—to save wild rivers, to improve water quality, to head off sprawl. I had vigiled with candles, marched *for* this, marched *against* that. Through it all, I had learned two glaring things: I could not save the world, and I could not just do nothing. Short of diving into another consuming cause, making causes my lifework, as many of my friends admirably do, the question for me has become how to live, day to day, with the over-whelming feeling of impotence in the tide of progress's debris. To stave off doomsday thinking, to reside in the positive, I have come to believe in doing my part, in an individual manner, on a regular basis: lining up behind con-servation efforts and social and economic justice while steadily making inroads, however small, in my consumption—buying shade-grown coffee, supporting local organic grow-ers, passing up spring's first trucked-in boxes of aromatic strawberries (waiting instead for the Bitterroot's to ripen), curtailing the purchase of things MADE IN CHINA, persistently yanking up knapweed. All with the idea (however unlikely) that if *everyone* did her or his ten minutes or half hour a day, with our collective small shifts—just as with the power of voting that resides latently within the masses—pressures would come to bear, mountains would move. One could only hope. I know many people who do their parts, many who never will give it thought, and too many who think seventy miles an hour is *slow*.

My "part" at this moment concerned weeds, the prevention of their spreading. With Pancho and Lefty in the cow camp corral, I dragged from a shed one of the four certified weed-seed-free bales Steve had trucked in for us. I pried open my pocketknife, severed the two strings of orange plastic binder twine, and broke the loaf into flakes. No tough stems here, just long blades of a deep green that still held the pungent smell of a fresh-cut lawn. To ensure Pancho's getting his fair share, I tossed the flakes around widely.

Audrey and I luxuriated in the cozy and not totally primi-tive three-room cabin—laying over two nights, playing cards, reading, washing hair in sun-warmed pails of water, and showering under our solar bag strung up on the corral gatepost. Audrey hiked; the boys took it easy. I napped, sinking into far-gone comas.

At the second sunrise, my traveling juices were again primed. After breakfast, I watched as Audrey meticulously layered sticks in the woodstove and the cookstove's firebox. "This is my trademark," she said, the leaving of a ready-laid fire for the next comer. It was a thoughtful thank-you for the hospitality extended us in this instance, but to the sojourner wet, cold, hungry, stumbling into a remote Alaskan shore camp—the coast Audrey had paddled solo for the past fourteen summers—a ready-laid fire might have weightier import. Late morning found us hanging on the front fence, cameras trained, watching a cattle drive slowly funnel down the road. We had been asked to wait until it passed: A jingling wagon might spook the hundred carefully collected and orderly ambling cows being brought down from the high country for the winter. Steve, in his broad-brimmed tan Resistol and red neckerchief, sat his horse as though he was never meant to walk—cowboying the sweetest of his worlds and what he knew best.

With a fine day of sunshine at our backs, we wound farther on up the Bloody Dick to camp in the pines. While we were cooking a huge dinner—warmed up butter-and-mountain-sage potatoes Audrey had baked the day before, a large fried trout given us by the cow camp neighbors, and a pan of black beans with freshly made salsa—Steve arrived with the nightly hay. We invited him to dine. He seemed a little stunned by the waftings of sage and fish and garlic, perhaps even the sumptuousness of the fare, and though plainly curious about black beans, dug in with us, appreciative and praiseful.

We chatted about the day to follow—the stretch that, unbeknownst to anyone else, had had a vise grip on my gut ever since I'd driven over it in the truck. Before the team could get warmed up, we had a steep, blind scramble out of nearby (oxymoron-named) Reservoir Lake, followed by a fairly steady six-mile climb to the pass. Then came the harrowing section, the first mile and a half of descent. Here one-lane switchbacks are closely hemmed in by lodgepole pine forest and berms of rock. The road surface itself is largely of blasted or chiseled rock, leaving succeeding humps, ledges, slides, holes, cuts. Behind the windshield, in first gear, I had bucked, swayed, dropped, fairly lurched into tree trunks. It felt like a wild high-seas ride. Since then, deep in the night my imaginings had the wagon's steel-rimmed wheels and the team's steel shoes alternately slipping and wedging in. There was potential for broken wheels, pulled shoes, torn tendons—at worst, downed horses with the wagon run over top. Steve and I had pondered various drag devices, one being to chain a heavy log to the rear axle. I had made no provision for this, and it looked as though Steve, who had thought to be available, was pressed for a day of cutting fence rails before winter, on up the mountain in a different direction: a case of chores for staying alive before frivolousness. When the time came for it, I would have to trust soundly in the Great Spirit, and another brake adjustment.

It was a cold morning, ice trimming the creek, and we broke camp, heading out in good time. Audrey waved me on. I chirped to the boys, starting them up the immediate brutal hill. They leaned hard into their collars, paired up their steps, and hauled me skyward. I trusted in their hearts but found their conditioning far advanced from what I'd assumed. As we leveled out, they fell comfortably back to their individual paces—Pancho to his big-boned, swinging stride from the Clydesdale Patrick and I suspected was in him, and Lefty, more the Percheron, finer leg bones and big-muscled chunk of a butt (our "body builder"), taking three tight steps to Pancho's two.

The route to the Big Hole Divide placed us parallelly east

and beneath the spine of the Continental Divide. On the winding ascent, Audrey regaled me with stories from yet wilder country: the grizzly bear that had worked on the doorknob of her Alaskan cabin; the killer whale that had surfaced a few feet from her kayak and rolled her an inquisitive eye. I had been thinking all along that the next few days, terrain-wise, and this time of year, posed possibilities for encounters with the largest animals of these parts, black bears. Beneath the lid clamped on my mind there had been simmering this further agitation—of what the horses, glimpsing a bear, might do. I needn't have worried. With their clompity-clomping reverberating off the hard-packed road, the jingling of harness and creaking of wagon, and Audrey's and my yelled directions and banter, any bear in the vicinity would have headed for lunch in Idaho.

In fact, during our traveling hours, no wildlife was in evidence beyond the occasional hawk circling on thermals and a few distant skittering deer. The countryside had a "species depleted" feel to it—a preview, as I thought about it, of the predictions on extinctions. Would we, *Homo sapiens*, remain so preoccupied with our own clompity-ing and jingling as to not notice? Or would we, inch by inch, adjust to losing things? The way folks I knew living with the crime rate in Los Angeles had accepted over the years not walking the streets after dark, not venturing out at night at all.

The last time I had visited the sprawling coastal metropolis, I was cautioned to keep my purse between my feet instead of tossed casually upon the bench of a booth where I sat in a benign enough looking cafe. A pall of fear hung all about. Gated communities that I drove past were status neighborhoods not solely for their privacy: They indicated a wherewithal to afford protection. I found my old San Fernando Valley home posted with three signs touting armed security patrols. On a friend's TV one afternoon, we watched live coverage shot from a helicopter chasing an assailant from some crime as he fled through double-decker freeway mazes, onto treed residential streets, eventually into a suburb cul-de-sac. With the helicopter hovering overhead, he jumped several backyard privacy fences before police finally pinned him. The running commentary had echoed the high-drama, who's-winning tone of a football game broadcast. "Chase the Criminal!" It was flat-out entertainment—who needed sit-coms? I was stunned. Had I so fast become a country hick naive to my previous world? Or did it take someone from the outside to see my city friends were gone mad, inured to such bizarre living—its having crept so slowly upon them they had registered no note of peculiarity, severity, sickness? Was I to suppose their loss in safe mobility had somehow been pacifyingly replaced by a gain in entertainment? Was some similar demise to be the fate of the world's animals—a con-tentment in our watching reruns on TV? Were our basically denial-happy and accommodating human natures to allow us no escape, from just lying down and embracing huge losses in species—making a million minuscule adjustments to, find-ing unknown delights in, demolished diversity? There are people who believe in preserving trains, not wanting their grandchildren to *not* know what a train is. If you never heard of a bear, would you care?

We broke into a small clear-cut and then a flat area that told me we were on the divide. It was time for a lunch break and a regrouping. Parked at the roadside, we unhitched the horses and tied them to the wagon. Audrey and I snacked on gorp and cheese, the boys on hay. All of us downed water. Having walked a good distance for our early warning sys-tem, Audrey stretched out on the wagon seat and slipped into a nap; I crawled under the wagon to pull cotter pins and adjust brakes within a hair of the wheels. In Patrick's and my touring, I had driven the uphill and flat stretches, he the pronounced downhills. This was because, at the normal brake adjustment of an inch gap, his extralong leg was needed on the center-front brake bar. To jam the brake on hard put me in a tenuous position, with my bottom off the seat and my braking foot extended well beyond the front of the wagon. Add to that the forward tip of the bed, and I was in imminent danger of taking the slanted front combing like a big slide and landing snarled in the doubletree and tugs. For this trip, I'd taken up the normal adjustment by half (reset after our day in the muck), and, for traction, I had mounted a piece of tire tread on the steel bar where I stepped on it. We could not camp on the pass all night—and to what avail?—and I was not of a mind for retreating. There was nothing for it now but to ratchet in, hitch up, and hit the downslope square-on.

Coming off the divide, we wound down into the thick of the forest with Audrey onboard. There was not a thing she could do for us in here on foot. There were only two skimpy places in the switchbacks where I could pull over if need be, and our blinking light, we hoped, strobing through the forest of skinny-trunked trees, would emanate some warning of our presence. We intended to pause occasionally to listen for engine roar.

Immediately the steel-rimmed wheels began to tool our trail into the stone. I kept Pancho and Lefty pulled in, giving them added tension on the bit to keep them taking it slowly, to offer them a forward point to steady upon while they fished for footing, and to communicate "Hey, hey, my sweets—heads up! I'm with you!" Staying unswervingly attentive to the business of braking (my noon adjustment was keeping my butt on the seat), I slowed the wagon's momentum, but not so strongly that it caused the horses to pull, just enough to hold the breeching off their bums and allow them to concentrate on keeping upright. The wagon did not lurch and buck in the manner the truck had. Its large-in-diameter wheels spanned the faults and holes; its beefy springs mellowed our ride. "Easy, big guys, you're doing fine." Had I not been so thoroughly focused, I might have laughed at their little Betty Boop steps in their fullered shoes—the bottom-side creases of which, packed with dirt, were affording them just enough traction.

No engines whined. We snaked through the shaded turns and, before we guessed it, flowed out the bottom into a sunny meadow. Audrey cheered, "That was great! I wasn't scared at all." She meant it as a compliment to my driving. But I was wondering if someone had smoothed out the road in the eight weeks since I'd seen it last. Wondering if night imaginings had gotten the better of me. Or if a team and wagon, after all, were better suited to a few things beyond just a rational pace of living.

A couple more miles—and a week into my trip—at Skinner Meadows, we met Rikki and Jon for a changing of my companion in adventure, and with the night's serving of certified weed-seed-free hay. We were a foursome for dinner, and Audrey had a fresh audience to regale with Alaska stories. My mind played over too many things to partake for long. I carried a bucket into the bushes for a bath and listened to the laughter from afar. Then I worked on harness and collars and readied the articles we would need for greasing the wheels. In the morning, after "Safe journeys!" were said all around, Audrey rode with Jon back to Patrick, who delivered her to the Missoula airport. It was Rikki and I who were feeding and grooming, harnessing and hitching and setting out.

The day ahead had more mileage than usual to it, but we were on the downhill run, and the boys took up a perky pace. Several vehicles met us, coming in from Jackson. From one, Rikki copped a beer. She'd been enjoying the warm autumn sun, scouting ahead on foot, telling drivers to watch for the wagon. Her dark, Gibson girl tresses, with wisps come loose and gone wild, coupled with her lanky-legged hip swinging proved too intriguing for a carload of early hunters to pass up pausing for a come-on. When I caught up, she flashed me a cockeyed smirk and said in her South African–flattened British, "Kauthleeeen—want hauf a warm beer?" I dithered for a second on my propensity for being a cheap drunk, half a beer could sometimes do it, and promptly settled on "Sure!" Then queried, "You managed to keep from them where we're camped tonight, right?" So wrong.

She climbed on until we came to the next cattle guard. Here, where a head-high pine sprouted in the middle of the gate opening and I was preparing to break out the saw, Rikki cleverly bent the tree over and rolled a rock on top. I took the challenge—perfectly between the ponies and between the wheels. There would have been chaos had it loosened and gone *boing*, but I was feeling pretty heady—the divide, the beer, and all. As the tailgate cleared it, Rikki pushed off the rock and swung the gate closed, leaving the puzzle for the next wagon. *When would that be?*

We were scheduled to camp at an unusually glorious spot, beside a pond and what looked like a small, deserted, charmingly weathered, two-story house but was in actuality two one-room schoolhouses—one atop the other—situated where the valley first opened up. When we arrived the sun was sinking behind the Big Hole's backdrop, a long bowing string of peaks, including Monument, Freeman, Homer Young, Ajax,* Center, Squaw,† Jumbo, and Sheep.

---

*Known once for its silver mine but more recently for the mountain fall taken by Hank Williams, Jr.

†Soon to be renamed. In Native American cultures, the word *squaw* carries sexually vulgar connotations.

But the gate was unexpectedly locked. We left, sorrowfully and without the boys' dinner, which I'd dragged inside the schoolhouses two weeks earlier. Scurrying against dark, we drove on to the main Dooling Ranch, two more miles. The ranch manager, George, informed us the lock we had seen on the backside of the gate *was* open, had we inspected it more closely. He directed us past houses and barns to a high hay-field, swathed clean, that offered a mouth-gaping, around-the-world view—no second fiddle in a campsite (and carload of hunters foiled!). Then he offered to run back for our specialty hay. The night was crystal clear and cold and, perhaps just in my imagination, still smelling sweetly of hay. The texture of the field's blond stubble might have been the bristles of a mammoth scrub brush. We crunched around on it, cooking dinner in the dark. Then rolled out our bedding beneath an inverted bowl of more stars than I have ever seen.

In the morning, Katya, with directions to the school-houses, found us from her name scrawled in bright crayon on a paper plate festooned with curly ribbons and stuck to the old yellow grader blade serving as the ranch's signpost. George's wife, Cindy, had welcomed us into their abode to help with strategic realignments and shuttle arrangements.

Katya brought news of the outside world. The United Nations' Fourth World Conference on Women was being held in Beijing and had produced a visionary prediction for the twenty-first century: "women no longer walking the earth several paces behind men." In traversing the valley floor, mountains now jutting up in all directions, we puffed up likewise in feeling ourselves the United Nations' Big Hole International Covered Wagon Contingency, representing three widely flung parts of the world: Norway, South Africa, Montana. This was a glory day—all sunshine, extraordinary open vistas, high spirits, girl laughter. Sometime in the after-noon, we came across seven head of Black Angus wandering the road from a sagging spot in a fence. At the sight of us, six vaulted back in, while one lined out wrongly and trotted down the road. It missed a couple more opportunities to return to its clan, and we began to think we might scare this hefty beast all the way into Jackson. I stopped the team, and Katya climbed down to "herd a cow" in her accomplished Norwegian way, but the animal was by now skittery as hell. We hoped to push it behind us, where it might sprint for home. Soon a van packed with men tourists appeared, one canted half out a window steadying a camcorder, capturing this Wild West scene to take home. Katya walked up to the driver's side and in her sweetest little Suzy Cream Cheese voice said, "Oooo, could you help us with this cow?" Later, mission accomplished, everything on video and the men driven on, Rikki and I teased Katya about employing her feminine wiles.

Late in the afternoon, we sat hip-to-hip on the wagon seat, too-cool grinning, rolling down the main street of Jackson—all of its two half blocks. Katya caught a ride with Cindy back to her car, and Rikki and I swung in and parked behind the Jackson Hot Springs Lodge, where a grand, massive old barn held our hay and a corral ran with a stream of clear water. The boys fed and settled, we checked into the resort. I had reserved a two-room suite with a fireplace. The unlikelihood of such lavishness and leisure on a wagon trip was not lost on me. It went with my stocking the wagon with Medaglia d'Oro instant espresso, watermelon pickles, macadamia nuts, dried papaya.

Unpacking, Rikki called from her room, "I brought my cozzy." Then she stood in the doorway, dangling from her forefinger a fetching black Parisian bathing suit—or, from the British influence in South Africa, a "swim costume." We had the outdoor hot pool all to ourselves, though I sat with only my toes in, having developed some gross fungus on the backs of my knees. No doubt a prairie woman's plague. Only conjecture tells us now what all unsoundnesses developed beneath those voluminous skirts at a time when to speak or write of ailments, including pregnancies, was not to embroider beyond "feeling poorly."

We denned up for two nights, dining in the resort restaurant, reading, writing postcards, and me running loads of laundry. I wasn't the first woman to do laundry on a wagon stopover, though my means and conditions offered decidedly more convenience. Westering women in the 1800s had washed clothes in creeks and hot springs and by hanging them out in the rain. Many managed even to iron, which was more than I was considering. Laundry was a recurring topic in *Covered Wagon Women*, the eleven volumes I had lately been reading of collected diaries and letters edited by Kenneth L. Holmes. Twenty-year-old Viola Springer, on the Oregon Trail, camped near Fort Hall, Idaho, wrote in her diary of August 6, 1885, after a previous day of washing: "We did not do any ironing yesterday. We have quit ironing." Yet the washing topic itself bordered on the obsessive. Her entry September 14: "We want to stop here and wash today but Martha and Alvin do not want to. We are going to wash some before we get in to Harney for we have no clean close for a change. Martha says they have some clean close and they don't haft to wash. They say they are not a going to stop to wash but I know that we are. We would wait though untill we get there if we had a change of clean close. We havent though only what is packed away." And the ironing revolt was short-lived. September 16: "We washed this forenoon. We all laid over. Martha she washed and so did Morna. Mrs. Murphy was not able to wash. She is better this evening. I ironed the colored clothes this afternoon. Morna brought her dress and bonnet here and ironed them. They have their irones packed away."

.   .   .

Wined, dined, rested, and ready to hitch again, we found ourselves standing in the middle of the Big Hole, trying on its morning vastness, when our most cherished men arrived. Patrick and Jon tossed their gear in the wagon, and the four of us set out for three days of gently picking our way across hay and range ground at the hospitality of more of the Hirschy family—Dick (Steve's father), Heidi, and Jack. I feel more than just a little fondness for western cattle ranchers, their hard, close-to-the-ground, colorful way of life—and their large landholdings. Creek degradation, water pollution, and unsavory cow-pie camping not to be made light of, wildlife still roams their vast acres. These are a people who love the western country, love the land, the animals, the rivers, as much as anyone. Portions of Big Hole ranches, I learned, have been put into conservation easements. These intact expanses—coupled with the Big Hole's harsh climate—stand, mercifully, and one hopes forever, as a stronghold against urban sprawl.

Aside from the gorgeous country, it was a grim three days. The skies opened up with a bitter driven rain, even hail. And Patrick and I were seriously out of sync. A few days of "getting away from it all" was not his idea of fun. He was, after a fashion, a reverse snob, turning up his nose at the elitism buried in the notion of "a vacation." To his mind, satisfying travel, true travel, could be had only by heading out with no home to return to. He would sooner hit the work world without sidetracking breaks, until the day we could leave for a year or two. Our philosophical differences on leisure-time needs had jumped right up between us. Moreover, from his perspective of chief home support coordinator— of phones and airports and sorting out the shuttling of hay, fresh groceries, blocks of ice—he already was seeing the staggering folly in my advance across centuries and millenniums. Altogether, he was in no fine humor. With a hurry-hurry, he dove into chores in a silent, maniacal manner—where he goes when troubled. I, instead of being undyingly grateful for my first real help, felt him moving in on my show. *Hadn't I been doing just fine?* I crept around the edges of his mood, aching for playful banter and romance, and working up a good being pissed. Not infrequently I glanced over at Rikki and Jon, who seemed never to be at odds over anything, but rather effervesced a constant, reciprocal adoration—a condition I generally viewed as toxic to a relationship, but theirs had never shown any signs of sickness, nothing but healthy, loving caring, and oddly mutual goals. I found myself falling into an old trick bag of mine, that of comparing, and then fighting the feeling Patrick and I were the ill-matched "ugly couple."

On the last day with the four of us together, we were climbing a seemingly endless rise when Lefty, in his inimitable way, served to loosen our moods. It is probably the effort, the extra strain, of his leaning hard into the collar when trudging uphill that causes him to explode in farts. Rikki, under the lap robes with me, broke out in astonished giggles. Walking at Lefty's shoulder, Jon turned and shot us a sideways grin, while the fourth of us continued pensively to plod at the other side of the wagon. I paused to let the horses catch their breath, and Patrick, evidently having been doing a little reminiscing, burst forth with a story. "When I drove tours on Mackinac Island there was a team of big Belgians, Ike and Mamie. Ike was great! He had a long-standing intestinal disorder, he never fully digested his grain. Every fourth or fifth step, he'd fart, and blow a puff of oat hulls at the passenger seated behind him."

A round of laughs.

Then another story. This one from Aspen. While running a sleigh-ride business, Patrick had been asked to bring a second sled to a winter wedding in the woods, and he'd hitched up a team with a notorious bay. "The minister," he said, "was just coming to the part 'Now, Bromley, do you take this woman to be your wife, to have and to hold, in sickness and in health,' and the big gelding's cheeks parted: The base tremolo of an African elephant! *Everyone* heard it."

"The horse that farts," Jon chortled, "will never tire." It was a recitation, we all knew this one.

All together now: "The man who farts is the man to hire."

"A man who hasn't farted when he's worked," Rikki exclaimed, "can't ever have really worked!"

And the woman who farts? Don't we get to fart? Jeez, Kathleen—not just now.

Puckering up, I blew Lefty a kiss. Patrick a bigger one.

With a steady cold drizzle settling in, we arrived at the hilltop and also a padlocked gate, where Jon and Patrick were already conversing with a man who had come from the other side on a four-wheeler. I had the immediate sense their confab was not progressing well. With three days' growth of beard, our men may have resembled gypsy vagabonds, but certainly not terrorists, and with women on the wagon seat in the background, it was a scene that—in the manner of Sacagawea with Lewis and Clark—exuded peaceful intentions. Soon the two of them trotted back to us and Patrick said, "He's not going to let us pass. Maybe you should try."

I stepped to the gate to speak to a man whose eyebrows were leveled into a steady glower at me. He was a ranch manager or caretaker, probably about my age, but it was hard to tell: He might have been cleaner had he just come from wrestling pigs. His ranch jacket and jeans did not carry their soil on the surface; dirt, sweat, calf scours, God-knows-what gave off an impression of being ground in over months, maybe years; the fabrics stood now to go *pffft* with any kind of cleaning. Not in thirty years had I encountered a person of quite this asocial caliber. Not since a girlfriend and I had clambered onto the only empty barstools in a hotel pool-room in the little town of Washington in California's Sierras, and found ourselves seated next to a hulking mountain man in a grizzly state of filth, his broken jaw (and maybe his skull and neck) wired up to pins poking out of his forehead, his big lips wrapped around a straw through which he suctioned beer, and grunted. He might have been the most upstanding man in the county, but at my tender age it took only a first-impression gander to catapult me off that stool. The man now planted before me—triply dirtied, I took further note with a wince, all about the crotch of his pants—I might have categorically slotted as *the* peerless despicable specimen hereabouts, had not my heart gone out to him at observing a dozen black, cancerous-looking growths on his lips, chin, and one cheek.

"Hello, sir," I said, trying for a respectful tone. I explained that our hay was in a shed at the other end of the ranch, that we had permission to travel on through and camp at the cow corral. He was having none of it. I quoted his boss as the man who had offered us the shortcut. "Never heard it," he said.

It was now time for *my* feminine wiles.

"Perhaps he hasn't had a chance to call you," I said, in a dulcet tone, going on that the weather (any fool could see!) was cold and stormy, that within the hour darkness would descend, and that it was probably more than ten miles back down this road and around the long way. My Mr. Triple Filthy, it turned out, had heartstrings as well, and I had plucked one. "Okay, go on through," he growled, with which his head tilted slightly, catching a different slant of light, and I noticed a glistening about his chin. His skin affliction, as it were, showed itself to be a copious slick of saliva, ferrying around rafts of chewing tobacco. But he was unlocking the gate, barking, "Turn right at the barn."

A winding two-mile tour through several more gates

brought us to the cow corral, where we unhitched. Patrick and Rikki pitched in with chores, while Jon disappeared in the dusk, hitching a ride to retrieve their pickup. All of them soon to drive off, deserters, heading back to the workaday world.

So, now I was alone. And cold. Suffering from dehydration. Dawn had flared up into daylight—the inside of the wagon was glowing like the *inside* of a lightbulb, blinding me through my eyelids. There was no more sleeping; nothing now but to brave it. Still with my Carhartts zipped up, I pulled on boots and mittens and crawled out the front, over the seat. One foot fishing down the side for the wheel top, I jumped to the ground. A bale of certified weed-seed-free hay sat by the corral gate. Breaking it open, I picked up an armload and pushed my nose in deep, taking comfort from its sweet smell. The horses were blowing big, gauzy trumpet clouds out their nostrils, and, pleased to see breakfast, they dove right in. I retrieved the water pails; they were empty, save for a coating of ice, and knocked about from the boys trying to extract drinks that weren't there. Across the road, I found a fast-running ditch, where I dipped in the buckets and then filtered a bottle of my own. The pumping warmed me up. A quart and a half downed and I began to feel better.

My next companion in adventure was Jan, member of the local ski patrol, horsewoman, and my hairdresser. I expected her about eleven o'clock. She arrived exactly on time, with four bales of certified weed-seed-free hay and the flu. Pulling her van off the dirt road, she stayed tucked inside with the heater running while I harnessed. Today's route was the one section I had not scouted. In part, because I had run out of time and, in other part, because I had been supplied a detailed map. "Can't miss it" were the words accompanying the description. It all seemed plain enough, beginning with: Turn east at the green gate.

With the sun warming the afternoon, Jan climbed on board and we started up Little Swamp Creek Road to trail in on a back entrance to the Ruby Ranch. Upon entering the timber, as described, we located a green gate and swung in. Before long we emerged from the woods and arrived at a washed-out bridge over a small, placid creek. Jan tugged on my gumboots, climbed down, and waded in. "The bottom's hard!" she yelled. I drove Pancho and Lefty down the easy slope, and we splashed across. These horses knew creeks and rivers; they had crossed many in Patrick's and my travels. Though on the present trip I had managed to avoid pavement, except for short stretches, and unless you count tire tracks through hayfields, the fording of this creek was our first true off-roading. Flinging up a big spray produced a pure joy in me and I sensed in the horses, too. This was serious adventure now, a day of unknowns lay ahead, and I found myself rising to the challenge and fun of it. But then abruptly, we arrived at a place of impassable faults, a perfectly odd sheered-off bank with a several-foot vertical drop, something an earthquake might leave, with no possible way forward. Wrong green gate. No rear door to the Ruby. Nothing for it but to backtrack.

Here challenge took on a new face and one, I daresay, more thoroughly matching that of long ago frontier travel— albeit it was not cholera one of us was down with. With Jan on the seat again, I swung the horses back alongside the wagon and spun us around, grateful for the fifth wheel's tight-turning radius. Maybe it was having to cope with disappointing changes at an ebb in my strength; maybe it was the turn in the weather or the something I ate for breakfast; whatever it was, it began working on parts of me like Drāno in plumbing pipes. Jan, sapped of all color now—even the lovely blond of her hair looked dull—was forced again to crawl down off the wagon. I snatched up the small, always-keep-it-handy ammo box containing toilet accoutrements, leaped to the ground, threw in the chocks. In my race for the woods, I left Jan to stand in front of the team. With her back turned to me, I chose the first likely spot to hang off the back of a downed log. Everything would have turned out fine in a matter of ten or so minutes, except there came twenty head of cattle moseying from the direction of the green gate and behind them, pushing them along, the vaquero strangely named Isabel (EEs-ah-bell). We had met him—"Hola!" "Howdy!"—only briefly on the road two hours earlier. I was about to meet him again, only this time with my pants down. What I hurriedly accomplished behind that log was not anything the author of the properest outdoor-crap manual would applaud. But by golly, I was back at the lines before the cows split and poured around the wagon.

Isabel had no idea how to get through to the Ruby. The day was getting away from us, and Jan was miserable. Her shuttle—the friend she had arranged with that morning to help her retrieve her van, a day earlier than planned—would soon be leaving home to pick her up at our evening's projected destination, ten miles from where we stood. Jan needed to get to a phone. With Isabel, and our rusty Spanish, we drew up a new plan—to bag the Ruby, head down the valley toward Wisdom, and park wagon, horses, and hay at Isabel's little abode, which sat beside an uncountable number of handy corrals. Jan, by van, would go on ahead to find a phone, then double back and deliver me to a motel in town.

Westwarding settlers of the 1800s when faced with delays had rarely taken shelter in paid lodgings, or, for that matter, come upon towns. Wisdom was to me a welcome sight, and with its 101 residents, 20 of whom attended the grade school, it was hardly a culture shock from horse-touring the backcountry.

"Feel better," I said to Jan as she left. And then I settled in at the Nez Perce Motel for a night of not freezing.

Patrick and I weren't due to rendezvous again until the Continental Divide. Before he could reschedule his shoeing appointments and drive to the Big Hole, I had laid over another day, hitchhiking—how many years since I'd last hitchhiked?—out to chat with Isabel, snag a few things from the wagon, smooch with the horses, stretch out their hay. My trip was fizzling out, but I didn't quite know it yet.

With Patrick preferring to stump alongside, I drove the team out of Isabel's and right up the main highway toward the mountains. It is only a two-lane, yet busy enough, with motorists honking, waving, pausing to click pictures and ask the perennial two questions: "Where did you come from?" and "Where are you going?" The sharp clatter of traveling on macadam pushed my splash through the creek back to a distant dream.

That afternoon we passed the Big Hole National Battlefield. It was here, on August 9, 1877, in a creek-laced meadow, that Colonel Gibbon and his Seventh Infantry jumped the sleeping family encampment of Chief Joseph and the Nez Perce. Though the creek still runs in gentle bends and the birds sing, I find it an untenable place of anguish buried in the ground, with unsettling rufflings of grass. Next we drove by the other entrance to the Ruby Ranch, with its garage still holding two moldy bales from my first hay run. Once into timber again, we pulled off to camp. I started the chores, while Patrick took a good downhill rip on his bicycle (carried in the wagon) to shuttle forward his truck and our infernal hay. The following day was approximately the same routine, landing me a mile up the mountain from May Creek Campground, where, awaiting my next companion in adventure, I was scheduled to camp for two nights in a meadow just down the embankment from the highway. Patrick unloaded four bales and kissed me goodbye.

The day was pleasant enough weather-wise, but otherwise a weird one. I spent it reading and lounging, an autumn sun warming my bedroll, which I'd thrown down on the wagon's off side. It was a pretty camp with scattered mature pines and the clear, burbling waters of alder-lined Trail Creek bordering its backside. A tall covered wagon, however, turned out to be a billboard to highway traffic and here, along a roadside, I began to suffer my return to civilization. So many people stopped and peered down at me, I started to get kind of crazed. In the late afternoon, two helmetless motorcyclists pulled off onto the shoulder, dug out binoculars, and for twenty minutes scoped out my camp. Hidden behind the wagon, I peered back at them through my own binoculars, poking the telescoping ends between spokes of a wheel. I thought at one point we locked gazes. Fear began to move in; I rummaged around for weapons. I had a sledgehammer and two hay hooks. It was after dark that I worried about. When the time came for bed, I crawled under the wagon, truncheon and spikes at the ready. I could not sleep. An hour went by. Headlights turned in, paused at the gate, and started down the meadow toward me. Best to be bold, I thought. Never having gotten undressed, I rolled out to meet the vehicle. Fast talk brewing on my tongue, I marched forth decisively. I kept in plain sight but out of the main beams, hay hook held behind my thigh.

Out of the night, rang a little voice. "Hi, Kathy! Sorry I'm late." I almost collapsed in relief. It was Linda, not due—by my schedule—until morning. She was new in the Bitterroot, a veterinarian come from Nebraska, and once cozy with a team of Belgians. Her man friend, driving, turned to me and asked, "How come you're toting around a hay hook?"

"I thought you were rapists," I said, though I really hadn't thought anything so precisely until he asked. Too freaked, I suppose, I hadn't allowed my mind to linger on just what types of weirdos would make a nighttime visit.

Linda threw out a small duffel, an air mattress, and two sleeping bags, one to stuff inside the other, and, as it was already late, her friend quickly departed.

We were soon settled in, and sleeping. Two hours later, I awoke to ponderous sloshings in the creek and immediately the horses were running. They took off crashing and splashing toward May Creek Campground, having broken through their fence. A moose, it was. Equally spooked, it, too, fled, though upstream, in the direction from which it had come. I cautioned Linda to stay put; the boys didn't know her well. Grabbing the halters from where I kept them under the wagon, I snatched up a pail, threw in two handfuls of grain, and headed down the meadow with a flashlight. Steel fence posts were bent cockeyed, and orange fence wire, ripped in several places, was strewn through willows and sagebrush like toilet paper strung by kids over trees and houses on Halloween. The night was clear and cold, no moon. I could hear my gee-gees still running, cracking branches, blundering along, fleeing with their fright—and they were a long way away. I threw them my high-pitched, yodel-yell "Yuooh-hoo!" Twice. Their running stopped. I couldn't believe it. I let loose a second double call. The running started up again. Damn! I didn't know what else to do but start picking my way through the brush and the myriad crooks of creek in their direction, or perhaps hike parallelly down the highway. I stood pondering for a moment and, in that time, noticed the racket they were sending up was getting louder. They were running toward me!

In the blackness of the night, their dark forms came like phantoms thundering past. I thought they must be seeing better than I was, but they didn't stop. They went straight for the wagon. I found them huddling in the bushes, jittering about. "Hey, you guys, where aaare you?" I cooed. "Are you all right? Ponch, Lefty, did you think it was Sasquatch?" They lined right up. I felt even Lefty's warm breath in my face. They were shaking, nervously snorting, looking for comfort, not grain. I hugged their heads and necks and slipped on their halters.

With Linda holding the flashlight, we mended fence for an hour; then all of us settled down to quiet for the rest of the night.

Though we got off to a late start, by early afternoon we were again on a dirt track, following the Trail Creek drainage almost to Gibbon Pass. A small, deserted campground became home that night. It would turn out to be my last. Linda's friend came to get her about the same time Patrick arrived with our rations of hay. The following day, we were planning to pop over the Continental Divide and wind down the long, snaking grade to Camp Creek Inn—a bed-and-breakfast horse operation.

After steaming bowls of oatmeal and raisins, coffee for me, we caught up the horses. While Patrick broke down the fence, I measured out grain. This morning I held the pails, one at a time, feeding first Lefty, then Pancho. Their big, soft lips Hoovered the handfuls off my palm. I had no one scheduled for a companion in adventure; nights were getting colder; a week of snow and rain was predicted. Yet the deciding factor was Pancho. Or my love for him. He was starting to sore up. His collar offered no more notches for me to

cinch on; it had become too big, so fit was he. The looseness
was generating a rocking motion that had rubbed the hair off
his skin. It wasn't blistered yet, but I knew he was hurting
deeper in.

I picked his feet clean and then, in a pleasuring of us both,
slowly groomed him, running the brush and currycomb over
his sleek coat, fluffing out his tail. When I lifted the collar to
slip it on, he raised his nose in the air protesting: Not today!
He laid his ears back. It was the silliest attempt to look mean,
and then agreeably he pushed his nose on through. This was
the last I could ask of him. The road ahead, but for a mile,
was all downhill; he wouldn't have to lean into his collar,
though it would still rock. I hoped the friction would not
open him up before we cleared the bottom.

Horses have historically dealt altering influences on travel.
Had I been a westering homesteader with no one along to
rescue me, I might have driven this team until they dropped
in their traces, or I might have spared them and settled on
the very piece of ground where I felt they could stagger no
farther. How many times had I seen the bleached bones of
homesteads tucked in the most out-of-the-way, unremit-
tingly inhospitable of nooks, leaving me to ponder: Why
here?

Yet incontestable were the things that had gone well with
my trip. Perhaps my friend with the planets would indeed
tell me they were not at their squarest. I had known enough
to *want* to inhibit knapweed's spread into the high country.
The broad sweeps of rolling range, the strings of muscled
mountains, the under-the-open-sky living had rejuvenated
my corralled soul. Pancho and Lefty and I had become an
enduring threesome: a Team. We could have survived the
machine-gunning racket of an engine brake simultaneously
from front, side, and rear. Were there no cattle guards ahead

and no national forest lands with certified weed-seed-free hay regulations, were it summer instead of winter coming on, intoxicated, I might have found myself restocking the wagon and jingling along until another September. There was no disputing that the withering little corn sprout of my personal power had grown thick and tall as a harvest stalk. Lastly—in our three weeks of slamming along slubby roads, through rock, brush, and creek waters, the gee-gees had lost not one of Patrick's shoes. His skill. My luck. Ah, risk. Adventure. A woman's fortune!

I took a long gander at the back trail and made the arrangements—to trailer horses and wagon home.

Addendum: A rough guess puts it at 287 gallons of gasoline to support my petroleum-free touring—due in large part, but not wholly, to messing with certified weed-seed-free hay. Most of the vehicles employed were pickup trucks. Counting all parties, and including beforehand scouting and researching, there were *two and a half* trips to Salmon, *four and a half* to Bannack, *one* to Dillon, *three and a half* to Horse Prairie, *three* up the Bloody Dick, *two* to Skinner Meadows, *three and a half* to the Dooling Ranch, *four* to Jackson, *four* to the Wisdom area, *one* to the Ruby Ranch and Big Hole National Battlefield, *three* to May Creek, *three* to Trail Creek, *four* to Camp Creek, *two* to the Missoula International Airport. Plus countless local runs for groceries, tack, gear, hay. And a cell phone.

Ever Changing, Ever Stuck

The Fading Rural

For ten years now, we have lived in the long shadow of the mountains strung north and south—on this corner, and awaiting a visit from real gypsies who would take us to task for our name, Romany. The sun continues to rise over the Sapphires and sink in Day-Glo riots behind the Bitterroots. The mountain peaks hold their craggy majesty. The barn persists in filling up with critters. Mammals of the larger mountain species carry on ambling up and down the watershed, albeit with increasing difficulty. The creek waters tumble ever faithfully to the river, which keeps on braiding back and forth—running with fish and gouging out heavenly swimming holes. Much remains unchanged. Yet I'm like a skittery horse ready to bolt.

What might have changed, to my way of thinking, has not, while the rest is turning over with such speed it renders me heartsick, sometimes rageful, and, in one respect, fully fearful for my life. (In the fight or flight syndrome, I've left out—someone might be thinking—wanting to fight. I did that already, for the greater part of six years with the campaign for a better highway design: one safer, more community friendly, less growth inducing.) In this regard, my feelings are not unique to the year 2000. Almost a century and a half ago, and at every juncture with *crowding* since, there have been valley residents to proclaim, in so many words: "The Bitterroot has gone to hell!" In 1866, it was Jim Simonds, known as Delaware Jim (a Delaware Indian). As recounted in *The Lost Horizon*—a local family history written by Glenn Chaffin—it was to Glenn's great-grandfather Elijah, returning from a yearlong trip, that Delaware Jim said, "Well, my friend, things is bad. The damned Missourians are coming in here so fast, they're about to push us white folks out of the country." *Things is*, of course, worse now. Though it's all in a person's perspective. New arrivals—no matter the year—will stand transfixed in awe at the montane beauty.

With that said and this chapter the end of my tale, I will begin close to home. Here life is good. Patrick and I are married, without the ceremony. In Montana, once you publicly present yourselves as husband and wife, you are considered legally married. Circumstances naturally arise when it is more advantageous to be husband and wife; there are just some people better left in the dark as to unwed arrangements. I think Mike, our wholesome-faced lad of a loan officer, was the first. (He has since been promoted to president of the bank.)

Patrick's and my relationship, in its state of being officially unsanctioned and theologically unblessed, might best be described by the Gaelic *sinn fein*, "together alone." I don't tell him how to shoe horses, he doesn't tell me how to write, though as the years accumulate we are becoming more open to suggestion. That, in itself, is something self-blessed and divine. Someday when we are flush with time and money, we will marry. Weddings, to my mind, are for the purpose of the asking and the answering, followed by a great good bash with friends. There has been but one problem for us with any of this—in my writing. Some women nonfiction writers relegate husbands to the dusty attics of their works; the reader barely knows a testosterone personality exists. That's one way of saying "These writings are mine." Patrick, however, because of the person he is, supplies me with a wealth of idiosyncratic material I can't leave alone. To soften his inhabitancy, I at first took to labeling him "my mate" and presenting him anecdotally without a name. When the manuscript for this book first circulated for publication, two high-powered New York editors informed me that *mate* would never fly—it must be *husband*. I gagged. And, truth be told, it's not easy to live with a man who can open his mouth and scream like a mountain lion while sticking out his tongue. I have settled now on using his Christian name, with a *mate* here and there.

It is a tough task for us to make our lips form the words *husband* and *wife*. We cringe at the conventional, which has to do with a long list of dysfunctional beginnings, better at this point left unaddressed. We have examined all the euphemisms: *spousal equivalent* (sounds like a math problem); *significant other* (I don't like being an "other"); *mate* (easily understood by young, across-the-border Canadians as a live-in "steady" of equal respect, but, in this country, I might be mistaken for the hockey goalie behind Patrick at guard, or even his seasick bunkmate); *POSSLQ*, pronounced "Pah-zul-Q" (cute, but a government label, the U.S. Census Bureau's acronym for "person of opposite sex sharing living quarters"); *companion* (brings to mind same-sex senior citizens sitting in the sand); *partner* (what, in business?); *girlfriend/boyfriend* (I'm too old for anything so fleeting); *sweetheart* (sounds sweet-sixteen); *lover* (too one-dimensional); and *honey* and *dear* (mightily commonplace). Nothing fits. In our hearts, we are lifemates. I call him my gypsyman, the Pastaman, my buckaroo and Booli-Q; I'm his Ursa Wonderfullis, his Boop and Pook-a-Lilly, his sex goddess, his Frijolita Roja (when I dyed my hair), his Little

Potato, and, on winter nights, his Arctic Blossom and Polar Pookie and Northern Nasturtium—not to mention his very own Cantankerous Cowslip and Crankus Horribilis. My sweet is evermore coining endearments of the moment. I can only *try* to keep up. (The Pastaman, at this very second, is standing over my shoulder, informing me I cannot put these terms in my book because he has plans to use them in *his* book, the one he has decided to write about *me!*)

Patrick's and my bonds may have deepened and broadened with our years in the barn, but the hulking wooden structure itself has changed little. The second year we put up the thirty-four-foot masonry chimney and installed a bigger and better woodstove. The following year—putting the gypsy-man's first credit card to immediate good use!—we graduated from campstove and coolers to a used, apartment-sized electric stove and a sparkling new Sears Roebuck refrigerator. The fourth year, in a tearful ceremony, we closed the outhouse upon learning that an underground bacterial plume in all likelihood extended into the creek waters; we tossed two boxes of enzyme-enhanced, microbial waste digester down the hole and in the barn installed an abominable flush toilet—an item, I'm certain, a man designed for a woman to clean. Though we were of like mind in abhorring our porcelain addition, we nonetheless had a horrific tiff over its installation—with my standing firm on protecting the creek and Patrick's jumping up and down that he would *not* shit indoors.

"I'll take the shovel and *dig a hole!*" He wasn't kidding.

"Be my guest, but the back of the bench is off limits. You'll have to hike out by the highway." Here all arguing fizzled, there being only a few waist-high bushes along the front fence.

Someone told me early on that setting up housekeeping

with Patrick would be like inviting a frisky fawn indoors to live beside the woodstove. In many respects, the description wasn't far off. Aside from the folding chair at his desk and the straight-backed chair at our eating table, he sits only on the floor, the cinder-block hearth, or on one of the odd, whimsical stumps I keep in the barn for end tables. Our living room furniture consists of two armchairs from my parents' collection, one a 1950s white Naugahyde, the other a red leather, and two more from my college days, a Kennedy rocker I once traded a guitar for, and a dilapidated white-cane wonder—secondhand-store vintage, MacAllister Street, San Francisco, 1964—that still bears the price tag of eleven dollars. A few times I've caught Patrick napping with a book in the cane chair, but if he were to relax into any of the others, I suspect a preciously cradled loyalty to his extreme austere beginnings would break like a dropped egg. This same loyalty, having been worked over now by his midlife years, rather than burning strictly as antiluxury, tends to manifest itself more as a fear: that soft seats, much like television, will dull the mind. There is also another element at work here, one of principle: living simply. The more his life resembles that of a long-legged fawn's, the less need he has for chairs and beds and such. We were three years living here before I dared lay down a few scatter rugs, so concerned was I that at the sight of them Patrick would up and depart.

Slowly we have diminished the nightmarish tangles of extension cords, adding more electrical circuits, a wall heater in the bathroom, and four baseboard heaters for emergencies. The heating of the barn has developed into nothing less than an ecological travesty, a combination of wood burning and propane and electricity. Exorbitant, when all going at once. Still there are winter mornings when I wake up exhaling gauzy clouds into a room two degrees above freezing, after not having hauled out of bed during the night to stoke the stove. Tomatoes, in these temperatures, begin to look like shrink-wrapped balls of red gelatin; bananas refuse to turn lose their peels but lose all their flavor. When it comes to *my* keeping warm, there is this brighter aspect: I haven't had need to resurrect my indoor snowsuit.

As for the floors and walls, stained pressboard and naked Sheetrock remain with us, although I've painted big rugs in the kitchen and dining areas (a mop is useless on bare pressboard) and wallpapered part of the kitchen in a collage of pushpins and favorite greeting cards from friends. The remodeling job most appreciated by yours truly, and I might add built by same, with the help of a carpenter friend, is an eight-foot-long wall of slab wood. It sets the front entrance apart from the bedroom. Anyone pushing open the front door now, despite my PLEASE KNOCK, PRIVATE RESIDENCE sign—people still think there are folks in here milking cows and assembling buggies—will not step directly into my bedroom. This is especially appealing when I'm lolling in late. But of equal attraction to my supine body: Baby bats can no longer sail over top.

The largest of our building projects needed to be farmed out to professionals. Last year on Halloween, the roof, which was already wearing thin enough for a few strategically stationed buckets, blew half off in a freak microblow. The storm uprooted more than two hundred towering pine trees in just the seven miles north of us, toppling them onto electrical wires and houses. We felt fortunate only to have approximately two thousand shreds of our asphalt roofing lying about the yard. Over our heads now is a snug new metal roof—a roof beneath which, as a matter of fact, *someone* could finish out a home. If I were to count up the hours I've spent sitting and staring at different corners of the barn, mapping out floor plans, designing cupboards and closets and bookcases, a kitchen with running water, I would be as old as

stones. Only recently have I come around to fully understanding that if I were actually to complete a makeover—
floors, ceilings, drywall mud, paint, window trim, sinks! for
God's sake—I'd have to move out. It wouldn't be home!
Beams adorned with bird poop and the chore of hauling
water for dishwashing grow on a person. There is a certain
irony that appeals to me in a former drywall taper's living for
ten years with raw seams and bare nails. I still muse sometimes on the whole place, at our departure, going back to
the mice. Moreover, I fill a few hours now and again spinning dreams of someday, somewhere, building a straw-bale
house—for its cheap, renewable material and nice fat-walled
insulation, to say nothing of lavish deep windowsills, for sitting in and reading.

Meanwhile, we are living again this year amidst a throbbing
nursery. Birds are a-flutter and a-twitter everywhere. The
barn sparrows nest all along the eaves, their fledglings coming to the feeders like tousled children just out of bed, little
tufts of baby fluff poking at odd angles out of their heads.
They squat on the tops of the feeders, flap their wings for
balance, and, beaks cocked open, peep incessant demands of
"Mom, feed me, I don't know how!" The creeks and ditches
float little balls of fuzz, the offspring of wood ducks and mal-
lards. Tending to their broods in the fields are killdeer and
meadowlarks. Flocks of red-winged blackbirds guard their
nurseries in the cattails. One day, I was digging out a waist-
high knapweed plant near the mailbox and discovered an exquisite little nest lined with a skein of horses' mane hair and
cradling a lone, cold cowbird egg. The female kingbird,
whose real estate it was (cowbird mothers are deadbeats, depositing eggs around for others to raise, a rapacious trick
having greatly to do with why they are a weedy species), had
perhaps a bit of wisdom under her head feathers and thought

better of raising a thankless cowbird that would push her own hatchlings out of the nest. Whatever the case, she had abandoned her handsome labors for better pastures.

At the scary thought of being cooped up in the stifling mow all summer, finishing this book, I set about cobbling together a table out of two sawhorses and half an old Dutch door. I found the door lying beneath the sleeping deck, forgotten in the weeds, where in our first months here it had served as the floor to our solar camp shower. In intervening years, it had grown a delicate coating of greenish gray lichen. I assembled the table next to the defunct outhouse (full now of gardening tools), right at the lip of the embankment. Using a huge drill bit, I bore a hole in the middle of the door and plunked in a patio umbrella—a flowered Martha Stewart design, the disgusting truth be told (for someone of unconventional taste, that is, and I'm whimpering this excuse: It was the one umbrella in three counties only *half* made in China). To complete my workstation, I dragged over a big stump of firewood for seating and settled onto it for testing. Off to my right there rose a skyline drawn with favorite Bitterroot peaks. The middistance was strictly an interruption of power poles and the whiz and scream of highway traffic, but thirty feet away a Clydesdale gazed at me over the fence. The remainder of the landscape within my view swung wide over the bottomland.

In the damp cool of my first June morning at the table, I cranked up my new, pale-green-with-pink-dogwood-blossoms umbrella, purely for ambience, and plopped down twenty pages of manuscript and a red editing pen. Immediately stealing my attention was a black-and-white flapping ruckus of squawking magpies, five or six juveniles vacating their nest, a bulgy wad of brush the size of a beach ball wedged into a thicket of alder beside the creek. My once having fed this species poisoned flies didn't seem to have cut down their numbers. Another weedy species, I thought, generalists feeding on most anything from cat food and grain to carrion, mixing it up easily with humans, and rearing large broods. Then my eye caught a twitch of movement closer in, from the camouflage of shady grasses at the base of another alder, a white-tailed doe with a new spotted fawn. Patrick had witnessed the birthing the previous evening, at the edge of the cattails below his shoeing shed. Though I had walked up to my table all within their view, I now carefully slid off the stump, ducked down, and crawled across the yard, returning in reverse manner with binoculars in hand.

I was wearing a shirt with a splashy print of pastel flowers—maybe I would blend in as though part of the garden. As I idly watched the doe and fawn, bumblebees buzzed a few feet away in the honeysuckle vine twining up the outhouse, and I had to shake off black-and-red ants crawling over my toes. I had been going barefoot again. My soles were toughened to the point where I could trot across the barnyard rather than assuming the posture of a hunchbacked burglar walking over tacks. While the doe took her respite in the deep shadows, with only her elongated nose and tall ears showing, the spotted fawn frolicked in the high, sunlit grasses, thirty-foot exploratory jaunts in various directions, but always returning for maternal licks and nuzzles. Hearing what sounded like the squeaks of a mouse, I took the binoculars from my eyes and turned to see a female rufous hummingbird sticking its needle beak into the slender orange honeysuckle blooms, one, then another, in rapid succession. The hum of its wings produced a soft blur to my eye. Its small fanned tail and fleshy rear part of its body pumped with the rippling motion of a swimming mermaid. Suddenly, the bird zoomed over to investigate the flowers on my blouse. Five, six times, it stood off a foot from me, treading air. Then it zeroed in, a quarter inch from the end of my nose, and hovered there. I froze. Cross-eyed, calmly, I studied its green iridescence, until it occurred to me the pretty wee thing might push its beak up my nostril. At that thought, grooves developing between my eyebrows frightened it away.

I had sat an hour at my worktable, and though my soul was fed to surfeit, rejoicing in paradisiac distraction, any writerly inroads on my twenty pages had gone lacking. I headed back to the mow.

The family of yellow-bellied marmots from our first years had long ago taken the hint and hied themselves out of here. The hint was our neighbor's conducting a spring cleaning (with his rifle) of about two hundred marmots and Columbian ground squirrels that were tunneling up his meadow. Though he spared sixty of them at the north end, over our way, for a seed colony, both species soon dwindled— perhaps at the hands of weasels and owls—or they just plain vacated. So it was that Patrick and I were amused when another pudgy Mr. Marmot, a loner, turned up last year. Sitting up on his haunches at the end of the front porch, he *pipped* pertly before settling into Our Apartments for a summer siesta. He arrived again this year in May, toting his crowbar and chain saw and pickax, and for two weeks went noisily about rearranging our foundation more to his liking. (We apparently aren't the only species that does this.)

One of our groups of year-round lodgers is very much in absence. For the first time, we are without skunks. An early and fairly benign mating season, as far as aroma goes, began on the seventh of January. After that, one female periodically trundled about, making trips to the bird feeders and creek, until the end of March. Expecting kits early, we kept ears cocked to the floorboards, waiting for the first murmurings. But we never heard a sound. And we never saw her again. I like to think she might have taken herself down the road to the Stumble Inn—for a last night on the town before being squarely saddled with family. Or perhaps, she was a *he* and had set off on a prowl. In any case, about this time a skunk was hit on the highway half a mile south. That the barn has not attracted other mephitine lodgers is perhaps connected with the neon vacancy sign's not burning as brightly these days: during high bear season, we've been keeping the mound of sunflower seeds raked clean.

Though Our Apartments might be on the empty side, up in the rafters the bat colony has been growing in numbers again, after a multiple-year slump, due probably to the raggedy condition of the roof. The new sheets of forest green Delta Rib have tightened up the big browns' quarters as well. Petite chitterings of pups—nearly inaudible even to my ear—began right on schedule in the fourth week of June. For the past few years, we've had fledgling flight season pretty well under control. No baby bat catastrophes, since we've learned to leave the mow lights burning in the evenings until after the bats depart for their nightly flyabout. But then, recently, in our flopping onto the downstairs bed for an afternoon nap, we found ourselves staring up at a small bat. Its presence was somewhat disturbing. We had no idea when or how it had come in—we hadn't napped on the bed for a few days—and it was hanging, in an improbable manner for a normal bat, on the beam directly overhead, just opposite the window in the most illuminated part of the room. A small-bodied specimen, smaller than our big brown youngsters, it was all black.

"Has it moved?"

"No," Patrick said.

"Maybe it's dead," I said, having not long ago read that bats, because they have a way of locking their legs into place, can keep right on hanging after they die, virtually until they disintegrate.

"Why would it be dead?"

"I don't know, I'd just feel better about taking a nap under it if I knew it wasn't going to cough, spit, or pee on us."

Patrick and I had been aware for some time that with all the contact we have with bats we should be vaccinated for rabies. (Rehabists handling vagrant or orphaned bats get vaccinated.) Just on the plain permutations of statistics and luck—we had had nine good years—we decided this spring to get shots. Yet there unfolded from this decision a whole set of quandaries and further questions, starting with: So great! We get our rabies shots and then what? Just let company take their chances? Maybe we shouldn't have company anymore. Then the shots were expensive. And we didn't want to be succumbing to inflammatory rabies scares. We also didn't want to die. In perusing information from the federal Centers for Disease Control and Prevention, I learned that humans can contract the virus from a rabid animal's "infectious material," such as saliva, by getting it into eyes, nose, mouth, or a wound. But we cannot catch rabies from a bat's guano, blood, or urine, or in touching its fur. In recent years, in a few mysterious instances, there reportedly have been people that died from bat rabies without having knowledge of being bitten. A few years back, a Montana man with no known bite died of bat rabies (the state laboratory, where they find the answers to these things, can pinpoint not only the general type of animal at fault but the species).

People who habitually handle wild animals can ensure against rabies by receiving the preexposure prophylaxis (a series of three shots). The rest of us, if we become exposed, can avoid getting the disease by taking the postexposure prophylaxis (a series of six shots) shortly after our exposure— *shortly* meaning several days, or time enough to have the animal tested. With the latter regime, there is this one catch: You have to *know* you've been exposed. Once you exhibit the symptoms—the snarling and foaming at the mouth that many of us remember from the movie *Old Yeller*—there isn't a scrap of a chance of living.

As I said, we had made our decision to get vaccinated.

Then the weeks drifted by, chock-full of other things. Now we had a bat, a gorgeous black bat with a mantle of silver; it looked perfectly healthy but was behaving strangely.

The plan became to catch the bat and send it in for testing. Because it was a Saturday, this posed a problem: The county extension office, where I would take the bat, was open only on weekdays. To get the most reliable test results, I was instructed by local rehabists to keep the bat alive up until—but not *when*—I delivered it to the office at two o'clock Monday afternoon. At that time of day, a cooler package was sent off to the lab in Helena. If the bat died before mail time, we had the choice of letting its tissue disintegrate, perhaps beyond hope of detecting the virus, or of preserving the tissue by means of freezing. But who wanted a bat—a possibly rabid one—in their freezer? And, according to the information at hand, freezing might promote a false positive test result. With the idea then of keeping our interloper alive until midday Monday, Patrick donned his leather gloves and, with his arms-longer-than-mine, grabbed the little guy and nudged him into a large peanut butter jar—peanut butter long gone. We screwed on the lid, which I'd punched full of holes. The jar went into a shoe box, supplying the bat with its preferred darkness (we hoped it would quietly sleep), and we set the box in the coolest place we could think of where the cats wouldn't think to investigate it—on top of the washing machine.

At the appointed hour on Monday, I pulled up at Judy Hoy's, and we settled down on her front porch, with the box. At the jar's first exposure to light, the bat flexed its wings and jumped. Judy pronounced it a silver-haired bat, a species recently discovered to be colonial in nature, and a rather rarer mammal than the big brown.

"Looks like a healthy bat to me. At least we're not killing a female."

"It's a male?"

"Sure, see its penis?"

With the bat's agitated flapping, my first ganders were too fleeting to be sure I had seen anything, or if there was anything to see. "Where?"

"Right there!" She tried to rotate the jar faster than the bat was moving to stay upright.

Finally I caught sight of something lying against the body in the right spot; it was furry, about the size of a grain of rice, but I couldn't be totally certain—and were those two minuscule balls? "That little thing!" I blurted. "I thought bats had tremendously *long* penises."

"Well, look at it. It's huge."

"Huge?"

"Comparatively. The bat's *only* two inches long. If you saw a penis that big on a deer, it'd be a giant salami!"

Judy opened the lid and tossed in a Q-Tip dipped in isoflurane, and we screwed on the other lid I'd brought, without holes. Within a minute, the little creature was stone dead. I zipped off to the county extension office, and in two days Patrick and I received a phone call. No rabies. A beautiful bat, dead for nothing. We were despondent.

Collisions of people and animals are not confined to the barn. Around the valley, the last two years have been the "Years of the Moose." This, all within two days last summer: Our farmhouse tenant, driving home after dark from Missoula, collided with a moose (her SUV sustained a hit on the side mirror—it's not known what happened to the moose, but with a sound *thunk* to a hip, it might not have lived long); a motorist, five miles south of us, totaled a vehicle in killing a female moose that had a calf (the baby was sent off to the state rehab center); and Patrick, half a mile north, just where the highway crosses Big Creek, barely avoided hitting a young bull moose sporting a small lopsided rack. Moose, or

PS- It's marked
"FIRST EDITION"
SO KEEP IT!!

Erik —

I read a review of
this book years ago &
have never found it —

It is special catalog
I showed up (on sale!!) so
I bought 1 for you & 1 for me

Hope it's GOOD!!

Alces alces, belong to the group of hoofed animals with antlers (head racks that grow from scratch every year, as opposed to horns that grow bigger). In their migration to the river, these particular Bitterroot moose had been attempting to cross Highway 93 at points where trees, bushes, and banks that constitute riparian corridors pinch down into culverts, through which only the creek waters pass under the road. The big animals had no place to go but up and over: After that, we saw or heard tell of one wandering moose or another for months. The young bull browsed up and down the river bottom until late November. Katya and I thought we shared him.

"Have you seen our moose?"

"Yesterday. He's probably headed back your way."

Arden's pond, down below, lured a female and calf. With binoculars, I watched their primeval-looking dark forms from our sleeping deck. Stories of hairy conflicts with charging moose filtered back from friends who ride horseback up the canyons.

This spring, the same week the marmot arrived, the Big Trio showed up: a she-bear with a new cub, a mountain lion, a moose. Two winters of light snowpack followed by a spring lacking notable rain may have sent them down early. I saw only the moose, wading knee-deep in the creek; it may have been last year's calf grown into a yearling. Arden called with news of the rest, in incidents that took place in the brush on his place, brush I gaze at from my writing desk. The lion killed a white-tailed deer. The bear took over the kill and hauled it back by the owl trees. I started keeping a vigilant eye but never caught a glimpse, and then Arden stopped by with an update: They had all moved off. Soon after that, last year's bull moose—we assumed anyway, with its larger and getting-on-toward-magnificent rack—settled into his browsing paces again. Then one day Katya called: "We have a cow moose with twins! They've made beds in the brush by the swampy place. The poop is very large—you must see it!" Moose twins, my Peterson's *Field Guide* says, are a rarity.

And what of the local insect life? It's not quite time yet for the flies' annual dive into the walls; they'll be awaiting fall and the arrival of cooler nights. Yet the clustering darlings have not been entirely out of mind. I recently took my fax machine in for repair. I'd been receiving complaints of its sending pages with a blank vertical strip down the left side. The next morning a service technician called with the good news. It was repairable. A couple of spiders had made webs inside and caught four or five flies. "Your blank strip?" he said, "The wing of one is right in front of the optical lens, blocking the scanned image." Only $87.50 for a good cleaning!

In placing the order for my yearly supply of Fly Scoops, I became party to a convoluted saga of business. The rights to the trademark had apparently been bought and sold several times in the past few years, and the current owners were no longer selling boxes of just the disposable sticky inserts—the plastic scoops I already had by the dozens. What's more, the company, it was rumored, was near financial collapse. Through a series of phone calls, I discovered that Victor Brand, "World's Leader in Poison-Free Pest Control," the company Patrick and I knew from our mousetrap days, had sent a letter of intent to acquire Fly Scoops. In a panic, not able to imagine living without this product, I called up Victor Brand to ferret out the breaking news. As I asked my questions and shared my story—"We live in this old dairy barn in Montana . . ."—I was shuffled up the line until I was talking with the vice president in charge of new technologies, a man who sensed immediately that he was speaking to someone who lived in ideal fly testing grounds. He will be shipping us—I can't believe this!—a variety of fly catchers in developmental stages, thingy-jingies on the technological cutting edge of fly control. One, he said, is keyed on a blinking light that flutters at the same rate as the wing beats of copulating flies, and the horny little buggers all dive for it. I'm not sure this will work with our cluster flies, as once they're inside the barn they seem to be into their reproductive dotage, but if it works—*What the hey, what we need around here are a few more things copulating!*

A brand-new set of relationships—intriguingly and appallingly—has been developing on our acres, in fact, on any property where deer mice and knapweed exist. I was recently prowling corridors at the University of Montana in Missoula, during the Fourteenth Annual Meeting of the Society of Conservation Biology, and quite cosmically stumbled onto a presentation in a small classroom. The speaker was Dean Pearson, a lanky, fair-haired man who's a wildlife research biologist with the U.S. Forest Service at the Rocky Mountain Research Station, housed on the UM campus. Pearson's interests center on the interconnectedness of species as they form communities of animals and plants and insects. His major area of study is what captivates me—the effects spiraling out from relationships between deer mice and knapweed and the gallfly.

It is a few weeks later that I catch up with Pearson for further discussion. We sit at a picnic table under a huge pine tree outside his office, and he tells me that it was within six years of the gallfly's initial introduction, as one of the biological controls for knapweed, that deer mice turned it into their primary winter food source. "One mouse can eat twelve hundred gallfly larvae in a night," he says.

"You must be kidding!" I cry, trying to imagine my little she-mouse and all her hordes of descendants racing up and down the stems of knapweed, stuffing their cheeks.

The scenario unfolds with the gallfly laying its eggs in the knapweed's seed head, where the eggs immediately hatch into maggots, or larvae. Unlike a butterfly larva, which makes its own cocoon, this maggot somehow knows to take advantage of the knapweed's being in summer seed-making mode, and it chemically induces the plant to make it a winter den—the gall. "It tricks the plant," Pearson says, "by saying, 'I'm a seed, make me into a seed.'" After which, having completed their good job of biocontrol—of robbing energy from the plants and occupying space in the seed heads, thus on two fronts inhibiting the production of seeds—the billions of little larvae snuggle down to winter over, for nine long months.

Deer mice, being the ultimate in generalists, the small-mammal versions of coyotes, will dine—it is true—on anything and everything. "Seeds of conifers and grasses, insects and fungi," Pearson says. Birdseed, bread and butter, Beautiful Soap, I add. But also, the species is ever eager to adapt its diet to a specific, plentiful food source—like gallfly larvae. (That deer mice had an appetite for gallfly larvae was not apparent when the insect first was brought to this country and put through the comprehensive testing that identified what *it* fed on.) Our northern winters, with their endless larvae picnic, now look a lot rosier for deer mice, which causes Pearson to postulate their populations are increasing. This leads him to speculate further that changes are taking place in connected communities of wildlife. As the weeds and flies move in, deer mice congregate to feast, and voles move out. Voles are small mammals, two or three times the size of deer mice; they are plump, easy to catch, and travel abroad day and night, as opposed to the nocturnal deer mice. Rough-legged hawks, northern harriers, and kestrels live mostly on voles. Long-tailed weasels prefer voles. "Voles are pretty dumb," Pearson says. "They are like little cows, versus white-tailed deer. A white-tailed deer is a lot smaller and harder to catch than a cow. If I'm making a living off cows, life is good. If I'm living off deer mice, I'm working hard, and not getting as much return." This means the predators may begin to require larger territories. Or that the number of their offspring may diminish.

We've talked for two hours when we rise to part. The results of Pearson's studies, ongoing in the Calf Creek area of the Bitterroot Valley, will not be completed in time to be included in this book, but I promise to keep in touch. Then, on the drive home, I do my own speculating. On the one hand, if deer mice populations were indeed increasing, wouldn't that then heighten the danger of people's exposure to hantavirus? *No more camping in knapweed!* On the other hand, with deer mice consuming major quantities of larvae, wouldn't there be smaller gallfly hatches in succeeding years? Then fewer deer mice? Wouldn't it perhaps all even out? But there's one thing Pearson mentioned that won't even out. Before knapweed spills its seed in the fall, there is a stretch of time when the seed heads simultaneously carry seed and larvae. Deer mice scampering through the knapweed fields and banqueting with abandon on their favorite morsels will accidentally ingest five to ten whole seeds in a night. A deer mouse might disperse these seeds in its feces for a range of half a mile. But here swoops in the great horned owl, consuming five mice in the same night and ending up with twenty-five to sixty seeds, which travel—in a viable state—right on through into a pellet that's dropped maybe twenty miles back in the Selway.

Another traveling weed has arrived in the Bitterroot. One day, Judy Hoy was weeding a garden for an elderly friend and came across something she had never seen before. She took it to a botanist in Missoula, who identified it as a tropical species. Quickweed. Where did it come from?

Who knows. Are there more around? Probably. The questions running around in my head are again endless. Is this summer—this year of hot and dry—quickweed's first run at Montana? Will global warming help it survive in a northern climate? Can it withstand a winter of snow? Is it a weedy species, having just been awaiting all its fine life a ski weekend special?

The old barn has recently hosted a new visitor and the valley one also, though neither is what could be called *altogether* new.

Patrick and I had just come home from a triple-header of movies in Missoula, taking full advantage of the gasoline that's required to get us there. It was two in the morning, and we were sitting at our dining table being little piggies, spooning through a carton of Häagen-Dazs mango sorbet. The spoon was in my mouth, when he shot me a "Pssst!" with a finger pointing toward the window. I looked over and saw nothing but night. We waited. Two dainty gray paws emerged and grabbed the bottom of the window frame. A pointy nose rose up, sunk back down, and rose again, until gradually a whole face appeared. A black-masked animal stared in at us. We didn't make a move. When the animal sank out of sight again, Patrick tiptoed out the front door to peek around the side of the barn. I stayed fixed on the window, and here it came up again until the frame was full with raccoon, the nose of a second pushing right along behind. Slipping in close to the back of my chair, Patrick whispered, "There's four of them. Looks like a mom and three younger. They're giving each other boosts up to the windowsill." We reveled in their antics for twenty minutes. At one point, two squeezed into the frame, vying for the best position to scoop seed from the feeders, which they set to swinging wildly. Then, abruptly, the window emptied out.

We jumped to peer out, and caught sight of them in the pale moonlight, scurrying past the outhouse and fast over the bank.

This brief encounter produced in me the strangest thrill of involvement—in the way that watching film projected on a big screen, with its larger-than-life immediacy, will suck you deep into a story. With the raccoons, it had to do with some amalgam of their proximity, a mere three arm-lengths away; the darkness of their background contrasted with our spot-lighted dining table; the lateness of the hour—the entire valley, or so it seemed, was asleep, letting me think I had dropped into a world before the advent of population centers; and then, the almost eerie slow motion of the animals' movements. This was not the close encounter of a bat on my nightgown, a fly in my soup, deer mice running past our ears; nonetheless, but for a pane of glass, for a few fleeting moments the raccoons were right in our lives, as we were right in theirs.

The valley visitor. After the 1996 reintroduction of gray wolves to the Greater Yellowstone Wilderness and the Frank Church River of No Return Wilderness, it wasn't long before members of this wide-ranging species, *Canis lupus,* found their way into the Sapphire and Bitterroot Ranges and right down to the edges of the valley where we live. Within a year, a pair had been sighted on the Ruffatto Cattle Ranch, a cow-calf operation of about eight hundred head on four thousand irrigated acres, a unique stretch of land extending from the Bitterroot Mountains clear to the river.

Wolves had been making headlines in the local papers, on and off, for a few years when I finally sat down with Tom Ruffatto to hear the story straight from the cattle rancher. You can't live in the valley long without hearing of Tom; he is active in his community, from the planning board to the conservation district. Patrick and I typically bump into him at our mutually favorite world-class eating establishment, Marie's Italian Restaurant.

I turned into the barnyard and parked near an old bunkhouse, a two-story clapboard affair with white paint peeling, chimney mortar missing, the trunks of two soaring old ponderosa pines growing into the overhang of the eves. The building hadn't been lived in for years, yet the well-soiled area around the front doorknob testified to the structure's role in a different era—before the advent of big machinery.

Tom was standing near his kitchen door, squeegeeing a huge bird poop off a window. He motioned for me to come in. The house was nowadays stucco, though originally a log cabin from the same late-nineteenth-century period as the bunkhouse; it sported a new metal roof and a recently rebuilt stone foundation. Tom's grandfather and grandmother had begun living in the house in 1916, when they worked for the landowner. Mario and Mary Feronato, each having made their way to America from Italy, met in Denver. Mario was digging ditches for water lines, Mary working at a never-ending job, scrubbing the marble steps of a big hotel. It was a Missoula-based sugar beet industry that brought them on to Montana, offering a boxcar to transport their worldly goods. The Feronatos, including two daughters (their fifth daughter would be Tom's mother), climbed on the train and made the journey in the company of their household furniture and their farming implements and the family cow. Tom's paternal grandfather, Joe Ruffatto, also came to Montana from Italy, but via the coal mines of Illinois. Management of the ranch had lately fallen to Tom and his brother, Cliff. Tom, a powerfully built man of fifty, with the sturdy hands of a toiling rancher and a full head of shinning black hair, fits the picture of his genetic and outdoor-labor heritage.

After a tour of the house, much changed from its original

look, with a floor plan of add-ons as the family grew, and a peek at Tom's extensive collection of Bev Doolittle paintings, we settled at his kitchen table, with its crisp, blue-checkered tablecloth.

The first fall of the wolves, Tom and Cliff had been riding horseback, chasing cows, when Tom looked down the field and said, "Hey, here come a couple coyotes." The animals, though, grew larger and larger as they kept coming. "Jeez, they must be dogs!" In the canines' passing of the riders, almost the way hikers might step by each other on a trail, there was no mistaking they were wolves. For several days, they hung around feeding on a dead cow Tom had buried with a backhoe. After tunneling down through four feet of earth, they raided the "icebox" daily, covering themselves with dirt and mud. Finally, perhaps looking for better pickings, they moved off and up the valley, into the Lolo drainage, where in the spring they produced five pups. Tom remembers thinking it was "kinda neat" to see wolves on his family's ranch—without having to travel way off to Canada or Alaska. The following fall a second pair arrived and decided to stay.

Though the Ruffattos knew they had wolves, it took more than their saying so to convince the federal agencies overseeing the reintroduction project.* Confirmation didn't come until a coyote trap accidentally snagged the male wolf—a rather passive animal for his species, or he would have been out of the trap—and federal officials were invited out for a look-see. The female wolf, soon to have pups, had already disappeared into a den a quarter mile off the

---

*Wolves released into the Frank Church River of No Return Wilderness, as part of the larger Northern Rockies Wolf Recovery Program, are managed in a joint effort by the U.S. Fish and Wildlife Service (Department of Interior) and Wildlife Services (Department of Agriculture) and the Nez Perce Tribe.

Ruffattos' back fence. With the male captured, and a federal offer to relocate the pair, Tom had an easy out. Yet in the reaches of his mind, he could hear the ringing voices of environmental groups: "The wolves were going to be 'good wolves,' but you never gave them a chance." He asked the federal agents to turn the wolf loose. The animal was collared and let go.

The Ruffattos are a ranching family already coexisting with more than a hundred elk and fifty to sixty white-tailed deer. These ungulates of the wild come in winter to feed alongside the Ruffatto cows when the daily hay is strung through the fields. With feed for three elk equaling that of one cow, and eight deer equaling one cow, without the wild company the ranch, feedwise, could have fifty more head to work from, yet the Ruffattos would rather "just get along." Tom enjoys seeing bears, frequently, the few moose that migrate through, the occasional mountain lion. Even the coyotes: "They eat lots of mice." (When coyotes become too many, he allows a friend to come and trap.) So why not wolves, he thought, why not see "if we can live together, too"? Of course with a caveat, which he gave me now in his large voice, "If they start chomping on my livelihood, then it's a whole new story."

When the mother wolf delivered an astounding eight pups instead of the usual litter of four to six, it patently became the "whole new story"—yet with a few chapters. Food sources rapidly vanished in the area surrounding the den, but the male in his scouting learned there was roadkill to be had on the highway. Daily, he made repeated treks down a long draw on the ranch, gorging himself on dead white-tailed deer and returning to the den. "We'd see him going down looking like a thin dog and coming back up with a big basketball in his stomach," Tom said, his hands drawing the rounded image for me. Sometimes the male wolf would eat too much and have to puke up a good portion of the half-masticated flesh and fur before arriving back at the den with the family's sustenance. The pups grew steadily larger and hungrier, and the father wolf was run ragged.

During this time, the Ruffattos' cows that were calving were kept in a field close by the house, but also bordering the draw. It seemed only a matter of time before the pups' provider popped over and snatched a newborn.

But meanwhile, an unusual pooling of resources and ingenuity was taking place among the managers of the wolf program, representatives from environmental groups, and local ranchers. In what way might they help this wolf keep his distance? Scare devices had previously been built and employed to keep coyotes in check, but they hadn't been fully tried on wolves. The apparatus used with the coyotes was geared to sound off at intervals, but animals tend to get accustomed to the regularity of a timer, much as we would to the bongings of a grandfather clock. A neighbor of Tom's, cattle rancher Ed Cummings, at a gathering of minds around his kitchen table, threw out the idea of keying the device to the radio collar on the wolf. This would create a greater surprise effect. Anytime the wolf approached, he would encounter a carnival of lights and sounds. John Shivik, leader of the Non-lethal Methods of Predation Management Project at Wildlife Services in Fort Collins, Colorado, set to work building the fancy new strobe-light-and-siren contraption. When the battery-operated setup was finished, they hung it in a tree near the top of the draw. It was keyed, like a tracking device, to the radio signal emitting from the male wolf's collar. The animal's venturing within a few hundred yards set it off: wild blinking and the tonal scream of a car being burglarized. Yet the gadget was triggered only by line of sight; as long as the wolf kept his head down, he could quietly pass close by in the draw.

So far, so good. No calves were lost. It was only later, when the calves, having grown larger, had to be moved to fields farther away (to keep from overgrazing pastures)—fields, in fact, up toward the wolves' den—that temptation mounted. The exasperation and ironies still vivid in Tom's mind, he said, "We just kept moving dinner closer to them!"

Calves, it seems, on top of everything, are a curious lot; and they will investigate almost anything. I knew this from the bunch that had spooked Lefty, running after us along the fence line on one of our training trips. Just *seeing* a wolf will pique a calf's interest. One afternoon Tom observed a scene that had all the makings of a classic fable: a wolf leading half a dozen calves across a field—"Come little dears, come with me to my cozy den!"—and then turning sharply into the brush. That day the calves tired of the game before entering the trap.

Then one morning, the inevitable: Tom came upon a pile of bones. It was at this point, he said, that the big controversies began. Federal officials are in charge of verifying the livestock deaths, after which the organization Defenders of Wildlife, out of its program called the Wolf Compensation Trust, pays for any animals lost to the wolves. "We would all be standing around kicking the bones," Tom said, "and I would say, 'The wolves ate it,' and someone else would say, 'How do you know it didn't die and then the wolves ate it?' "

After dickering over a couple piles of bones, Tom came across a calf with a five-pound roast eaten out of its buttock, canine marks all around the wound. It wasn't something you could doctor and have grow back. The animal was hamstrung. Tom felt he had to shoot it. Yet *because* of his shooting it, the verdict came back that he would be paid only half its worth. (Somewhere there's a page of bureaucratic rules, needed actually, to stave off Defenders of Wildlife's paying for every calf gone missing—with a broken leg, upset stomach, sense of wanderlust—from ranchers who see wolves only in their dreams. I hadn't been there, of course, at Ruffattos' at the time, so this might not be fair, but I *was* thinking, *You must be kidding! With a verified wolf den overstocked with youngins just a quarter mile off?*) Calves at this age, depending on their weight, bring between four and six hundred dollars.

The loss of Ruffatto's stock was news to me. None of it had hit the papers at the time.

"You just didn't say anything?" I asked.

"Well, you don't have to *call* the papers," he said. "I didn't want to stir up a hornets' nest."

But soon a neighbor lost a few calves and, down the line, Ed Cummings started losing a calf a night. The wolf pups had grown big enough to be left alone, and the parents were effectively hunting as a team. Dean Pearson suddenly came to my mind, his description of voles—"If I'm making a living off cows, life is good!"

The time had come to relocate the whole bunch. It took about a week to trap them all. "They did a good job," Tom said evenly, a steady look in his brown eyes. But I had seen him the day the last wolves were caught. I was in a crosswalk in Stevensville when his big ranch pickup stopped for me. To his rolling down the window, I shouted, "How's it going?" "The wolves are gone," he said, "they got the last two pups." His shoulders said more—a huge heave accompanying his sigh of relief. Like the raccoons in our window, the Ruffattos' wolves were another rural fringe case of "wildlife right in our lives"—more precisely, right in the *groceries* for Tom and the wolves.

The tragic part of this story came after the wolves' capture and transport to an Idaho holding facility. A veritable wail went up all over the Bitterroot at the headline: WOLF DIES IN CAPTIVITY. In a caretaker's trying to doctor a wound on the male wolf, a loop restraining device accidentally jammed, choking him to death. Shortly thereafter, three of the pups died of a virus. But the tale goes on to end, or begins once again, on a heartening note. The mother wolf and her remaining five pups were eventually released in the Spotted Bear area of Flathead National Forest. At first they were placed in a pen, constructed of twelve-foot-high electrified plastic mesh, allowing them time to acclimate to their surroundings. The very next morning, large wolf prints were found *outside* the pen. Soon a courtship of howling started up. It was the beginning of mating season and a new wolf pack.

A few weeks after recording Tom's story, I went out to see him again—to take this thoroughly Italian man some of my homegrown garlic. "I forgot to ask," I said. "Would you do it again, with the wolves?"

"Sure." No hesitation.

This was the time of year adolescent wolves were kicked out of the packs. Tom had been waiting to see if one or two showed up. Wolves stake out wooded territory by peeing on trees. When the pee is fresh, any passing wolves will likely move on. The pee on the Ruffattos' back acres was, by now, old. "The no-vacancy sign is out!" he said. *Was Ruffatto's sign neon, too?* "Some ranchers think we're dumber than a box of rocks, but I love to see the animals. I'd just as soon see wolves as more people."

In allowing my gaze to rove over the vistas of southwestern Montana, I'm quickly able to take in where the change, which we lack in the barn, is concentrated. Over in the Big Hole, Troutfitters has a fine new fly-fishing shop, bigger and better, and there is evidence of a small influx of residents—a few new houses tucked around the valley, at least two of which rear up ostentatiously from the riverbank. But it is in the Bitterroot where change, development, that thing called progress, has run unleashed. A person can see it in little ways: in the lines at the bank and grocery store; in the parking places stuffed with vehicles; in the espresso huts and bars that have swept Montana until they are two to the block. (There is, of course, the upside to the latter: I can easily get a fine cup of coffee.) Change can be judged by the menu at Maggie's Wild Oats Café and Coffee House. We are now being served, right here in the hardscrabble Bitterroot, simple little dishes like game hen with "a sauce of natural juices, gin, thyme & juniper berries" and "grilled focaccia with caramelized leeks," in addition to food items with the intriguing names *aioli, coulis, puttanesca, tagine, blinis, cornichons,* and moose turd pie à la chevrolet foo-foo! Patrick and I eat there often. The waitresses are accomplished at rattling off the specials in the proper accents, as well as patient and unwincing when folks, not excluding us, ask, "And what's that, exactly?"

Delights of espresso bars and caramelized leeks notwithstanding, they are only a small part of a much larger package. In recent years, Ravalli County has captured the dubious statistical distinction of being not only the fastest-growing county in Montana (containing the top two fastest-growing towns, and two more in the top ten) but, I also read somewhere, the fastest growing, percentage-wise, in the country. Largely for reasons of property rights—that fierce instilling of the Old West's "No one's going to tell me what I can do with *my* land!"—a comprehensive plan for county growth never comes to fruition. Not without irony, but certainly with bottomless sadness, I say this next: The folks hereabouts so disdainfully intolerant of Californians now have sprawling at their feet a tremendous start on a San Fernando Valley of their own, yes, in the great state of Montana. Drive up a mountainside at night and the valley spreads below in a sea of lights, recalling for me early views from Mulholland Drive. When we first arrived—drove in with the U-Haul and, indeed, increased the population by two—I could count all the twinkling lights in a minute. Last week, I heard this shocking assessment: "Missoula to Darby in twenty years? Another Seattle-Tacoma."

Just to remain evenhanded here, there are those people I suspect could only have come from southernish California who clearly exhibit signs of birth defects, or at least of having no sense of transplant aesthetics among their genes—or is it their jeans? They are the home builders who throw up against an indescribably glorious wild mountain backdrop something on the order of a Barbie doll–pink house with a white crushed-rock yard. Worse yet—perhaps not in visual design but in jarring ways just the same—are the things a forging of ignorance and big money can buy: fancy log homes in the floodplain and getaway cabins with floor space approaching that of an opera house, perched high up the mountainsides—the latter not just lordly blots on everyone else's view but serious encroachment on wildlife rhythms, not to mention hell on UPS deliveries and fire truck access. During one of my fresh-air exercise walks, I met a woman who summers in one of these cabins. Tan as a walnut from, I would guess, swimming and playing tennis in other parts of the world, she had hiked down the mountain to retrieve her mail from the box on the county road just as I was coming along. In a neighborly manner, I held my tongue while she effervesced, "We just love our view, we can see right down into the canyon!" *Yup, and you are so nicely now smack in others' enjoyment of the mountain.*

Certainly private holdings in the valley still retain expansive chunks of undeveloped land: natural and tilled. Even the developed acres, if you think of them as fabric, might resemble a loosely hand-crocheted scarf thrown casually about the shoulders, as opposed to that of metropolitan acres—an oxford cloth shirt, trussed up tightly with button-down collar and knotted necktie. But pressures on land use are continually increasing, with the reverse flow to rural living and the ever-burgeoning county population. In the twelve years between 1987 and 1999, the number of real estate offices in the Bitterroot jumped from 12 to 45 and pages in the real estate promotional directory from 8 to as many as 230. Replacing the failed ten-acre orchard of the 1800s is the ten-acre mobile home ranchette, fenced, cross-fenced, gobbling up landscape with a fervor equal to that of knapweed. Migrating animals, in ricocheting off the new fences and barking dogs, end up in terrifying places—scary for them, scary for us. They race down paved streets and lurch suddenly into a backyard, seduced last by the taste of petunias, ripe apples, dog food. With the larger ranches breaking up, acre-lot subdivisions are becoming common. While the million-dollar trophy houses creep up the hips of mountains and in along the riverbanks, more modestly priced subdivisions spread across agricultural fields, in a seemingly unheralded quest to sink their inedible roots—concrete foundations and septic systems—into the most fertile soil. Altogether, it is a spectacle resembling the grand advance of mold. I mentioned this to a friend, and she looked at me askance. "Please don't denigrate mold. I think it's beautiful!"

Topping off the august forward march of development is the valley's first gated community. Erected grandiosely out of prime winter elk range, it is designed not for the purpose of locking out rampant Montana crime but plainly for that of bestowing prestige. To be considered for "Membership in the Club" (a 17,000-square-foot log lodge with restaurant, bar, swimming pool, tennis courts, eighteen-hole golf course, not to mention a men's locker room in singular grand old tradition, with bar and poker tables), one must show a net worth that exceeds $1 million or an annual income in excess of $200,000.

Sleepy and bucolic are veering toward postures of the past. Everyone's in a hell of a hurry. Twenty-first-century Bitterrooters we are and witnessing clashes of new and old, of asphalt and agriculture, of human society and wildlife society. A newcomer woman who sleeps in a bedroom adjoining a farmer's hayfield is incensed at a few nights of tractor lights sweeping her walls. In response, farmers band together with a "first rights" ordinance: We were haying here before you came sleeping. Another woman, with a robin bashing headfirst into her window, calls 911, irate that a bird is destroying her property. It's pooping and bleeding on her window ledge. An emergency dispatcher refers her to a rehabist (of wildlife, in case anyone's wondering, from whom I got the story). The hysterical woman was told to tape a plastic garbage bag to the window to eliminate any reflection for a few weeks—the bird, full of testosterone, was territorially dive-bombing itself—and then to take the hose to her window ledge, which would make it good as new. At these suggestions, I understand, she tersely replied, "I draw the line at attacks on my property!" While I'm on the topic of birds, I might as well confess: I often catch myself now flipping them to untold numbers of slack-brain, homicidal drivers. I'm becoming what I left behind twelve years ago.

Faced now with another influx of population, potentially a huge and unending one, the Bitterroot is poised on a brink. The brink, this time, is sheerer and higher; it holds huge monetary gains for the few and threatens dear losses of community for the many. I know some folks praying for a killer winter, thinking it will send passels of the lightweights packing. I hold out no such hope. Barring the county's going broke first (supplying infrastructure on a negative residential tax flow), it seems destined—even with all the good souls riding hard to turn the herd—to sideslip, as on runny cow fops, into an increasingly minimalled hodgepodge of urban, an extended Missoula bedroom and highway strip, a faceless march of housing, and taking with it, through haphazard sprawl, massive swaths of the rural fringe. As well as bringing to the mountains themselves a high-use invasion.

The value in our Romany Forge corner, when looked at purely in monetary terms, is no longer agricultural or residential. The metamorphosis first began when the dairy broke into smaller and smaller fields, commercial businesses then sprouting to the north and south, the power company's substation appropriating the opposite corner, the water rights vanishing. The yet-quiet rural corner that we purchased has evaporated like boiled milk, leaving a scummy pan. In our tenure, the noise level has risen perhaps triplefold. With the highway soon widening to five lanes along our frontage, with its rolling right up through the fence and into the paddocks, the noise, as well as the carbon monoxide, will take another giant leap upward. *How long will we be able to last?*

Over the years, my concerns with selling the place have narrowed to saving the bat colony and a hundred-and-twenty-year-old ponderosa on the back of the bench. Nonetheless, it will be a wrestling match with my conscience: a duel between our walking away with a break-even investment by peddling the place as a deed-restricted, lovely old-timey but noisy, ill-located, single-family dwelling and "please like the bats," which would leave me feeling nobly righteous but also victimized, or our selling the front property for its commercial potential. Commercial potential, what's that? Something as charming as another gas station? Patrick, if he exercised his druthers, would give the whole mess back to the bank and pack his backpack. I, by contrast, with an identical nonexistent retirement plan, keep having full-color visions of the wire grocery cart I might one day be pushing down grim back alleys.

Now comes the fully fearing-for-my-life part. The anticipated words here no doubt will be *Ursus horribilis*, grizzly bears! The ones under discussion for reintroduction into the Bitterroot-Salmon-Selway Wilderness. I can't say as I'm altogether enamored of the idea of a tête-à-tête with even a small hundred-pound grizzly on some squeezed-down bend in the path, one of those many trails that run along the bottoms of the Bitterroot Mountains' typically steep-sided canyons: a roaring creek on one side, drowning out our oncoming presence to each other, a sheer rock wall begging ropes and carabiners on the other. Yet a hike of this sort is not required of me to reach the grocery store and post office. I have already commandeered, along with the others of my species, the entire valley floor. The whole planet is available to me for hiking—trains, planes, bicycles, SUVs to get me there. If I personally am too hysterical to hike in grizzly territory, then so be it. The mountains belong to the animals first. Those "backyards, front yards" again.

Fears, for many of us, spring hard into being with a name. In the case of grizzly bear, the very words conjure up the worst—nonetheless, it is the highway, *Car-wreckius instant deathius*, that has me paralyzed. Yes, the 34.2-mile highway improvement through the Bitterroot.

There are those who will say my bringing this topic up for discussion at this point sounds a bit like the old adages "sour grapes" and "spilled milk." The lawsuits by citizen groups (all lost) were fought on the unaddressed issues of land use—the "pave a big road into the middle of nowhere and in twenty years there will be a metropolis"—and on the cumulative effects, things like air pollution, consumption of groundwater, and such. These continue to be serious concerns, but there was one other. Safety! So, never mind that enlargement of the highway—indeed just the thought of it—drives development; never mind that once you start in this vein, of adding a lane in each direction, studies show they will be full in five years and needing again two more; and never mind that the days of the fast Hamilton-to-Missoula commute, in truth, are over (exchanged for the congestion of population increase, strip development, frontage roads, traffic lights): It is the actual motoring down the finished pavement that has me wildly unnerved.

An undivided four-lane highway presents the potential, with a head-on collision, for involving two more lanes than does an undivided two-lane—or said PRAY FOR ME, I DRIVE 93. Then, when you start thinking about folks who will be stopped in the fast lane making left turns, well . . . there you have it. An undivided four-lane is, in fact, a fine road design, I understand—appropriate for speeds of thirty-five to fifty miles per hour.

Approximately half of the 34.2 miles will end up as the sorry undivided four-lane. The rest is planned as a five-lane, with what's been called the suicide lane in the middle. Oh! for a grassy median, one wide enough to accommodate left-hand-turn lanes and with a swale to push winter's snow into and, for added safety, a guardrail at the bottom. Thus it is more than just the highway's widening right into our paddocks, right into our laps in the barn: It is the configuration of the lanes themselves that threatens to chase me not only from our corner but from the valley entirely. The gypsyman, of course, is always poised and ready to go. "Let's blooow this pop stand!" Though I must say Patrick, more than most, is ready to take nonmotorized or public forms of transportation. He is ready to walk.

Howsomever, I mention all the above by way of coming again to the animals and their greater plight on the rural fringe as it barrels faster and faster toward sprawling *urban fringe,* or—the newly bantered term—"urban-wilderness interface." On Ravalli County roads (extrapolating from some known figures), we're clobbering upwards of a thousand deer per year.

Because of Highway 93's alignment—its run parallel with the main river plain—it crosses every western Bitterroot River tributary within its stretch. What happens at these junctures is crucial to the well-being of wildlife, and people. In the two-thirds of the improvement project yet to be constructed, "what happens" is still (and will be at the time of this book's publication) marginally correctable—even with taking into consideration the intractable mind-set and the budgetary constraints of the Department of Transportation. The situation boils down largely to a push-pull scenario between two state agencies. Fish, Wildlife and Parks, with their mandate to protect fish and wildlife, is the agency issuing permits to anyone building roads across creeks and rivers. The Department of Transportation is that *anyone* wanting to build across those watercourses. The folks at the DOT are an enthusiastic but inveterate lot, always raring and ready—in the absence of extreme outside lobbying—to dash ahead with some 1950s thought-out plan.

Thus there is a third entity mixing it up in this tug-of-war: the ever-present well-schooled citizen group, giving over lives without salaried compensation—in this case, organized around on-site studies of each crossing, assessing reasonable needs, and making thoughtful, detailed recommendations. In the ideal: All the smaller drainages and the wetlands bordering the road would be furnished amply large culverts equipped with raised internal ledges for the smaller migrating mammals and reptiles—to name a few, turtles, frogs, muskrats, mink (a species that moves up and down every little seep), weasels, and raccoons. At crossings of more substantial tributaries, nothing short of single-span bridges—long enough for creeks to go naturally about their meanderings and tall enough that ranging moose and bear might consider ducking *beneath* the highway—are sufficient. Were even the best of the best to be built at every juncture, still there will be a highway with speeding vehicles, and animals trying to cross it. Cover vegetation of a beckoning-to-wildlife character and whatever additional funneling lures can be dreamed up notwithstanding, there will be animals to go up and over. It's not as simple as: UNDERPASS QUARTER MILE ➜

A farrier friend of ours, Ben, who's a retired-to-the-Bitterroot highway patrolman, coming from thirty years' service in California, pointed out something a while back that stuck with me like pine pitch in a wool mitten. He described an undivided four-lane he once watched being constructed for high-speed traffic. When it was finished and major carnage erupted for motorists and the cries of "Do something!" went up, the only solution was to resort to emplacement of a Jersey barrier—a sectioned concrete median. Though the barrier provides safety for opposing speeding traffic, it also plays havoc with wildlife. Deer are capable physically of jumping the divider, but, perhaps because of its solid and beveled nature, the animals don't seem to know this, and they end up instead turning and running down the highway. I recently heard about a female moose crossing a Jersey barrier. She sprang over, but her calf couldn't manage to follow. Two people got out on the road to help the calf, preparing to halt semis while also dodging a frantic adult moose. "All's well that ends well" might describe the case in specific. But in general, this situation is treacherous for all species involved.

The Latin word *urbanus* has its origins in the definition "a palisade of hurdles." In turn *palisade* describes a rather stouter ancestor of the picket fence: "a fence of pales or stakes . . . pointed at top, a number of which are set in the ground vertically or obliquely in a close row as a means of defense." In the Bitterroot, it is not just the wildlife's paths to the river but their biological corridors—those least-cost migrating routes* to other large wilderness areas—that are becoming palisades of hurdles. Animals crossing the north valley must navigate the new four-lane highway. At the valley's southernmost end, at the pass, recent improvements to Highway 93 have resulted in substantial widening and straightening (though no additional lanes), and the ski area has expanded its runs and capacity. For those wider-ranging mammals needing contact with larger gene pools, "least-cost" is turning increasingly expensive.

When I step back and take a longer view—on the continuum of evolution and changing land formations—I see that the building of this highway plays a curious role. The other day I stood before the sixty-foot-high, exposed internal wall of a west-side bench, once an alluvial fan of sand, mud, and angular stones, formed at the tail end of the last ice age, some 10 million years ago. Colossal machinery has been hacking it back now, the way one knifes pats of butter off a stick. We are mining the substance of the bench for use in the new roadbed. The folks greatly enamored of the road improvement may be charmed to hear of its novel connection to the valley's geological beginnings. Overall, this is definitely a graphic piece of evolution in which we are involved. Evolution indeed—but is it *progress*? Do we believe this? When we might have been getting not only a more safely designed road, but in this unique geographical loca-

---

*Remembering, "least-cost" refers to the safety of the animal.

tion, a road with a leg up on reinventing our relationship with wildlife?

Finding myself in need of a different long view—more a perusal of the planet's future than a surveying of its past—I called David Quammen and asked if he had a little time. He was between trips to Romania, Kenya, and East Africa.

I drove over to Bozeman and met him at an upbeat espresso joint, where we chatted to the whirring of milk being steamed in little stainless steel pitchers. I didn't recognize him at first. The tousle of dark hair that I remembered was now clipped short and gone to a salting of gray. Looking every bit the outdoorsman and the writer of landscapes with their tenuous inhabitants, he wore a plaid shirt and Polarfleece vest, and his identifying large-lens glasses. Quammen and his wife, Kris Ellingsen, were just finishing building a house, with Kris doing much of the building. It was a story that intrigued me, not solely because of my building background.

They had been living for thirteen years in a small, turn-of-the-century bungalow with a dirt-floored basement, situated on a narrow city lot of an eighth of an acre. Finally itching for more living space, they came directly up against the state of the bungalow, its need for updating in wiring, plumbing, roofing, you name it. After careful consideration, having to do largely with their not being people to buy twenty acres of pristine backcountry and carve a new road up the side of a canyon, but also because they liked their neighbors, they chose to stay on their little lot. They tore down the old bungalow, methodically, and saved everything usable. Much of the old wood was cleaned up and remilled. The original pine roof boards, nail holes and all, became ceiling boards. Building in this manner turned out to be somewhat expensive in terms of money, more expensive in terms of time, but two years later they had a house with doors, bookcases, tables, counters, floors—all shaped out of pieces of the bungalow.

In all of this is a heavy point of principle that Quammen gave to me now. "We both really believe," he said, "if you love the landscape, live in town."

I opened my notebook to where I'd stuffed the copy of his essay for *Harper's* magazine, "Planet of Weeds: Tallying the Losses of Earth's Animals and Plants," which was in a tattered and multicolored state of underlining from my different readings of it. Sitting with the light streaming over us from a big window at my back, I pointed to the third page, where he had written that, though many experts remain hopeful about our being able to brake the planet's descent into mass extinctions, his own view was "we're likely to go all the way down." Then I pointed to the thirteenth page, on which he had recorded a prominent paleontologist's thoughts on the prospect of our ability to pull back from our presently charted human course, perhaps lessen the overall loss of species, bring it down to 35 percent. Quammen had asked the paleontologist if he were hopeful. The man had replied: "Yes, I am." But the next paragraph began again in the author's voice with a curt "I'm not."

"It's been two or three years since you wrote this," I said. "Are you still of the same mind?"

"Still pessimistic? If anything more so."

For a book he is working on, Quammen told me he's been tracking the populations of three species of large predators, as models for preservation, in coexisting amid a crunch of humans. The Asiatic lion is one, two hundred animals living in a small forest reserve in, of all places, India, where we think of there being tigers rather than lions. The brown bears of Romania are another. The third is a saltwater crocodile. The question of interest is: Will there still be wild populations of the big predators fifty to a hundred years from now?

"The more I travel, the more I read, the more I talk to people," he said in his quiet, steady, thoughtful manner, "the closer I look at situations that I used to think offered hope, the less hopeful I am about those situations."

"So here you are literally without hope," I began with my second question, "and yet *behaving* in a way"—referring to the manner in which he built his house—"that is hopeful. How do you explain that?"

His voice carried a charge when he answered. "I'm not yet despairing to the point where I think we should all just kick back and burn all the fossil fuel we can and consume all the habitat we can."

I was talking with a man who firmly considered despair a futile emotional condition. The essence of Quammen's reply suddenly reminded me of my father in his last months of fighting lung cancer. On my first visit to him after he had been told of his terminal condition, he asked me to locate the Hemlock Society to learn about a "death potion" and be prepared to have some ready for when he would need it. If I would do this, he said, he would not buy a gun. I agreed immediately, not wanting ever to come upon the aftermath of him shooting himself. I promised. I did my research. I had a recipe on hand and the means to quickly obtain the ingredients. Three days before he slipped into his final coma, I sat by his bedside, wondering if he were reachable even then. He was under heavy doses of morphine yet still having to endure fierce pain at times. (These were the early days of hospice in Los Angeles, working with doctors not fully onboard.) Perhaps he had forgotten there was a way out of this, I thought; I probably should ask him if now were the time for the potion. Taking his hand, caressing the long fingers that looked so like mine, I posed the question. "No!" the word came stabbing the low light of the room. He had barked it with a great force, though he didn't seem able to elaborate.

Humans, as a whole, are like the Ruffattos' calves, a species curious, always wanting to know what's coming next. Typically we are willing to bear nightmarish pain, disappointment, and marginality to extend slightly the moments, weeks, years—of Life.

Quammen, ever reluctant to candy-coat his pessimism, nonetheless added, "The battle is so important that even if there's little likelihood we can do more than slow the inevitable, it still seems to be *very* important to try. More important than anything else I can think of."

Living in the old dairy barn, a place imbued with the presence of randy-natured occupants—weedy species all of us, except for the bats—I find it almost impossible to believe perhaps that while I'm hanging up the laundry we are losing a devastating amount of the living world. Prominent scientists say the current extinction rate in mammals and birds has risen to roughly a hundred times the background rate (again, that rate at which the evolution of new species normally provides a steadying counterbalance—or, in the course of a million years, a loss of about one in every major grouping). With rainforest species, the extinctions have risen to a thousand times the background rate. Tropical regions stand to lose the most because they contain the highest density of species, an astounding number of which are disappearing before we can even catalog their existence. The day will inevitably come when we look around Victor, Montana, and places like Daytona Beach, Florida, and Oakland, California, and Bangor, Maine, and Winona, Minnesota, and Churchill, Manitoba, and notice great holes in what we have known. The bears will go first, particularly the brown bears, I'm told. And the polar bears and the lions. As much as 30 percent of the world's bird species are expected to vanish within the next thirty years.

As I sat at this small coffeehouse table with David Quammen, it became clear to me that if humans wanted to change these predictions in a big way, it would take a damn sight more than my boycotting of huckleberries, passing up out-of-season strawberries, buying shade-grown coffee, yanking out knapweed—and with the First World, heavy-consumer areas working at it hardest. To use Patrick's term: Consumer-puking would have to end.

My last question for Quammen was again along the lines of coping. I was aware that his career took him zipping around the world in search of the breaking news on extinctions and also that his extensive traveling is something about which he's had his moments of remorse—airplanes are public transportation but also resource hogs. He could stay home, he has said, "and write bad poetry."

I, for one, am glad he does not, and yet I have wondered how he withstands—on a blood-and-tissue cellular level, on a spiritual level—being the person whose inadvertent networking among the world's scientists allows him to know, possibly more than anyone else, what is taking place. "How is it that all this news doesn't destroy you?" I asked.

His answer came quickly, without contemplative sip of his blond coffee drink. "It's *fascinating* to me, even when it's depressing, because I love the landscapes and the creatures that are disappearing—and they're not all gone yet. Just the dire drama of when they *seem* to be disappearing is important, and therefore riveting." It's like being a war correspondent, he said, in the middle of a frightful, heartbreaking drama. "There are people who are junkies for it. They get up every morning ready to go out and see some more of it, and that's kind of the way I feel."

Quammen's writings serve a valuable purpose; they are crucial in bringing a far-flung, deeper truth to those of us who are at home slapping together the peanut-butter-and-jelly sandwiches, carting out the garbage.

And a war it is. In a very cruel sense of the word. Between

us and other species, between introduced and native species, between us and us—all interconnected and with casualties lying around virtually everywhere. It occurs to me, as we move further into extinctions (for anyone listening who's looking for a career), we're going to need rafts of mediators and boatloads of conservation biologists. In addition to more writers with the tenacity, the piqued intellect, and the intently searching, blue-green eyes of David Quammen.

A mid-July night. Finally, we were down to sleeping with a thin covering of sheet. Ursa Major prowled the northern sky, hidden from us on the deck by the vault of the barn. In the summer months, the three-star, dished head of Scorpio keeps us company, the arachnid's long, curling tail diving into tall cottonwoods on the southern horizon. Sagittarius, my own trapezoid and triangle, treads on Scorpio's heels. And the Milky Way spills down toward them, carrying in its braided flow the great Swan.

"Good night, Poopie. I love *you!*" This last was delivered in Patrick's three-notes-up-the-scale stage voice that I so adore.

"Poopie? What kind of name is that?"

"One of the utmost endearing, dear one."

I felt his big grin in the dark, and I remained wisely silent.

Long ago, I had lost on the issue of nose hairs because I expressed my displeasure too fast and too loud. Now I can rant and rave—"They're disgusting!" "Appalling!" "How can you walk around like that!" "Boogers live in them!" "Grow up!"— all to no avail. I've tried everything. Shocking. Shaming. Demanding. Ridiculing. He smiles. In the warmer months, his trailing whisk brooms are on display front and center, as good as being under spotlight, because his mustache is gone;

he shaves it, religiously, on Mother's Day and begins growing it back on the Marine Corps' birthday. There is something of undying critical significance in this that continually
escapes me. Probably similar in its origin to his rotation of
the china—ours a gallimaufry of Cost Plus relics and Fiesta
Ware. When Patrick empties the dish drainer, freshly washed
plates and bowls go to the bottoms of the stacks, allowing for *even* wear, he says. Rather than a sensible pairing
of patterns. Which means, when I am three-things-in-one-
hand setting the table for dinner, of the two dishes I'm
after, invariably, one is on the top and the other, two up
from the bottom. Yet with mustaches and dishes—whatever
the spurring compulsion or tradition or military training—I
wave the behavior by. With nose hairs, since he wears them
on his face, and since we go about together, I am definitely
involved. At the slightest indication that we might be on the
subject again, Patrick is prompted to root up in one orifice
and resolutely tug each hair to its maximum length. "I'm
working in particular on this one"—feigning seriousness, he
juts his nose into my face—"see, right here." He has ahold of
a white one that's been curling up the outside of his nostril
like a honeysuckle vine. Drawn out straight, it almost
reaches his lip. *Criminy!* He *will not* cut these hairs. Only when
we are headed to a place of blue-blooded atmosphere and at
the last minute, when it's certain to make us late, does he
grudgingly succumb to *my* cutting them for him. I drag him
to the light of the bathroom window and go after them with
nail scissors. Carefully, of course. It is a tedious job, and
there is always one long one he has hidden, stuffed way up
inside, pasted against his septum, to be teased back down tomorrow. Periodically I threaten to present him with one of
those stainless steel, battery-operated, nostril-sized weed
whackers, advertised in a catalog we get in the mail. But I
fear he will be brokenhearted at the game's being over. And

besides, I am, I suppose, as quaintly and dysfunctionally tied to this ritual as is my double-broom-nosed sweetie.

Normally, my beloved's is a bimonthly schedule for new moniker creations, but, as anyone might guess, the barest hint at this point of any real displeasure and the sobriquet Poopie could stick for five years.

I slapped at a stray mosquito, one tickling a landing onto my eyelid, and drew the sheet over my shoulder. Under the soundless swooping of mother bats—some coming, some going—we dropped asleep.

"Jesus, fuck!" A loud, blearily disgruntled voice carried to us on the night air, following a sharp screech of tires. "Christ! Came out of nowhere!"

We bolted to a sitting posture in the bedroll. Patrick's clock read two-fifteen. Down the road one light shined. A pickup truck was stopped, a man stumbling around in the beam. He appeared alone, chastising the state of his world, struggling to drag the dead deer from the lane.

After the man drove off, Patrick dropped back asleep. I lay awake, listening to the distant hooting of an owl. It is the great horned that hoots strangely—Arden had told me it was not a different species. *Hoo hoohoohoo hoo hoo* instead of the typical *hoo hoohoo hoo hoo.* I'd taken a walk with Arden the week before to check out the bases of the trees in which the great horneds sleep away their days. We had picked apart the furry pellets the raptors expel. One yielded a muskrat's wee leg bone complete with ball joint; the toe claw of a bat; one vertebra large enough to be a pheasant's; ten tiny, graduated-in-size, snake vertebrae. *Nothing belonging to a deer mouse!* The night vocalizations of another resident-of-the-peculiar sometimes reach us on the deck—a coyote that runs alone. We hadn't heard him for a while. He sends up a series of macabre cries, as though being tortured just short of death. Arden, also familiar with the coyote, says: A case of disabled voice box, from birth.

By this hour Scorpio had swung over to the west, ready to dive behind chiseled peaks. The moon was up and high. I could hear the grinding of a horse's teeth on the salt block. The biting smell of cow manure began drifting in from the neighboring dairy. My first inhalation of it always makes me sit up and take note. "Whew, what *is* that?" It is an odor decidedly unlike that of horse manure. Once I recognize it as not life-threatening, I'm able to relax into it, though it will never be as pleasant a smell as the whiffle of skunk.

My thoughts rolled on, from one thing to the next. Patrick had been shoeing one day this week fifty miles northeast of Missoula, in Ovando. It's a long way; he generally takes another farrier with him; they like to shoe a barnful. During summer's hottest weeks, probably for a clear and understandable-to-someone reason, Ovando is host to a horsefly olympics. The big black-and-yellow biting machines emerge in droves. Trying to shoe a horse that's jumping and kicking after horseflies can be dangerous. Jeff, the farrier with Patrick, had been a windmill all afternoon, snatching them out of the air, flinging them into the forge. *Flies truly are a bother. What is their purpose on this earth?* Bats don't eat them: flies are not active at night. Sustenance, maybe, for swallows? Frogs and lizards surely grab a few, but I'd never seen any lizards around here and there weren't enough frogs to balance out the flies. Flickers act interested. They hop along the window ledge, pecking at what they can't reach behind the glass. I recalled a photograph from many years ago, most likely from *National Geographic*, showing the people of a tropical country eating burritos stuffed with live flies, a few escapees lighting on big smiling faces. But as far as I know fly burritos haven't caught on farther north. I'm familiar with only one instance of fly tacos. So, with the exception of wounds that in dire circumstances have been medically cleaned with fly maggots, what possible good were these little beasts? What gave them their prestige in the food chain, their value in the delicate ecological balance of things? Well, obviously, I had overlooked a few items. Without cluster flies, earthworms would grow to rule the world. Moreover, it was the itty-bitty darlings that had sparked the building of spine, character, and ingenuity in a few people (*ah hem?*). Come to think of it, the cluster fly with its ebony luster was directly supplying a regular cornucopia of material and, indirectly, actual food on the plates of at least two people. One, a writer of sorts. I should lighten up on these guys.

But *mosquitoes* it was just now! My face by morning would resemble a batch of lumpy Cream of Wheat. Our pleasant night breeze had gone still. The air was heavy. Suddenly the bull frogs were croaking and the coyotes singing. For the latter, it was their first time this summer. With pups in the den, they had been quiet. That coyotes are a weedy species deserves, in my opinion, the response "Thank the Great Creator!" Though I am well aware there are those folks who consider coyotes as I consider cluster flies.

I nudged Patrick: It is our ritual to awaken each other to enjoy the chorus. "Oh yeah," he whispered, appreciative, then faded out again.

But I knew I could chat with him. Patrick has this queer ability to carry on a conversation while asleep, and well beyond the rudiments of "um" and "ah." A version of his talent is evident in our hours spent reading aloud to each other. When he is the listener, he has a tendency to drop off (which, I might just note here, has nothing whatsoever to do with my delivery skills, dramatically animated as they are). Reading along, I will peripherally sense he has slipped into the even peace of slumber, and in my glancing over, I'll see his eye wrinkles have relaxed, his jaw gone slack, his mouth opened a slit.

I'll jiggle his arm. "Did you go to sleep?"

"Only a little bit," he mutters.

"Should I continue?"

"Um, a lit-tle more."

In a minute, he's again gone. I jiggle.

". . . on-our-way-to-Alice-Springs." He almost shouts it, perfectly enunciating the last words of the last sentence I just read, without a scrap of context.

It had been two weeks earlier that we'd lain here conversing—the usual, Patrick asleep, me pondering—about the lack of mosquitoes, how they definitely had thinned out over the years.

"You *do* think so too, right? It's not just a quirk of my mind?"

"Ba-t-s doing a great job."

"Bats don't eat mosquitoes, remember?"

"Som-e-one is."

Now in my walloping away at them, socking myself silly, I was wondering just why we had *so many.* The heat was prompting hatches? Patrick had said the temperature was 102°F this afternoon where he was shoeing, and tonight it wasn't cooling off even to 60°. But weren't mosquitoes thickest in the wet years? This was a drought year. Maybe I just didn't recall their ferocity from year to year? Perhaps it took the infernal whining in my ear, the maddeningly itchy welts on my forehead, knuckle, wrist, elbow, knee, three on my belly, two on one little toe, one granddaddy on the back of an earlobe to refresh my memory.

Patrick rolled over. His taking the sheet with him wouldn't have mattered—I was hot—except that I needed it for cover. To my tugging it back, he groaned, and, with that, I assumed a particle of him was conscious.

"Why is it that a mosquito will buzz around my face and,

only when slapped silent, give rise to another's coming along?" (Such mosquito behavior can go on for hours. Their sequential arrivals could be timed to something like an even two minutes. Time enough, anyway, that I'm just winding unconscious when the next one in line skewers me.) "Do you think mosquitoes could be territorial, like bears?"

"What!" He brayed, jerking upward, as though some danger threatened.

"Sorry, sweet," I said. He'd been more zonked than I had thought.

"Oh."

"So, what do you think? Could mosquitoes be territorial?"

"Whadda-ya-mean?"

"Well, they only attack me one at a time, like they possess some social etiquette about not moving in on another's territory."

"I-dun-no."

"It's such a dry year, you'd think by now they would be finished."

"L-o-tza species, 'member. They hang out in tall grass-es."

"From how far away do you think these buggers sense our body heat?"

"Oh *hundreds* of miles." No sleepy sag to his hyperbole.

But I was on a mission by this point, figuring out how to get some sleep without all the time retreating indoors. "Do we have any standing water around the barn? What about your slag bucket?"—the oak tub of water in which he cools hot steel—"Are they breeding in it?"

"P-o-opie, we've got all this slow water just over the bank." He was coming awake.

From where I lay, my Irishman's profile inclined crisply against the night sky—the principled swell to his brow, the curve of his eyelashes, his bold nose. I rolled to him, set my cheek against his shoulder, and, as in Taj Mahal's "Cakewalk into Town," threw my big leg over him.

"Yeah, I suppose. The cattails. The swamp." Yet I was not satisfied. "There must be a lot we don't know about mosquitoes."

"Worlds."

The next night, hurdling ten years of memory lapse, we unearthed Patrick's bridal veil netting. Stringing a line from railing to railing, we secured the netting to it with clothespins. No need now for Meryl and Robert, Kate and Bogie. We crawled expectantly into our wispy conjugal tent— to bare skin to the moon.

Afterword

All over the world are countless causes deserving of our attention and donations. Here, I list three. By contributing to the following projects, you can help large predator species to live in the wild and compensate ranchers for losses of livestock. Consider an annual donation to one of the following as just part of the package—in this day and age—of eating hamburgers, steaks, and lamb chops. Vegetarians, in all good conscience, may send their monies elsewhere.

Wolf Compensation Trust
Grizzly Compensation Trust
Proactive Carnivore Conservation Fund
    —Helps finance projects designed to *prevent* loss of livestock. For instance: contributing to the cost of building scare devices; sharing the cost of purchasing livestock-guarding dogs; sharing the cost of electric fencing to construct secure pastures in high predator areas; purchasing hay, which allows ranchers to relocate and feed stock that might otherwise be grazing close by a wolf den.

Make out your check to Defenders of Wildlife, noting on it which fund you would like to support, and mail it to:

Defenders of Wildlife
1101 14th Street NW
Washington, D.C. 20005

ABOUT THE AUTHOR

KATHLEEN MEYER was born in New York City and raised on the New Jersey shore and in California's San Fernando Valley, coming finally to the intermountain West to live in 1989. A longtime outdoorswoman, she is the author of the bestselling *How to Shit in the Woods: An Environmentally Sound Approach to a Lost Art.* She makes her home now with Patrick McCarron in the Bitterroot Valley of western Montana.